Writing Step by Step

Easy Strategies
for Writing and Revising

WRITING
STEP BY STEP

Easy Strategies
for Writing and Revising

ROBERT DE BEAUGRANDE

University of Florida

HARCOURT BRACE JOVANOVICH, PUBLISHERS

San Diego   New York   Chicago   Atlanta   Washington, D.C.
London   Sydney   Toronto

ISBN: 0-15-598258-3

Printed in the United States of America

To the Instructor

WHAT I BELIEVE ABOUT LEARNING TO WRITE

Every composition textbook author—consciously or unconsciously—has a particular idea of what it means to learn how to write. These are my convictions, which have informed my writing of this book:

✔ Anyone, of any background, can learn to write at least well enough to meet his or her aspirations in life, and we shouldn't form hasty advance judgments about a person's chances for success.

✔ One's writing can always improve, given a workable method. People with special problems need special methods, even if those methods diverge from the way we usually do things.

✔ Failure as a writer is not a statistic at the bottom of somebody's "grade curve," but a social and personal tragedy.

✔ Writing errors and problems are signs of unfamiliarity with the medium, not of low intelligence.

✔ A good writer is not so much the one who doesn't make bad choices or mistakes as the one who can evaluate and revise bad choices and mistakes.

✔ Good writing is not writing that conforms to strict standards of usage, but writing that is readable, interesting, and relevant for its audience.

✔ A piece of writing should be judged on both its strengths and its weaknesses. A grade based on counting up "errors" ignores the positive effort of the writing, an effort that may be considerable for an unskilled writer. The grade should reflect what that writer is capable of at his or her particular stage of development.

✔ Too much emphasis on minor points is inhibiting. Students who must worry about such niceties as "which" versus "that" may not have enough time and energy left to pay attention to the major points in an exposition or an argument.

✔ Many issues in writing are genuinely a matter of personal choice. An instructor should not try to impose a "rule" for every issue, but should try to negotiate standards in light of what the students want to do with their writing. Even many of the traditionally "bad" choices, such as passives and contractions, have some legitimate uses, and it's better to learn where certain choices are appropriate than to throw them out altogether. *

✔ The authority of the instructor can be a two-edged sword. On the one hand, students need explicit assignments; on the other hand, undue coercion is out of place in a creative activity such as writing. Writing should be construed as a useful craft, not as busywork, and standards for grading should be flexible and reasonable.

✔ Insisting on fixed numbers of words or paragraphs in an assigned paper fosters an unrealistic and limiting attitude about purposes and audiences. Students should learn to fit the length to the occasion.

✔ Literary style, with its large, often Latinate vocabulary, is a valuable goal, but only for writers who already command a plain, generally readable style. Students should not be rushed into a literary style before they have that essential foundation.

✔ As much as possible, the correcting and editing of papers should be done by the students. They need the practice far more than their instructors do.

Whether or not you also believe these things, you probably know how hard it can be to find materials and methods that both incorporate your beliefs and work well in daily practice. I do not claim to have found the ultimate solution, but I have tried hard in this book to fill the gap, at least provisionally, with some workable tactics.

SPECIAL FEATURES OF THIS BOOK

On the whole, composition textbooks have changed their format very little over the years. Although we should not pursue innovation for its own sake, we should be willing to try out those innovations that can be justified with straightforward

---

*In estimating current usage and its motives, I have followed the authoritative *Grammar of Contemporary English*, whose 1984/85 edition I carefully read in manuscript; it is based on the most extensive survey of actual usage ever undertaken for English.

arguments. It is no secret that traditional composition textbooks have not been ideal for everyone.

Nearly all of the examples in this book are taken from *actual student writing or speaking* (sometimes with slight modifications appropriate to the point under discussion). Printed sources such as newspapers and essays were also used. If students are to learn how to work with their own writing, they need true-to-life samples. Moreover, practicing on other students' writing is helpful in classes where students check one another's work—a method we've found to be very useful for students and time-saving for instructors.

For convenience, the *examples are numbered* in parentheses; to prevent confusion, square brackets are used around the numbers of items in the exercises and quizzes. Abundant exercises and quizzes are distributed through the book—including review quizzes in a tear-out format suitable for handing in if desired. The accompanying Instructor's Manual gives answers to exercises and quizzes.

Every quiz is immediately followed by a *review quiz* with the same instructions and the same kinds of exercise items, so that students who have trouble with a quiz can try again. Because less skilled writers do best if they know exactly what they are supposed to do, every student assignment is carefully explained with *directions and steps to follow.*

Traditional multiple-choice and fill-in-the-blanks tests were avoided in nearly all areas. Educational research has raised serious doubts about the efficacy and validity of such tests, which encourage a narrow focus on details rather than a broad consideration of context. Moreover, those same tests are largely responsible for the drastic reduction in the amount of writing students do all across the curriculum.

As far as possible, the exercises were designed to approximate the natural activities of writing, especially the activities of the crucial stage where plausible ideas and provisional sentences are being worked out. This stage, which is curiously neglected by many textbooks, is a common source of discontent and writer's block. If we can offer a map of what happens during the hard early stage of writing and explain what to do about it, we will provide a great help to the ordinary writer.

All the same, not every problem can be attacked via totally natural activities. Real writers do not label sentence parts or punctuate a whole passage in one pass. Nor is it probable that skilled writers commonly use explicit steps to achieve a specific result. But by using such steps and doing such tasks, we may be able to clear up the points that typically preoccupy unskilled writers.

The order of the material in the book evolved according to what topics proved more or less pressing. Chapter 1 starts right off with a demonstration of how students can use their spoken language skills to get at their writing. After that, the progression is mainly from smaller toward larger concerns: assembling clauses, then sentences, then paragraphs, until a complete paper has been developed. This design meant delaying the coverage of punctuation until fairly late in the course; however, if punctuation is an acute problem, it might be moved up and taught along with other material.

So far, I have been quite pleased with the success rates of the approach. Most students not only have become better able to deal with their problems, but also have developed a more positive attitude about their chances of becoming adequate writers. Overall, the benefits of this procedural approach have heavily outweighed the drawbacks. It has been especially helpful in promoting a working consensus about what we are trying to do with composition in its broader context.

I am grateful to these reviewers for their valuable suggestions: Stephen D. Atkins and John Elder, Sinclair Community College; Barbara Beauchamp, County College of Morris; Audrey Roth; and Carolyn Simonson, Tacoma Community College.

RdB

To the Student

This book was developed during several years when I was studying my students. Many of them didn't like to write and thought they were "bad" writers. I gradually became convinced that they felt this way because they had no clear idea of what to *do* when they were supposed to write something—they had no map of the route between the blank sheet of paper and the final product. Of course, any job looks hard if you don't know what to do in which order, and you have no way to be sure you'll ever get it done.

So I began looking for and trying out some steps anyone could follow, mainly just by knowing how to *talk* English. Of course, you aren't supposed to write down exactly what you'd say if you were talking. But you can use your skills as a talker and work from there toward becoming a writer.

Also, remember that your skills will never improve if you're so scared of making "mistakes" that you don't even give writing a try. Writing is no different in that way from riding a surfboard or playing the drums. The main thing is to stop worrying about making "mistakes" and learn to find and fix them yourself—before you hand anything in for a grade, or send it off as a job application, or whatever. It might help to think of your paper as a computer program with "bugs" in it; as long as you can *debug*, you can count on getting the job done. You should not rely on your instructor to mark your papers or fix them up. That's the most important part of your job, and *you* have to learn to do it.

Once you aren't afraid of making mistakes, you won't need to be discouraged or embarrassed about your rough drafts. It's perfectly natural for drafts to be disorganized when you're writing on the spur of the moment. You make hasty choices or change your mind. You can't plan very far ahead, or remember very far back. You haven't decided exactly where you want to go, so you try this or that. Not everything turns out the way you wanted, or you suddenly realize that you should have tried something else. No matter what your problems are, you're better off if you don't worry about all of them at once—they're normal and hard to avoid. As long as you know how to rework your draft, you'll be all right.

So don't expect writing to be as easy as talking, but don't expect writing to be impossibly difficult, either. Your problems or mistakes in writing are not a sign of low intelligence. They are natural side effects of the way writing operates, as compared to talking. People have certain limits on their energy, attention, memory, and so on. It would be an inhuman strain on many people to be letter-perfect every single time they write. But you can overcome your limits by writing and rewriting in stages, rather than trying to get everything exactly right the first time. The hardest time in writing comes when you actually have to put something on the blank page. You'll do yourself a favor by loosening up and jotting things down freely. Then select a few problems and work on them—as much as you feel you can handle. Eventually, a reasonably good product will result. You'll reach your destination if you take small, safe steps. It's up to you to decide how many steps you need, so suit your personal rhythm.

There's no doubt about one thing: *Writing does matter*. Unfortunately, many people's careers are severely limited by a lack of writing skills. The national economy has shifted drastically toward administrative or technical jobs that require you to spend a lot of time writing. Only large businesses can afford to hire writing specialists who take care of revamping other people's writing. Smaller businesses can't pay for the extra staff—if you can't handle your own writing, they won't hire you at all. Besides, members of many higher-paid professions, such as lawyers, sales representatives, consultants, and engineers, have to write in order to give people their professional opinions. You should learn to write well enough not to miss out on good jobs.

And that's the point of this book. It shows you simple steps for finding and solving the problems most student writers have. These steps have all been tested in the classroom and redesigned until I felt sure they worked. In general, students not only improved their writing but also increased their confidence about their own ability to write. Most of the language samples in this book come from student papers or public sources, such as newspapers. The steps for writing are explained as clearly and simply as I could manage. I hope you'll have no trouble with them, and that the total task of writing will become easier once you've understood and practiced them. Then it will be entirely up to *you* whether your writing is successful or not.

Contents

2. Putting Clauses Together 73

4. Putting Paragraphs Together   219

1.

Talking
Versus
Writing

Preview

In this chapter, we look at how writing is different from talking. Your habits as a talker naturally tend to carry over into your writing. Not all habits of speaking work well in writing, however, so you should learn what to watch for and what to do about it in your writing. Talk typically has more extra words, and repeats things more often. Also, the statements of talk are often less consistent and less precise. You'll be seeing some examples of these tendencies as they turn up in people's writing. When you've learned some steps for fixing the problems, you can make better use of your talking abilities to help your writing, rather than to interfere with it.

■ A. GETTING STARTED

You couldn't even begin to learn how to write if you didn't already know your language. If you're like most people, you've come to know English mainly by taking part in everyday conversation. You feel more confident about your ability to talk than you do about your ability to write. You have probably noticed that when people write, they don't just put down on paper exactly what they would say in a conversation. But you're not so sure what the differences are or should be between writing and talking. This workbook is intended to make those differences clear enough so that you can use your talking abilities to aid your writing.

Talking and writing are different tools because each one is made to fit the situations where it's used. In conversation, your tone of voice, facial expressions, and gestures help to make sure you get your message across. You often talk to people you knew beforehand—friends, family, people from your school or town, and the like—who already have some idea who you are and what you'll say. And if they don't understand you, they can stop you, ask questions, repeat your message in their own words, and so on. Under these conditions, you can talk freely and not be too picky about choosing your words.

When you write, you don't have such direct contact with your audience. Writing doesn't convey your tone of voice, facial expressions, or gestures. Your readers are often people who don't know you personally and who may not have any idea who you are or what you'll say. And if they don't understand you, they usually can't ask you directly. Under these conditions, you need to be much more careful about deciding what to say. You need to be clear and well-organized and to take care of possible problems in advance, before the message gets to the readers. Communicating by writing is like selling something in a buyer's market: you have to accommodate your customers and give them a reason to want your product. Otherwise, they won't spend the time and effort reading what you wrote, and they won't do what you want—take your advice, carry out your requests, approve your report, interview you for a job, or whatever.

When you talk, people expect you to keep going until you finish what you're saying. When you write, you should allow yourself more time. Slow down or stop to think things over. Go back over the paper and check what you did. Whatever you've put on paper stays there, so you can keep your materials right in front of you to work with as long as you need. Don't get discouraged because your paper doesn't come out perfect on the first few tries. Each draft helps you see what the problems are and where you should go next. Don't forget, you have as many chances as you like to get it the way you want. All you need is practical steps to follow, and you can feel confident about getting there. In this chapter, we'll learn about some of those steps.

■   **B.   A DEMONSTRATION OF TALKING**

Let's start off with a demonstration of my point about talking and writing. Here is a transcript of a tape recorded by a freshman at the University of Florida telling how to get from the Interstate to her dorm. The sample shows what happens if you write down exactly what you would say in an everyday conversation. Since people don't talk with punctuation, let's use two dots for a short pause and four dots for a long one. Stressed words or word-parts are in capitals.

>   (1)   you..TAKE the INterstate north..from where to GAINESVILLE....and
>   ..you'll see TWO..a SIGN telling you that there's three exists to Gaines-
>   ville....aaannnd..you'll get off at the EXIT that....um..that's the HOSPI-
>   TAL exit..aannd you turn RIGHT onto ARCHER Road..I hope that's
>   Archer....and..you follow the road you'll see a..a RAX..a WENDY'S..on

the RIGHT and you'll see..a SHOPPING center on the RIGHT..aannd
....it's QUITE a bit down the road before you..REACH where you're
going....um....you'll see two HOSPITALS the V.A. on the..RIGHT and
the..Sh- and SHANDS on the LEFT....and..there's a RAILROAD crossing sign..next to a STREETLIGHT..which is the light that you turn left
on....and it's RIGHT before Shands Hospital so you turn left..down that
road....aand..you'll HIT a stop sign practically immediately....um..THEN
..right after that you TURN right into the PARKING lot of Shands...
aand..you hit a STOP sign..and turn LEFT up Newell Drive....there's the
hospital right..the front of it is on the right and you can't miss it so you
turn LEFT up Newell Drive and you get the first STREETlight..and..
there's a POLICE station right there..and you turn RIGHT onto MU-
SEUM Road..and..you....and JENNINGS HALL is right next to the police station and across the street from..the TENNIS courts..and you can
there's two big towers called Beatty Towers..right next to it

Talk looks strange written down, because writing normally has a different organization. Once a message gets written down, we notice the exact words and phrases
more strongly. Our freshman uses the same words over and over, for example,
saying "right" no less than thirteen times in one passage—sometimes she means
"directly" and other times she means "on the right-hand side." She links up
everything with "and" (twenty-one times), no matter how the various statements
are related to each other. She stops in the middle of a phrase and then goes off in
a different direction, as in: "there's the hospital right..the front of it is on the
right"; or "and..you....and Jennings HALL is right next to the police station."
She raises her voice to emphasize key words ("HOSPITALS," "POLICE station,"
and so on) and contrasts ("RIGHT" versus "LEFT," and so on). If she were writing the same set of directions, she should not repeat words confusingly, begin
every phrase with "and," nor leave a record of how she changed her mind. And
she'd need other means besides raising her voice to emphasize the important
words.

It is interesting that most people's everyday talk looks like our sample (1),
whether they are experienced writers or not. For example, here is a transcript of a
recording made by a professor of English whom I had been filming while he wrote:

(2)   Okay..yeah..I was..I was always AWARE I think that you were there..and
      I MIGHT have..I MIGHT have actually pulled back a bit..gotten up..and
      walked around and sat down again..because what I DID I thought was very
      hard for me to do..which is the very BEGINNING..of something that I
      had not REALLY..THOUGHT ALL OUT.... [then I asked him to tell me
      in talk what he had just written] I'm interested in HORROR..uh..I'm in-
      terested in....what HORRIFIES us....what we voluntarily and commu-
      nally seek out to be terrified by....I'm NOT interested in what is REALLY
      frightening in other words the difference between..what we KNOW hap-
      pened at Auschwitz and what we see in a movie like Hitchcock's *Torn Cur-*

tain where Paul Newman..shoves the body of a German spy into a GAS oven..or the difference between..here's where I had some trouble..how the little boy..felt..who....cried wolf..and then SAW the wolf....and how the people who heard the story....enjoyed hearing it again..but I had TROUBLE with that and I was gonna have to go back and..and fix that ..the difference between....uh....what he..FELT..when he knew the wolf was not there and then what he felt when it really WAS..horrible and then what the AUDIENCE..FELT when they HEARD the story and IMAG-INED how it must feel....and THAT'S....I don't know what I said toward the end

This particular professor is known for writing well and frequently. Still, like most people's, his talk doesn't come across like writing. Just as the freshman did, he keeps using the same words—for example, "felt" (four times) and "interested" (three times). He too has lots of "ands" (fourteen). He stops in the middle of something and starts over: "I MIGHT have..I MIGHT have actually pulled back a bit." He admits that putting into words something he hasn't "thought all out" is "very hard"; that he "had some trouble" he would "have to go back and fix"; and that he couldn't remember what he had just written "toward the end." If an accomplished writer has these problems getting the words right, you certainly don't need to be embarrassed about your troubles.

Many problems students have with writing come from the influence of their talking habits. Students who didn't have to write very much in school have not yet developed a special set of writing habits. Hardly anybody writes *exactly* the way they talk; at least nobody writes down all the "ums" and "uhs" we have in samples (1) and (2). But some influences still come through, and we'll be learning how to deal with them.

■ C. THREE WAYS TALKING INFLUENCES WRITING

Talking habits can influence writing in at least three important ways. One way is the tendency to pile up EXTRA WORDS in talking. In order to keep moving ahead without long pauses, talkers often insert extra words that don't add much of anything to the message. Also, since talk is not preserved like writing, talkers tend to repeat things they've already said, as a reminder of what's being talked about.

A second kind of influence is found in INCONSISTENCIES—things which don't fit together—that come from talking without preparation. Talkers choose something they later turn out not to need or want after all. They get caught between more than one choice and produce a mixture. They drop what they've started and go on to something altogether different. If a writer does things like this, people will notice because it's all put down on paper.

A third kind of influence is found in DOUBTFUL STATEMENTS that present, in addition to the intended message, some other message you don't want. Even though readers can usually guess what you really meant, they are likely to be confused, distracted, or amused. They'll think the writer is naive or careless. Like extra words, doubtful statements become far more obvious when they're written down for everybody to see.

Keep in mind that the tendency to imitate these talking habits in your writing is entirely natural. You can see from sample (2) that even English teachers do not instantly come up with a finished product—the professor still hadn't gotten down to what he really wanted to say. Most of the time, you don't reach the finished product until you've done some revising. So this chapter will point out some steps for revising the most common problems that talking habits can cause a writer. Once you learn to recognize what's happening, it's easy to do something about it.

■ D. EXTRA WORDS

D.1 Fillers

One sort of **extra words** that are typical of talk is **FILLERS**, that is, words that fill gaps in the stream of talk and don't convey much of anything. Fillers keep people from interrupting while you're still thinking about what to say. Short, common words with many uses, such as the **linking words** "and" and "but," are often used as fillers; as I pointed out, there were twenty-one "ands" in sample (1) and fourteen in sample (2). You can even lengthen the sound to fill up more time—just what our freshman did with "aannd" in sample (1):

(1)   You'll see a..a RAX..a WENDY'S..on the RIGHT *and* you'll see..a SHOP-PING center of the RIGHT..*aannd*....it's QUITE a bit down the road before you..REACH where you're going....

The same linking words show up as fillers in student writing. One student wrote:

(3)   I went to register at the appointment time they gave me. *And* when I arrived, there were long lines. *And* when it came my turn, all the courses I wanted were closed.

She could just as well have left the "ands" out:

(3a)   I went to register at the appointment time they gave me. When I arrived, there were long lines. When it came my turn, all the courses I wanted were closed.

You certainly shouldn't begin every sentence with "and." However, sometimes you have good reason to do it. You can start a sentence with "and" if you want to get the effect of: "on top of everything else" or "that's not all, there's more," as in:

(4)   The diplomats were seized and held at gunpoint. Some of them were interrogated for hours. *And* after all that, the Iranians called them "a threat to peace."

As in most decisions you make when you write, there's no hard and fast rule to follow. It doesn't help to say: *never* start a sentence with "and." We should rather say: don't do it *without a good reason.*

Words like "okay" (or "O.K."), "well," "let's see," "anyway," and "anyhow" are also commonly used as fillers. In talk, these words are signals that you've figured out what's going on or what somebody else said and you're going to make a statement about it. Those signals are not necessary in writing, where you have all the time you need to get your statement ready. They turn up sometimes when students are telling a story, as in these plot summaries for the Charlie Chaplin movie *Caught in a Cabaret:*

(5)   Charlie put on a dress suit and away he went. *Well*, the people attending the party thought he was a baron. He stayed much too long. *Well*, his boss back at the bar didn't appreciate that.

(6)   There was a tremendous fight with the ladies, the townspeople, the dachshund, and the thug, and nobody knew what was going on or who started it. *Anyway*, the woman invited Charlie to her party.

These signals aren't very suitable for writing unless you're imitating a conversation. In (7), for instance, George Burns is re-creating in print the talking style he made famous on the stage:

(7)   *Let's see*, I told you about Gracie and me in vaudeville, about our radio days, and about our feature movie careers. *Oh my goodness*, I forgot that we were in television. *Well*, that's understandable, we were only in it for eight years. [George Burns, *The Third Time Around*]

In your own writing, you'll have to decide whether being conversational will suit your audience. Otherwise, you won't want these fillers. If you use them, it may be because you haven't made your message as clear as it should be. So take out the fillers and try to clear things up—for instance, by changing (5) and (6) into (5a) and (6a):

(5a)   Charlie put on a dress suit and away he went. *When he arrived at the party*, the people thought he was a baron. He stayed much too long. *Meanwhile*, his boss back at the bar didn't appreciate that.

(6a)   There was a tremendous fight with the ladies, the townspeople, the dachshund, and the thug, and nobody knew what was going on or who started it. *After the confusion cleared up*, the woman invited Charlie to her party.

When it's plain how the story fits together, you don't need to say "well" or "anyway."

Fillers like "that is," "you know," or "if you know what I mean" are often used in talk to check up on whether the audience is following what you're saying. A student wrote:

(8)   We are living in the age of anxiety, *you know*, but I find it rewarding.

In writing, the audience isn't usually there to check up on. Why not leave out these signals and find more exact ways of backing up what you say:

(8a)   We are living in the age of anxiety, *filled with tensions and complications*, but I find it rewarding.

"I mean" turns up when you are afraid you didn't get your point across:

(9)   It wasn't the service we expected, *I mean*, a five-star hotel should have better meals than what we got.

You could drop the filler and make one statement out of two:

(9a)   Our meals were not up to the service we expected from a five-star hotel.

Here are some more ways to make improvements:

(10)   My family moved to Florida when I was very young. *Let's see*, it would have been around 1966.

(10a)   My family moved to Florida around 1966, when I was very young.

(11)   The compound isn't hazardous. *I mean, after all*, it won't burn in air *or anything*.

(11a)   The compound isn't hazardous, because it won't burn in air.

(12)   There was some dispute, *well*, about interest rates *and that sort of thing*.

(12a)   There was some dispute about interest rates.

The versions without the fillers are clearer as well as shorter.

When you're writing, try to be clear enough that your audience can tell right away what you mean. Then you won't need the kind of fillers you use in face-to-face conversation. Take them out and then look for any remaining problems you ought to fix.

1. EXERCISE *on removing fillers and clearing things up*

To fix these passages, get rid of fillers and make compact, clear statements.

Example:
> The next question is how to remove the bolt. Okay, you can get it out if you get some oil to put on it and loosen it up.

You could fix it like this:
> To remove the bolt, put some oil on it and loosen it up.

[1] This campground isn't too good. I mean, it's terribly primitive and uncomfortable.

[2] The shipment came too late. Let's see, it must have been about two weeks overdue.

[3] She isn't worried. That is, she doesn't care one way or the other about the election.

[4] The airline kept delaying the paychecks for a whole month. Well, they were doing it to avoid bankruptcy.

[5] As soon as we moved to town, Greek rush started. And we thought we should try it out. And we had friends in some of the fraternities. And our friends made sure we got a lot of invitations.

[6] The left riverbank is more valuable. I mean, the soil is more fertile on that bank.

[7] A lot of financial problems came at once. Anyhow, we managed to keep our credit rating all winter.

[8] The architect tried to plan ahead, if you know what I mean, and made the windows strong enough to stand high winds.

[9] The descent down the mountainside lasted all day. O.K., first we had to cross a glacier, you know, made of solid ice. Well, it was very slow going.

[10] The Asian flu is going around, you know—it's very contagious. Anyway, all my roommates had it.

Phrases such as "needless to say," "I need hardly say," "it goes without saying," and "as everybody knows" are also popular fillers. If you stop to think about it, these fillers are a contradiction, because you *are* saying it. Either your statement is necessary, or you're wasting time. You probably mean "obviously," "naturally,"

"as would be expected," and the like. For instance, (13) would make be
if you changed it to (13a):

> (13) In the final seconds of the game, Berkeley scored the winning
> down. *Needless to say*, the fans went wild.

> (13a) In the final seconds of the game, Berkeley scored the winning touch-
> down. *Naturally*, the fans went wild.

Or you can leave the phrases out when it's obvious how the statements go together:

> (13b) In the final seconds of the game, Berkeley scored the winning touch-
> down, and the fans went wild.

The point about fillers should be plain enough. If they just take up space, remove
them and try to clear up your statement. Only for special reasons, such as imitating conversation, should you keep fillers in your final drafts.

☐ 2. QUIZ *on fillers*

Revise these passages to get rid of fillers.

Example:
> Most days are cloudy, well, overcast actually, and it rains all the time, that
> is, once a day.

You could fix it like this:
> Most days are overcast, and it rains once a day.

[1] Well, we had to take out the whole engine, you know, to fix it, the bearing.
I mean, to get at it and fix it.

[2] Anyway, I started by taking off the air filter. And then I took off the carburetor. And then we started pulling the wires. Needless to say, the job
soon got very complicated.

[3] It was a great vacation. You know, just what we'd hoped. Well, it began
kind of dull, not too bad I mean, but not great, I suppose. Anyhow, things
got better after the first week.

[4] My little sister has always been sociable, I mean, the sort who likes people
and goes to parties, and that kind of thing.

[5] You know, I've always wanted to be an artist. I don't mean just any artist,
but a painter or a sculptor. Well, the other day I heard about a special
course for learning to draw.

[6] Okay, that sounded like the chance I've been waiting for to be an artist.
And I went in to ask and they said to come back next season. That is, they
didn't have any more room or anything this season.

[7]   In my junior year I joined the staff of our school newspaper. Well, I didn't have much experience, you know, though I was able to cover a great variety of stories. Anyhow, I got to be sports editor. And before long, I was running the whole paper.

[8]   Our swimming team is really one of the best, you know, in the state, or maybe in the entire southeast. Anyway, it's famous. So it goes without saying that I was proud to be chosen as captain. Well, I didn't expect that could ever happen. I mean, I only started swimming in the last year of high school.

[9]   The United Nations had the task of persuading the two warring armies to cease their fire. Needless to say, this was extremely difficult. Let's see, there were delegates from five different sides, or something of the sort.

[10] Our technology has done some wonderful things, as everybody knows. Well, there are a few serious drawbacks, you know. I need hardly say that having more machines doesn't always make people more human.

◻ 3. REVIEW QUIZ on fillers

Same instructions as on the previous quiz.

[1]   The water-skiing tournament, well, the preliminary rounds actually, finally started. Okay, I was ready. After all, I'd been practising for three months, I mean, I was in top shape.

[2]   Anyway, I got my equipment loaded into the car for the drive to Miami. And some friends came along for the ride. Well, really they wanted to see me fall on my face, if you know what I mean.

[3]   And so here I was with these two guys in the car partying all the way. And I couldn't party because I had to be in top shape for the competition, that's obvious.

[4]   Anyhow, we made it to the motel and I went out to see the water, like, to see how the conditions were, you know?

[5]   Well, it was windy, and that makes water-skiing a lot tougher, especially if you're in slalom and jumping, and stuff like that.

[6]   So anyway I went back to the motel feeling kind of nervous. Well, my wonderful friends were partying again and making noise. And the place was filling up with smoke and empty cans and all that good stuff.

[7]   Well, I had to do something, you see. And so I suggested we all go have dinner in town. Okay, so off we went.

[8]   We found an Arby's. And there were these girls sitting at an outside table and my friends said that's the place and so of course that's where we went, where else?

[9]   And the girls were into water skiing, well anyhow, into the beach. Anyway, we ended up following the girls in their car to the disco just down the road, a pretty nice place after all.

[10] And once the disco closed, next thing we were back at the motel partying again, only by now, I was partying more than everybody else, if you get the idea.

D.2   Hedges

HEDGES resemble fillers in that both unnecessarily use up time or space in a message. But in addition, hedges soften a statement by showing that you feel uncertain or hesitant. Hedges are normal in everyday conversation, where you can't be running off every minute to check on facts and figures, and where you may not be sure, on the spur of the moment, how much responsibility you want to take for a particular statement. In writing, however, you do have a chance to check things out before you finish your paper, and you can make up your mind about what information you can rely on. It follows that you shouldn't hedge in your writing except where you really are in doubt and can't decide one way or the other. Otherwise, your writing will seem vague and wishy-washy, as well as loaded with extra words.

D.2.1   *Statement Hedges*

Statement hedges can be inserted almost anywhere to tone down a statement. These hedges include "kind of," "sort of," "more or less," "just about," "like," "pretty much," "basically," "in general," "by and large," "for the most part," "a little," "a bit," and so on. These hedges leave an escape route open if somebody challenges your statement. But if you hedge a lot, people will think you're too lazy to get the facts. Imagine that Rachel Carson had written not (14), but (14a):

(14)   The chemical warfare is never won, and all life is caught in its violent crossfire. ["The Obligation to Endure"]

(14a)   *Basically*, the chemical warfare is never won, and *just about* all life is *pretty much* caught in its violent crossfire.

Statement (14a) is so hedgy that we don't know whether we are expected to believe it or not. Rachel Carson is careful to hedge only where she feels that the facts call for it, as in:

(15)   The pollution is *for the most part* irrecoverable; the chain of evil it initiates not only in the world that must support life but in living tissues is *for the most part* irreversible.

She wants to make clear that *some* pollution can be reversed, but *most* of it can't.

Student writers put in many hedges they don't need. These statements would be better with the hedges taken out:

(16)   In many homes, TV *sort of* substitutes for family life.

(16a)   In many homes, TV substitutes for family life.

(17)   When the cease-fire was not ratified, it was *pretty much* a tense situation.

(17a)   When the cease-fire was not ratified, it was a tense situation.

(18)   *Love Story* is *basically* about how two people from different backgrounds get married.

(18a)   *Love Story* is about two people from different backgrounds who get married.

You can take almost any statement and stick hedges in it. Most of them are useless, or even annoying, as we see from (14a). Sometimes, though, a hedge serves a good purpose:

(19)   Einstein's theory is *basically* concerned with the relativity of quantities like speed and mass.

(20)   *In general*, Americans are anxious about the future.

(21)   The university's policies on student parking privileges are *somewhat* unfair.

Statement (19) offers only the "basics" about an extremely complex theory; (20) is true only for Americans "in general," not for every single citizen; (21) tells us that the policies are "somewhat," but not totally, unfair. In each case, the hedge shows that the writer is trying to be precise, not just to avoid the issue.

Some hedges are used for pasting together the parts of the statement, such as: "is something that," "is one of the kind who," "is the kind of thing that," "is the sort of person who," and so on. These hedges are common in talk because they give you time to think about what you want to say next. In writing, you're usually better off leaving them out. Here are some statements that improve when we remove the hedges:

(22)   My roommate *is the kind of person who* worries about everything.

(22a)   My roommate worries about everything.

(23)   This vandalism *is the sort of thing that* should be severely punished.

(23a)   This vandalism should be severely punished.

(24)   A solar eclipse *is something that* doesn't happen every day.

(24a)   A solar eclipse doesn't happen every day.

Only rarely are such phrases useful. For instance, (25) is obviously a more likely statement than (25a)—

(25)   My brother-in-law *is the kind of person who* was criticized in the president's speech on tax evasion.

(25a)   My brother-in-law was criticized in the president's speech on tax evasion.

—because the speech wasn't directly about your brother-in-law, but about people who, like him, evade taxes.

In any case, when you do have a good reason to hedge, once is enough. (26) should have one hedge removed, as in (26a):

(26)   *Basically,* Americans are *pretty much* a nation of pioneers.

(26a)   Basically, Americans are a nation of pioneers.

One hedge is plenty to let people know that you're limiting your statement.

Again, the point isn't that you should *never* use hedges, but that you shouldn't hedge *too much* or do it on statements that *don't need it.*

4. EXERCISE *on telling useful statement hedges from useless ones*

Cross out the useless hedges and circle the useful ones.

Example:
   ~~By and large,~~ everybody is human, but a few people are (almost) perfect. [Reason: Everyone has to be "human," but "*almost* perfect" is as far as you can go.]

[1]   The sudden rise in violent crime is a little bit alarming.

[2]   When winter is over, spring is pretty certain to come.

[3]   New Mexico is a place that gets continual sunshine.

[4]   In general, human beings can't live forever.

[5]   Politicians are the sort of people who adapt to changing circumstances.

[6]   Southerners generally prefer a leisurely pace of life, by and large.

[7]   For the most part, people have to get by with jobs they don't like very well.

[8]   Jogging is something that will improve your health.

[9]   The new theory had become more or less accepted when it was abruptly proven wrong.

[10] This is one of those kinds of stereos that play quadrophonic sound, basically.

D.2.2 *Verb Hedges*

Verb hedges are like statement hedges, except that they are verbs and therefore are usually concerned with an event—why and how it happened, when it started or stopped, and so forth.

One common type of verb hedge indicates the EFFORTS or DECISIONS involved in something that happened. Instead of writing that someone *did* something, you write that someone "tended to," "decided to," "proceeded to," or "tried to" do it. The trouble is that if someone did something, it's plain that they *must* have tended to, decided to, proceeded to, or tried to. Unless the circumstances were unusual, the verb hedges don't add anything. The following statements say just as much with fewer words when the verb hedges are taken out:

(27)   In high school, I *tended to go* to football games on weekends.

(27a)   In high school, I *went* to football games on weekends.

(28)   In college, I *decided to stay* home more often.

(28a)   In college, I *stayed* home more often.

(29)   After we moved to Pittsburgh, we *proceeded to buy* a house.

(29a)   After we moved to Pittsburgh, we *bought* a house.

(30)   When the charges were brought, the suspect *tried to deny* them.

(30a)   When the charges were brought, the suspect *denied* them.

Like other hedges, verb hedges can be useful sometimes. You can say "tend to" if you mean that something happens often, but not always. If you want to say that most, but not all, people in a group do something, you can make a statement like (31), which says the same thing as (31a) in fewer words:

(31)   Politicians *tend to* make promises they have no intention of keeping.

(31a)   *Some* politicians, *though not all*, make promises they have no intention of keeping.

"Decide to" is helpful if you're more concerned with the decision (making up one's mind) then with the action (doing it), as in:

(32)   After a long dispute, the union *decided to* continue the negotiation.

"Proceed to" can be used when it's doubtful whether something would get done. One example is when a person does a thing in spite of obstacles or good reasons not to, as in:

(33)   Scientists believed that the light bulb was an impossible idea, but Edison *proceeded to* invent it all the same.

(34) Even after severe warnings, they *proceeded to* release the report.

"Try to" makes sense if the attempt failed or if we don't know the outcome, as in:

(35) The settlers *tried to* raise vegetables, but the climate was too dry.

(36) The city has been *trying to* raise the water rates for a long time.

Of course, one hedge is enough. Don't say (37), say (37a):

(37) *Mostly*, middle-aged people *tend to* dream of a better life.

(37a) Middle-aged people tend to dream of a better life.

Once again, we see that writers should use hedges only when they have a good reason for doing so.

5. EXERCISE *on telling useful verb hedges from useless ones*

Cross out the useless verb hedges and circle the useful ones. Be sure you have no more than one hedge on any statement. Make any other changes you need, such as "tended to do" → "did."

Example: tried
    After the elections, our congressman ~~proceeded to~~ (try) challenging the vote. But he had to admit defeat. [Reason: He only "tried challenging," so you need that hedge, but not the other one, "proceeded to."]

[1] In the morning, I proceed to get up and go to work early every day.

[2] Whenever there isn't much to do at the office, I tend to go home early.

[3] When the deal was mentioned, their broker tried to pretend he wasn't interested.

[4] My friends mostly tend to be named Susan or Scott.

[5] I've been trying to reach the office all day. It was very frustrating when I tended not to get through.

[6] Once he decided to enter the competition, he proceeded to train with a real effort.

[7] Some football coaches, though not all of them, tend to act like little dictators.

[8] The rains were so heavy that we didn't even try to harvest the wheat.

[9] She proceeded to sell the land for much less than its value.

[10] Even though they tended to fight all the time, they couldn't decide to get a divorce until three years later.

Another common type of verb hedge deals with BEGINNINGS and ENDINGS. Here, instead of saying that somebody (or something) *did* something, you'd say that they "started," "began," "ended up," or "wound up" doing it. One student got carried away writing (38), where (38a) would have been much better:

(38) The doctor *starts to* run home. His colleagues *start to* chase him. He *ends up* running as fast as he can toward his laboratory. Inside the laboratory, he *starts* preparing the formula.

(38a) The doctor runs home. His colleagues chase him. He runs as fast as he can toward his laboratory. Inside the laboratory, he prepares the formula.

Like other verb hedges, these too can be used for a good reason. You can use "start" or "begin" if something didn't get finished:

(39) We *started to* cook dinner, but the electricity went out.

(40) They were *beginning to* close the gates, but we got out just in time.

You can use "end up" or "wind up" when the event comes after a long or complicated development, as in:

(41) We hired a lawyer and fought it out in court, but we *ended up* paying the fine anyway.

(42) After all the votes were cast and counted up, the meeting *wound up* not having a majority for any of the proposals.

You have to know when beginnings and endings make a difference for what you're saying. If they don't, you don't need the verb hedges.

◼ 6. MORE EXERCISE *on telling useful verb hedges from useless ones*

Cross out the useless verb hedges and circle the useful ones. Be sure you have no more than one hedge on any statement. Make any other changes you need, such as "tended to do" → "did."

Example:

                                                got
After the law went into effect, we ~~started getting~~ a raise. But since we moved to a higher tax bracket too, we (ended up) earning about the same amount. [Reason: you "ended up" after a long and complicated process. But you didn't just "start getting" a raise—you got it.]

[1] The sun started to rise this morning in a clear blue sky, and it's ended up being a beautiful day.

[2]   The fullback proceeded to break through the opposing line, and began to rush for the goal line when he was violently stopped.

[3]   After we got engaged, she started telling the whole town about it.

[4]   The party was dull, so we wound up leaving early.

[5]   When it began to rain, everybody started running inside.

[6]   Just because sometimes I didn't tend to make it to the office on time, my boss started getting mad.

[7]   It was a hard battle, but we ended up winning by one run.

[8]   As the soldiers began to arrive, the protesters proceeded to disappear into the crowd.

[9]   I always wind up having to wash the dishes at our house.

[10] The riot ended as suddenly as it had begun.

D.2.3   *Opinion Hedges*

Opinion hedges plainly identify a statement as the writer's personal opinion, rather than as a generally accepted fact. These hedges include "I guess," "I think," "I suppose," "I imagine," "I feel," "in my opinion," "it's my belief that," "it seems to me that," "if you ask me," "the way I see it," "as far as I'm concerned," and so on. Here, too, you should be careful to use a hedge only when you need it. If you say something, people normally assume that it's your opinion, and that you believe it. So you'll want to hedge only if your statement is personal or controversial, for instance:

(43)   *It's always been my opinion that* patience is the most valuable quality a person can have.

(44)   *It seems to me that* money is totally unimportant.

(45)   *I feel* life isn't worth living.

But there's no point in hedging a statement that nobody would be likely to argue with. These statements work better without the hedges:

(46)   *In my opinion,* modern society is very complex.

(46a) Modern society is very complex.

(47)   *It's my belief that* war wastes human lives.

(47a) War wastes human lives.

You should follow the same policy for using "seem" and "appear." If you're fairly sure about your statement, you'll do better to leave the hedges out, as in:

(48) Inflation *seems* to eat away at people's buying power.

(48a) Inflation eats away at people's buying power.

(49) The sunny climate *appears* to attract people to Arizona.

(49a) The sunny climate attracts people to Arizona.

However, when you want to let people know that you're just judging by appearances, hedges are helpful, as in:

(50) Vermont voters *seem* to be voting against their own best interests this time.

(51) Public schools *appear* to have lost touch with reality.

Here, too, one hedge is plenty. Don't say:

(50a) It *appears* that Vermont voters *seem* to be voting against their own best interests this time.

The same conditions apply to words like "apparently," "seemingly," and "it looks like."

7. EXERCISE *on telling useful opinion hedges from useless ones*

Cross out the useless verb hedges and circle the useful ones. Be sure you have only one hedge on any statement. Make any other changes you need, such as "seems to be" → "is."

Example: looks like
    The sun ~~seems to~~ (look like) it's rising and setting, but actually, the earth is revolving. [Reason: we are dealing with mere appearances, but one hedge is enough.]

[1] Their whole situation seemed to be under control, but it was really about to blow up.

[2] In my opinion, you should be allowed to marry more than one person at a time.

[3] I guess nobody seems to live forever.

[4] Though we're only in the first half, it looks like the challenger appears to be winning the fight.

[5] I think people should stand on their heads every day to relieve tension.

[6] It seems to me that if we pollute the whole world, we'll be in serious trouble.

[7] From the way he's acting, I imagine his attitude has apparently improved.

[8] If you ask me, we'll win the title next year, I'd say.

[9] Time never stands still, I suppose.

[10] The way I see it, no human being is the height of perfection.

No matter what kind of hedges you're dealing with—statement hedges, verb hedges, opinion hedges—the point is the same. Use them sparingly, and only when you want to let people know that you're being precise or uncertain. Otherwise, your writing will look wordy, vague, and wishy-washy.

8. QUIZ *on hedges*

Cross out the useless verb hedges and circle the useful ones. Then rewrite the statements. Make any other changes you need, such as "tended to do" → "did." Be sure you have no more than one hedge on any statement.

Example:
> Windsurfing ~~is a thing that I guess~~ I never (tried) to do. ~~It seems like~~ I never had a good opportunity to learn how. But ~~I suppose~~ I would like to learn if ~~there was a situation where someone who was~~ a good teacher was available.

You could fix it this way:
> I never tried windsurfing, because I never had a good opportunity to learn how. But I would like to learn if a good teacher was available.

[1] As I see it, not everyone's life is the same. Life seems to offer many opportunities which I think should not be ignored. But I guess some people do appear to ignore them.

[2] Both the United States and the Soviet Union tried to put a human into space. They started building enormous rockets. Eventually, the U.S. ended up launching a space shuttle to place useful equipment in space for other projects.

[3] When the rocket was ready, the control tower proceeded to run the countdown. After that, the rocket started to take off. Its flight lasted three minutes, and then it began to descend. It ended up landing just two minutes later. The whole time it was in the air, it tended to be slower than planned.

[4] Filing an income tax return is one of those things that I basically don't enjoy doing. It seems like I always tend to wind up filing it right on the very last day. Figuring the deductions is something that I more or less detest. I never seem to know exactly how much I can claim. I suppose this kind of worry is what makes me nervous when I start to file my return.

[5]　The future of today's college graduates seems uncertain. Many jobs are apparently starting to disappear, you know. In my opinion, a college degree is not something that makes a wise investment.

[6]　Since I've been in college, I get the impression that I tend to be pretty tired most of the time. I guess this all might have something to do with the fact that I don't sleep too much. Basically, I always seem to have things I think are more important or fun to be doing than lying around snoring all night, if you know what I mean.

[7]　Once in a great while, it seems as if the world can't last any longer. The human race appears to have lost all its incentives and motivations. Yet somebody ends up finding a way out after all. Both scientists and philosophers are people who discover these solutions.

[8]　Parallel parking is the thing that is the hardest when you learn to drive. If you ask me, cars just aren't designed the way they should be. With all our technology, it seems to me that we could start inventing a way to make a car go straight sideways. Parallel parking is something that can go wrong in so many different ways that it's pretty nearly hopeless.

[9]　Disco music is one of those things that changes its style frequently. I'm the sort of person to stay in touch with the latest fashions. So needless to say, I usually end up buying a huge amount of records, if you see what I'm saying.

[10]　My philosophy of life is a thing I have developed in the last four years. I believe a good deed is a thing that is its own reward, even if nobody begins to appreciate it.

☐ 9. REVIEW QUIZ on hedges

Same instructions as on the previous quiz.

[1]　As the party went on and on, I guess I sort of passed out, like for real. The next thing I knew it was morning. And there was my friend who was trying to tell me to start getting up.

[2]　I began to get up and try to pull myself together. I need hardly say that that was a thing I had a hard time doing, seeing as how I was so wasted from the night before.

[3]　We sort of kicked the girls out and told them to meet us at the beach or whatever. As far as I was concerned, it was all their fault that I was in that kind of condition at what I thought was altogether the wrong time.

[4]　We proceeded to pile into the car, but I was still sort of groggy and half asleep. The whole way out to the beach I tended to be almost asleep at the wheel.

[5] I pretty well knew for sure I wasn't in the kind of shape that you should be in when you're going to be in a water-skiing tournament.

[6] I began to picture myself doing things like falling on my stomach as soon as the boat started to move. Or maybe it would be something worse, like not being really able to stand up on the skis at all, or something like that.

[7] No sooner had we arrived than the wind started to get stronger. It seemed almost like the whole world must have been in a plot against me.

[8] I wound up drinking several cups of strong coffee. That was something that should have sobered me up. It did do that, but it also proceeded to make my nerves ten times worse than the way they were before.

[9] I turned out to be first in line and before I had any kind of a chance to get prepared or anything, I was starting to take off toward this big old ski jump that seemed to look like a mountain or something.

[10] I proceeded to go up it at some speed that must have been way too fast, it seemed like. My mind must have just about switched off then, because all I remember now is a crowd of all these people telling me afterwards I'd set some kind of a record for that ski jump.

D.3 Restating

RESTATING is another cause of extra words. When you're talking, you often go back over the things you've already said in order to remind yourself and your listeners of what you're talking about and to make sure you're getting your point across. But when you're writing, you don't need to restate so much, because the writing is preserved on paper and anybody who needs a reminder can reread it. So when you're writing, you should make sure you aren't restating too much.

In extreme cases, students forget what they're already written and write it again in exactly the same words:

(52) *At the party*, Chaplin and the girl spend all their time together *at the party*.

(53) Nuclear energy is a power source *for* which people pay *for* with their lives.

Less extreme, but still very tiresome, are cases where the first part of each statement is taken up with reminding us what was said in the previous statement:

(54) Once there lived a hero named *Charlie*. *Charlie* was your average poor person and he *worked* in a restaurant. After *working in the restaurant* for a while Charlie was able to get a *one-hour break*. On his *hour break* Charlie took his dog and went for a *walk*. While *walking* he saw a man and woman fighting. [57 words]

Reading this is like trying to move ahead by taking two steps forward, then one step backward. There's no need for so many reminders. The student should have written something more like:

> (54a) Once there lived a hero named Charlie, your average poor person, who worked in a restaurant. He was able to get a one-hour break. He took his dog and went for a walk. Soon he saw a man and woman fighting. [43 words]

Though you might not be aware of your restatements when you're writing the first draft, watch for them when you're revising. Your main strategy is:

TAKE OUT THE DUPLICATIONS OR EMPTY WORDS AND KEEP THE KEY WORDS.

Duplications are the parts that cover the same things you said before. **Empty words** are those that don't say much to begin with, like "something," "thing," "this," and so on. **Key words** are the ones that add something new or important. If you had to send a message with the least number of words possible, you'd pick the key words; for (52) and (53) you might get:

> (52a) party...Chaplin...girl...all time together

> (53a) Nuclear energy...power source...people pay for with lives

Now suppose you had to fix the restatements in (55):

> (55) You might spend a lot of time in court to resolve a situation. Sometimes, just talking face-to-face could resolve the situation. It's senseless going to court in a case like that.

The words "resolve the situation" are an obvious duplication. "A case like that" is a good example of empty words. If we leave the first statement as is, then "just talking face-to-face" and "It's senseless" are the key words in the next statements, that is, the words that really add something. So you could fix the passage like this:

> (55a) *It's senseless* to spend a lot of time in court when *just talking face-to-face* could resolve the situation.

You might need to experiment with various ways of saying something until you find one where you're not repeating yourself. Although you don't need to struggle for the absolute minimum of words, you should avoid long or obvious restatings and focus on the key words.

10. QUIZ *on not restating things*

Circle the key words. Then rewrite so that you don't restate so many things.

Example:

In reply to your question, I would say that it is not an easy question to find a reply for. It's a very hard question to answer. I should warn you about that right away.

You could fix it this way:

I should warn you right away that your question is very hard to answer.

[1] Many people in today's society are people who prefer a casual life style for today.

[2] Right away, a letter was sent without delay. Soon after the letter was sent, a telegram arrived with the reply.

[3] Those trees don't look healthy. You have sick trees in your yard, I'd say. There's something the matter with them. Call a tree surgeon to see what's the matter. You should do it soon.

[4] The bank refused the money with which we wanted to buy the house with. We were disappointed that they refused the money.

[5] Service will be terminated if the bill is not paid by the date shown on the bill for terminating service. This will happen immediately.

[6] Now and then, the secretary sometimes forgets to pass along or relay messages.

[7] The astronauts landed on the moon. Once they were on the moon, they set up an emergency station. As soon as the emergency station was set up, they radioed to all nearby spacecraft.

[8] The problems will be solved if we can carry out our new methods for solving our problems.

[9] When you're in the army, it's important to appreciate what it means to be in the army. Army personnel have special responsibilities which the army expects them to assume.

[10] The repairs were very expensive and cost a lot of money. The mechanic said our car wasn't in good condition—in fact, it was in bad condition. Even so, the size of the bill surprised and astonished us.

11. REVIEW QUIZ *on not restating things*

Same instructions as on the previous quiz.

[1] To enjoy scuba diving, you must be someone who can adapt to the environment and can change to fit the circumstances.

[2] You should look for surprises and watch for the unexpected. It's essential that you do this.

[3] The initial check-out is the procedure when you check all your equipment out to see that it's in good working order and it's all okay. The check-out is a very important procedure.

[4] On my first real dive the sensations I remember most were the feelings of fear. I was so scared, my mood was bordering on panic. I vividly remember that.

[5] Not only did the weight of the wetsuit hinder movement, there was also the weight of the other equipment besides the wetsuit to get in the way of my movement.

[6] The air tanks were very heavy, and also my buoyancy control device was also heavy, the more so as I had a brick inside it to make me heavier going down. That added some weight.

[7] The visibility under water was only five to ten feet, so I couldn't see any farther than five to ten feet.

[8] That visibility is good for New Jersey coastal waters but it was not good if you're used to the clear waters of the diving school, where the visibility is much better.

[9] Even though I was told over and over again not to get scared or frightened, fear is the thing that came over me in spite of what they'd told me.

[10] We checked out the wetsuits and we checked out all the equipment until there was nothing left to check and we were all finished and it was time to head for the water.

Now let's have a closer look at two kinds of restatements: REPEATED WORDS (the same words used over again) and REPEATED CONTENT (same meaning stated over again, but in different words). Since both kinds are common in everyday talk, you should be on your guard against them in your writing.

D.4 Repeated Words

REPEATED WORDS are easy to spot because the writer keeps using the same words. Frequent, obvious repetitions soon get irritating for readers.

The first thing you can do to fix this problem is to mark all the repeated words. Then you can try one of these three methods:

1. OMIT the repeats—that is, simply leave them out.
2. VARY the repeats—that is, say the same thing in a different way.

3. STREAMLINE the passage—that is, fix it to say the thing only once, and save on words.

Of these three, *omitting* the repeats is the easiest method:

(56) Many *nurses* are given boring *nursing* duties in their *nursing* school training.

(56a) Many nurses are given boring duties in their training.

(57) There are eight *regions* and each of these *regions* has a *regional* manager.

(57a) There are eight regions and each has a manager.

Varying repeats is fairly easy if you can find good substitutes for your repeated words, as in:

(56) Many *nurses* are given boring *nursing* duties in their *nursing* school training.

(56b) Many *nurses* are given boring *hospital* duties in their *professional* training.

(57) There are eight *regions* and each of these *regions* has a *regional* manager.

(57b) There are eight *regions* and each of these *areas* has a *local* manager.

Varying is a good method when you can't just omit the words you'd repeated. You can vary short, common words too, such as "go" in (58) and "very" in (59):

(58) The day *goes* better if you *go* for a swim before you *go* off to work.

(58a) The day *goes* better if you *take* a swim before you *leave* for work.

(59) The girl, who was *very* rich, was *very* grateful and asked the poor man to come to her party. He accepted, which made her boyfriend *very* mad.

(59a) The girl, who was *very* rich, was *extremely* grateful and asked the poor man to come to her party. He accepted, which made her boyfriend *furious*.

One common kind of substitute is the PRONOUN—which we'll be talking more about later in this chapter (see pages 48–52 and 54–60). In (60), "our team doesn't win the game" can be varied with "it doesn't":

(60) Sometimes our team wins the game, and *sometimes our team doesn't win the game*. My whole family goes into severe depression when *our team doesn't win the game*.

(60a) Sometimes our team wins the game, and sometimes *it doesn't*. My whole family goes into severe depression when *it doesn't*.

Streamlining isn't quite so simple as the other two methods, but it's often the best. For instance, when you stop to think about (60), you can say the same thing with fewer words than we used in (60a). The whole first statement doesn't tell us much, since every team wins sometimes and doesn't win other times. So why not streamline the passage down to the essentials? That way, "our team wins" only has to be said once:

(60b)   My whole family goes into severe depression when *our team doesn't win.*

If you streamlined (57), about "regional managers," you might get (57c):

(57)   There are eight *regions* and each *region* has a *regional* manager and three assistant *regional* managers.

(57c)   Each one of eight regions has its own manager.

Or take (61), which is written on a sign posted on a pier in Florida. You don't have to say something is "illegal" if you warn people they'll be "fined" for doing it. So you could streamline the statement (and make a smaller sign), as in (61a):

(61)   Fishing sharks off the pier is illegal. Anyone who fishes sharks off the pier will be fined.

(61a)   Fishing sharks off the pier is punishable by a fine.

In general, if you can cut out words that don't add any meaning to your statement, that's all to the good.

It's tricky when you'd have to say things in unusual ways in order to avoid repeats. In (62), the problem is how to get rid of two out of the three "park" words. You could omit the word "parking" in "parking space," since cars wouldn't normally be "parked" in any other kind of space. Then, you can vary one of the other two "park" words, as in (62a) and (62b).

(62)   We *parked* our car in the nearest *parking* space to the city *park.*

(62a)   We *left* our car in the nearest *space* to the city *park.*

(62b)   We *parked* our car in the nearest *space* to the city *recreation grounds.*

There's always another way to say something, but don't go too far out of your way. "Recreation grounds," for instance, is a little showy if all you've got is some grass, four trees, and a bench. Even a repeat is usually better than a weird or confusing replacement. For example, if you've said "man" three times in (63), changes like the ones in (63a) are clumsy and confusing. Omitting and streamlining is much neater, as in (63b).

(63)   The society woman, grateful to the *man,* invited the *man* to a party at her mansion. The *man* accepted.

(63a)   The society woman, grateful to the *man*, invited the *hero* to a party at her mansion. The *protagonist of our story* accepted.

(63b)   The grateful society woman invited the *man* to a party at her mansion, and *he* accepted.

Still, there are times when avoiding repeats really makes a big difference. You should try not to repeat the *same word* when it has a *different meaning* with each use. In such cases, you'll do better to vary the word:

(64)   There are three places you could make a *right* turn. Watch for the *right* place *right* before you pass the yellow farmhouse on the *right*. [confusing]

(64a)   There are three places you could make a *right* turn. Watch for the *correct* place *directly* before you pass the yellow farmhouse on the *right*. [much clearer]

(65)   The *mean* rate of consumption is not a good *means* for telling what these figures *mean* in each case. [confusing]

(65a)   The *average* rate of consumption is not a good *basis* for telling what these figures *mean* in each case. [much clearer]

(66)   You won't be able to *place* your product in the community if you don't *place* your store in a commercially good *place* in the first *place*. [confusing]

(66a)   You won't be able to *market* your product in the community if you don't *open* your store in a commercially good *location* in the first *place*. [much clearer]

Avoiding confusing repeats means being considerate of whoever is supposed to read it. The point is not whether readers can puzzle out your statement, but whether you ought to put them to the extra trouble involved in doing so.

Though repeats can be unnecessary and irritating, you will have to use them when only one word will do the job. For example, **scientific and technical writing** calls for the **special terms** that are established and accepted in a particular field (see also Chapter 3, Section A.2.2). If you're writing a technical manual, you'll want to stick to your special terms, as in:

(67)   PEEK *returns* the *numerical* code stored at a certain *location*. At most *locations*, PEEK only *returns* a *numerical* value. [*The Applesoft Tutorial*]

"Return," "location," and "numerical" have special technical meanings in computer science, and "PEEK" is a command in the Applesoft Basic language for accessing the computer's memory. You can't substitute other words just to keep from repeating yourself. The result would be very strange:

(67a)   PEEK *returns* the *numerical* code stored at a certain *location*. At most *places*, LOOK only *brings back* a *mathematical* value.

This version is hard to follow. Conveying the message depends on sticking to the same technical terms all the way through. Here are some more examples from technical instructions:

(68) On the BMW 3.0, the early models have *carburetors* and the later models have *fuel injection*. If your engine has a *carburetor*, you should install the standard *emissions controls*. Engines with *fuel injection* require modified *emissions controls* in some states.

(69) If your *amplifier* has one *set of inputs* for *auxiliary*, connect the first tape deck to the tape monitor input and the second one to *auxiliary* 1. If your *amplifier* has two *sets of inputs* for *auxiliary*, connect the first deck to *auxiliary* 1 and the second one to *auxiliary* 2.

Repeats like these are not at all like the unnecessary repeats of everyday words like "right" in (64).

▮ 12. QUIZ *on repeated words*

Circle the repeated words and then try to omit, vary, or streamline. Leave repeats of special or technical terms as they are.

Example:
> In baseball you have the (major) (leagues) and the (minor) (leagues). The (major) (leagues) get all the good players from the (minor) (leagues).

You could fix it this way:
> In baseball the major leagues get all the good players from the minor leagues.

[1] Some colleges are better than your college, such as my father's college.

[2] It doesn't matter if you use nickle cadmium batteries or alkaline batteries to run the tape player. But only nickle cadmium batteries can be recharged.

[3] The service people aren't very punctual when they service people.

[4] I asked the secretary to finish typing the letter as soon as possible. I mailed the letter as soon as she finished typing it.

[5] In the computer industry, you have three types of computers. These three types of computers go from small to large. The smallest computers are the micro-computers. After that you have mini-computers. The biggest computers are the mainframe computers.

[6] The fire starts blazing and is allowed to blaze wildly until we bring it down to a small blaze.

[7] The girl is deeply grateful for Chaplin's rescue and invites him to her party. This causes deep anger and jealousy to the girl's former escort. The jealous escort vows to get revenge.

[8] Watch what my watch does when I press the button. The alarm sounds with a really alarming sound.

[9] Our old disk drive used floppy disks. Our new disk drive uses rigid disks. A floppy-disk drive is much cheaper, but a rigid disk drive is much faster.

[10] In our school, when the teacher and the students disagree, the teacher always wins the disagreement, even if the students are right and the teacher is wrong.

⬜ 13. REVIEW QUIZ *on repeated words*

Same instructions as on the previous quiz.

[1] There were several things I had to think about. I had to think about the air pressure in my oxygen tank. I had to think about the amount of weight in my buoyancy control device. And I had to think about the depth of the water where I was diving.

[2] The inlet was not like the pool at diving school, because the inlet was darker, deeper, and more dangerous than the pool was at diving school.

[3] Despite the weight pulling down, I had to struggle to stay down the whole way down to the bottom.

[4] As we went deeper I did my best to breathe deeply, but my feeling of gloom got deeper and deeper.

[5] Soon the panic I was feeling changed into a feeling of excitement, and I could feel my whole outlook change for the better.

[6] I began to look around at the plants and the fish around me, and I began to swim around.

[7] It was one of the most exciting experiences I have ever experienced, and probably the most exciting experience in my life.

[8] I had never seen so many kinds of fish in so many different colors and in so many different shapes and sizes.

[9] The fish weren't about to bother me as long as I wasn't about to bother them. Besides, I had no reason to bother them.

[10] The first dive got better and better. And each dive after the first dive got better than the dive before it. The dives just kept getting better.

D.5   Repeated Content

The other main way of restating things is **REPEATING CONTENT**—that is, saying the same meaning over again in different words. When you talk, you often repeat the content in order to make sure you've gotten your point across and to keep the topic in mind. This same tendency can be a disadvantage in writing, where you're supposed to keep working until your point is clear enough when you say it only once. After all, you have the text down on paper to remind your readers of what you're writing about. To test for repeated content, ask yourself whether a statement—or a part of a statement—adds anything to what is already known at that point. In (70), for example, it's obvious that anyone who's "poor" is "not very rich," so let's take out one part:

(70)   The busboy was not very rich—as a matter of fact, he was poor.

(70a)   The busboy was poor.

In (71), anybody who "gets very drunk" has probably "had a lot to drink," and we can streamline the statement:

(71)   Charlie proceeded to have a lot to drink. He got very drunk.

(71a)   Charlie got very drunk.

Readers don't enjoy being told the same things over and over. Compare some passages from students' papers with their streamlined versions:

(72)   These new machines are very complicated and confusing, *and they are hard to figure out.*

(72a)   These new machines are very complicated and confusing.

(73)   You often don't know what the teacher wants *in many cases.*

(73a)   You often don't know what the teacher wants.

(74)   In the old days, we *used to* go to football games a lot more often *back then.*

(74a)   In the old days, we went to football games a lot more often.

(75)   In 1982, we found the answer, *settled the question,* and *solved the problem.*

(75a)   In 1982, we solved the problem.

In each passage, the italicized words say something anybody could assume from the rest of the statement. Again, test by asking yourself whether anything is being added to what's already been said. In (72), "complicated and confusing machines" are of course "hard to figure out." In (73), whatever happens "often" must be true "in many cases." In (74), something that took place "in the old days" obviously "used to" go on "back then." In (75), "finding the answer" is much the same as "settling the question" or "solving the problem." So the students got rid of all the repeated content.

14. QUIZ *on repeated content*

Circle the repeated content and then streamline the statements.

Example:

It (often) happens that students (frequently) put off their homework until the (last minute). They (wait to do the assignment) until (they can't wait any longer). When the (last minute) comes, they have to do a rush job.

You could fix it like this:

Students frequently put off their homework until the last minute and then have to do a rush job.

[1]   You could begin your inquiry by asking the opinions of the dorm residents and trying to find out what they think for a start.

[2]   When the building was finished, we were terribly glad it was all over and done with, and we didn't have to do anything more.

[3].   If you wish to come in person and attend the meeting yourself, your presence there will be gratefully appreciated.

[4]   Anyone causing loud disturbances or making noise in the dorms will be subject to having to pay a monetary fine.

[5]   Our contemporaries of today tend to suffer from a frequent compulsion that often forces them, against their will, to feel worried and anxious.

[6]   This car is engineered from components with high standards. All its parts are of high quality.

[7]   The whole difficulty with our entire problem is that some state employees have a desire to want to try to get by without working hard.

[8]   She constantly follows the latest fashions in clothes and always dresses right in style.

[9]   We took our places at the table and sat down and proceeded to enjoy the banquet. We really liked the meal. It was very good. As a matter of fact, it was splendid.

[10] The last three sports events take place at the same time and are therefore simultaneous. So you can't participate in all three at once. I don't see how you could, with them all going on side by side.

15. REVIEW QUIZ *on repeated content*

Circle the repeated content and then streamline the statements.

[1]   That summer, I made up my mind and came to a decision to join a summer farm camp in England. It lasted from June through August. It took all summer.

[2] It was located near a little tiny town and situated in the midst of a beautiful and lovely countryside.

[3] The quarters and lodgings where we were going to stay were not exactly fancy. In fact, they were a primitive place to be lodged.

[4] The rooms are so small that there isn't any place to put any of your things or belongings. You can't store anything anyplace in there.

[5] The daily routine is very similar from one day to the next, and there isn't a lot of variety each day. Everything stays the same.

[6] It was hard to wake up in the morning and get out of bed that early. I had a terrible time getting going at that hour.

[7] Then I got to the showers and took a shower and got clean. Next, I got my clothes on and got dressed.

[8] The food isn't the greatest. In fact, it's so terrible, you can hardly eat it. It's that bad. And I do mean bad.

[9] Some days I decided it was better to do without, that is, to go hungry and not eat anything by passing up breakfast altogether.

[10] The days are devoted to berry picking. That means filling your bucket full of berries while you gather as many berries as you can, and eat as many berries as you can.

General quiz

on fillers, hedges, repeated words, and repeated content

16.

▼

We have now gone over the first major influence of talking habits on writing—the tendency to use **extra words**. You should be able to fix problems with **fillers**, **hedges**, **repeated words**, and **repeated content**. In the following quiz, circle the extra words of all kinds and rewrite the statements so as to omit, vary, or streamline.

Example:

It is up to each team member to use his best capacities and abilities to do his job. You know, the game cannot be won by ten guys doing their job. It takes all eleven men doing what they are expected to do, to win the game. That's what I think.

You could fix it like this:

Each of the eleven team members must use his best abilities to do his job if the team is to win the game.

[1]   Well, maybe the test will be easy and maybe the test will be hard. Anyway, we'll know tomorrow when we go over to campus and get there. We'll find out how hard or easy it is.

[2]   I knew somebody was in the yard, because I could hear someone making sounds out there. There were these noises I kept on hearing, you see, like a person moving around in the dark. That's how it seemed.

[3]   In recent races run over the last few seasons, I'd say our runners have been running some really good races, if you know what I mean.

[4]   If you fail to receive by mail a letter of notification from us or our offices

within the space of a period of two weeks' time, you should be sure that you try to contact us with an inquiry.

[5]   Not long ago, we found out something, well actually, yesterday. We found out where you write in order to get on national mailing lists. We got the address you write to.

[6]   Soon the personnel belonging to the work crew began to arrive and started to clear the area of the place of debris. When the debris was cleared away, the work crew left and went home.

[7]   In reference to this university it must be said that it sort of has an image as if it is very competitive in sports, if you ask me.

[8]   When I was in high school, it seemed like it didn't often happen in those days that we had to write very many papers back then, well, at least not·a lot anyhow.

[9]   To borrow a book, look up its number, locate the book on the shelf, take the book to the main desk, fill out the book borrowing card with the book's title and number, and show your book borrower's permit.

[10] The boss proceeded to initiate an inquiry asking about the nature of the problem that was causing us trouble and creating the difficulties we were encountering.

Back-up general quiz
on fillers, hedges, repeated words, and repeated content

17.
▼

Same instructions as on the previous quiz.

[1] In my opinion, the hobby that is the one I consider to be the most exciting hobby is dove hunting, I think.

[2] It's something that's very important for people in today's modern world to have a sport which makes it possible for them to escape the monotony and sameness of their everyday routines in daily life.

[3] Anyhow, to get started, you begin by buying a hunting license, purchasing some boxes of ammunition, and acquiring a shotgun.

[4] To hunt down a hearty meal of dove meat, the dove hunter must constantly be alert and watchful at all times, keeping his eyes open and not overlooking anything, you see.

[5] An example of how patient you have to be is the way that you have to sit patiently all day, well for several hours anyway, in the hot sun without even seeing one dove, let alone a whole flock of doves.

[6] All at once, ten doves suddenly fly overhead and you begin to take aim, pull the trigger, and shoot, and you find out you've ended up shooting two doves that come falling out of the sky and hit the ground, landing about a hundred feet away, more or less.

[7] Okay now, doves have come up with ways and means of survival in order to stay alive and not be hunted down by dove hunters who are out to kill them.

[8] You see, the doves change their flying habits and switch over from flying in even, closed ranks over to flying in uneven, open ranks.

[9] One of the kinds of things that it's important for a dove hunter to remember is to be sure that you hunt with another experienced hunter who's been hunting a lot.

[10] Well, a hunter who isn't the kind that has a lot of experience will probably end up shooting in your direction, and that isn't exactly the thing you want to have happen to you and spoil your day or even spoil you. It just isn't, that's all.

■ E. INCONSISTENT STATEMENTS

A statement is INCONSISTENT if the choices a writer makes don't fit with each other. Everyday conversation has many inconsistent statements, but hardly anyone notices or worries about them. We saw some of them in the transcribed samples on pages 2–4, for instance:

(1a) you'll see two..a sign

(1b) there's the hospital right..the front of it is on the right

If you pay close attention to exactly what people say, you'll notice that their statements don't always make complete sense. One student made an announcement (76) in class, when she meant to say (76a):

(76) Our teacher's mother passed away and won't be with us this evening.

(76a) Our teacher's mother passed away and *he* won't be with us this evening.

As usual, the problem isn't so bad in casual conversation, where people overlook these slip-ups as long as the sense can be figured out. When you write, however, you're expected to check that you've been consistent before the paper gets to its readers. The readers can probably guess what you really meant to say; but if you say things carelessly, you still look dumb for having suggested something you didn't mean.

E.1 Leaving Things Out—Confusing One Thing with Another—Putting Things Together the Wrong Way

Since most writers produce at least a few inconsistent statements, we'll be looking at some common types and at some ways to fix them. Statements can be inconsistent when you LEAVE SOMETHING OUT. Newspaper headline writers sometimes have this trouble:

(77) New Jersey to Be Moved [*Johnstown* (Pa.) *Tribune-Democrat*, July 25, 1981]

(78) Murder Delayed [*Daily Times and Chronicle*, Aug. 1, 1980]

To fix these, you have to figure out what's missing and put it back in, for instance:

(77a) New Jersey *Oil Refinery* to Be Moved

(78a) Murder *Trial* Delayed

You may have to make a guess about what the missing item should be.

Statements can also be inconsistent when you CONFUSE ONE THING WITH ANOTHER. Words that look similar get mixed up, as in these newspaper items:

(79) Reverend Jones Will Be *Concentrated* Today [*Lancaster* (Pa.) *Intelligencer Journal*, Sept. 10, 1977]

(80) The senate introduced a bill that would require *restrooms* to post a sign if they serve oleomargarine. [UPI broadcast wire]

To fix these, you have to change the mistaken words to the right ones:

(79a) Reverend Jones Will Be *Consecrated* Today

(80a) The senate introduced a bill that would require *restaurants* to post a sign if they serve oleomargarine.

Or, statements can be inconsistent when you PUT THINGS TOGETHER THE WRONG WAY. Students wrote that a "crime" got "executed" (81) and that an "accident" got "hospitalized" (82):

(81) Even if the person did not commit the crime, it has been known to be unfairly convicted and executed.

(82) The accident severely injured several people and had to be hospitalized.

To fix these, clear up who did what:

(81a) Even a person who did not commit the crime has been known to be unfairly convicted and executed.

(82a) The accident severely injured several people and they had to be hospitalized.

Let's see if you can fix a few samples yourself.

18. EXERCISE *on fixing inconsistent statements*

Here are some more inconsistent statements. Make your best guess about what's missing, confused, or put together wrong. Then fix it.

[1] Museums Utilizing TV to Attack Visitors [*Fort Worth Star-Telegram*, Feb. 7, 1981]

[2] Power Outrage Hits [*Silver City* (Nev.) *Daily Press*, Dec. 22, 1979]

[3] In the long run, the metric system will simplify our lies. [*Tulsa World*, April 28, 1977]

[4] Mental Health Prevention Begins with Children [*Valley News-Tribune*, May 9, 1978]

[5] If you live in the dorms, you hear cars starting and running through the halls at all hours.

[6] Nicaragua Sets Goal to Wipe Out Literacy [*Boston Globe*, Oct. 1, 1979]

[7] Montreal police don't hesitate to use whatever laws they need to control morality in the city and prevent it from getting a foothold. [*Toronto Globe and Mail*, Sept. 21, 1977]

[8] Police Brutality Postponed [*Mishawaka* (Ind.) *Enterprise*, Oct. 1, 1981]

[9] Officials said Cynthia Hamann was in good condition, although she was examined at Memorial Hospital in Clarksville. [*Nashville Tennessean*, March 28, 1978]

[10] Any information leading to the arrest and conviction of persons making threatening telephone calls will be punished by law. [*Las Vegas Daily Optic*, Jan. 12, 1978]

E.2   Bad Placement

Another source of inconsistent statements is BAD PLACEMENT: putting words in the wrong place, so that the statement doesn't actually make sense, as in:

(83) After years of being lost under a pile of dust, Walter P. Stanley found all the old records of the Bangor Lions Club. [*Bangor* (Maine) *Daily News*, Jan. 20, 1978]

(84) Bound, gagged, and trussed up in a denim bag, with plugs in her ears and tape over her eyes, Cleveland teacher Linda L. Sharpe told yesterday how she was kidnapped to Florida. [*Cleveland Plain Dealer*, June 14, 1978]

Obviously, the "records," not Mr. Stanley, were "lost under a pile of dust" in (83); and Ms. Evans couldn't be "telling" her story while she was "bound, gagged, and trussed up in a denim bag" in (84). The writer should have put things in places where they fit together:

(83a) After years of being lost under a pile of dust, all the old records of the Bangor Lions Club were found by Walter P. Stanley.

(84a) Cleveland teacher Linda L. Sharpe told yesterday how she was kid-napped to Florida, bound, gagged, and trussed up in a denim bag, with plugs in her ears and tape over her eyes.

Some of the inconsistent statements students write result from shyness about using "I" or "you" in their writing. In fact, however, many good writers don't hesitate to say "I" or "you" when they need to. Certainly, it's better than going such a roundabout way as this:

(85)   Tennessee is a small state when travelling vertically.

(86)   My high school records were not considered for admission to college.

when you would make more sense if you said:

(85a)   Tennessee is a small state when *you travel* vertically through it.

(86a)   My high school records were not considered *when I applied* for admission to college.

Don't say lifeless objects did the things that were really done by people.

Some badly placed phrases are apparently intended to provide background and to set the scene. For example, students might begin a statement with an "-ing" phrase that indicates some location or circumstance, as in:

(87)   Soon after crossing the border, my stomach sickness got better.

(88)   Being a nice, fairly hard dirt road, I decided to do a couple of doughnuts.

Technically, though, an "-ing" phrase at the beginning of a statement goes with the **subject** of the sentence (on how to find the subject, see Chapter 2, Section B). The students wrote—although they didn't mean it—that the "stomach sickness crossed the border" (87) and that the writer himself was a "dirt road" (88). To fix these statements, you could give up the "-ing" word, as in (87a); or keep the "-ing" word, and fix the rest so that the phrase fits the subject, as in (88a) ("I" was "on" the "road"):

(87a)   Soon after *I crossed* the border, my stomach sickness got better.

(88a)   Being *on* a nice, fairly hard dirt road, I decided to do a couple of doughnuts.

It's natural to let a few inconsistent statements slip by once in a while. Though you can't always prevent them, you can fix them later by following simple techniques.

First,

READ BACK OVER YOUR WRITING
AFTER SOME TIME HAS PASSED.

When you no longer have your meaning so firmly in your mind, you are more likely to notice statements that don't strictly make sense.

Second, it helps to

ORGANIZE SCENES AND EVENTS
AROUND THE PEOPLE DOING THE ACTIONS,

even if you have to say "I" or "you." Otherwise, you may get landscapes (85) or parts of the body (87) running around on their own. For example, don't say (89)—say (89a) or (89b):

(89) Walking out on the football field, the booing of the other fans was now easily heard.

(89a) Walking out on the football field, *we* could easily hear the booing of the other fans.

(89b) As *we* were walking out on the football field, the booing of the other fans was now easily heard.

Paying attention to who's doing the actions helps to keep you from placing the wrong things together:

(90) Before being siphoned out of the tank, the engineers tested the fuel for safety.

(90a) Before *siphoning* out the fuel, the engineers tested it in the tank for safety.

(91) When totally disconnected, we have to use the neighbors' telephone.

(91a) When *our telephone* is totally disconnected, we have to use the neighbors'.

Third,

PUT THINGS NEXT TO EACH OTHER
THAT FIT TOGETHER.

Don't say (92) and (93)—say (92a) and (93a):

(92) They dumped all the dirty towels into *the bathtub they brought from the beach.*

(92a) They dumped into the bathtub *all the dirty towels they brought from the beach.*

(93) Texan accused of *killing local man to get hearing* [*Missoulian*, Sept. 22, 1978]

(93a) *Hearing is set for Texan* accused of killing local man

Finally,

DON'T MAKE THINGS TOO COMPLICATED.

You're likely to get mixed up yourself. The law officer who wrote (94) wouldn't have said something so silly if he or she had used simpler language, as in (94a):

(94) Any information leading to the arrest and conviction of persons making threatening telephone calls will be punished by law.

(94a) Persons making threatening telephone calls will be punished by law. We are requesting information that helps to arrest and convict such persons.

You shouldn't try to make things any more complicated than necessary. It's inconsiderate to your readers, and you're likely to get mixed up yourself.

⬛ 19. EXERCISE *on fixing inconsistencies due to bad placement*

Now try fixing some more inconsistent statements from newspapers and students' writings:

[1] Complaints About NBA Referees Growing Ugly [*Chicago Sun-Times*, May 23, 1979]

[2] After being tested on mice, Dr. Kline tried the protein on psychiatric patients.

[3] A hand grenade exploded on board a train, killing a soldier who was toying with it and two passengers. [*London Times*, March 27, 1982]

[4] With hearts pounding and fingers crossed, the rocket rose into the air.

[5] At the age of seven, my parents got divorced.

[6] While on vacation in Hawaii, our house was broken into.

[7] The adenoid is about the size of a pecan nut in childhood.

[8] They keep all reports of unsolved murders in the back office.

[9] The campus tour includes seeing the rare books famous people left behind when they died in the University Library.

[10] Mrs. J. Hawood Evans unearths the candelabra for the presentation doorway through which debutantes enter to be introduced from attic storage. [*Durham* (N.C.) *Morning Herald*, Dec. 25, 1977]

☐ 20. QUIZ *on inconsistent statements*

Revise the following statements so that they make complete sense. Remember: pay attention to the people doing the actions; put things next to each other that fit together; and don't make things too complicated.

[1]   In the control chair, the roar of the fire vibrated the pilot's body.

[2]   Vance's demanding tasks have kept him away from his family, which includes four daughters and a son, far more than he would like. [*Time*, April 24, 1978]

[3]   I had been driving for forty years when I fell asleep at the wheel and hit a tree.

[4]   When first discovered, Dr. Li could find no use for the protein.

[5]   The innkeeper is not responsible for any loss to a guest, not being a horse or live animal. [sign in an old Canadian hotel]

[6]   Huey Newton said he will testify at his trial on charges of killing a prostitute against his lawyer's advice. [*Cleveland Plain Dealer*, March 8, 1979]

[7]   You stand there with your fans backing you up along the sidelines.

[8]   While in first grade, my father insisted I should learn to read.

[9]   The photo shows a coffee service supported by chicken legs which belonged to Mrs. Abraham Lincoln. [Associated Press, April 2, 1980].

[10]   Crowds Rushing to See Pope Trample Six to Death [*Peoria* (Ill.) *Journal Star*, July 9, 1980]

☐ 21. REVIEW QUIZ *on inconsistent statements*

Same instructions as on the previous quiz.

[1]   Fish and Game Will Hold Annual Elections [*Berkshire* (Mass.) *Courier*, Dec. 24, 1974]

[2]   Patrolman Sarno admitted striking a man who later died at least once while quieting a public disturbance. [*Woodbridge* (N.J.) *News Tribune*, Jan. 21, 1976]

[3]   For the President or other leaders, the FBI has plans to handle any future assassination. [*Wenatchee* (Wash.) *World*, Nov. 11, 1978]

[4] Cure Is Sought for Rural Health [*Kansas City Star*, Dec. 2, 1976]

[5] Accused Rapist Finds God in Jail [*San Antonio News*, Nov. 20, 1975]

[6] Driving in a heavy cloudburst, a flash of lightning struck a tree near the road.

[7] A baseball game has the goal of scoring more runs.

[8] After getting a good hit, the bases are run all round the field and home again.

[9] Four outside pitches go to first base with no hit.

[10] A fielder catching a fly ball does not need to be thrown to first base.

■ F. DOUBTFUL STATEMENTS

A DOUBTFUL STATEMENT is one that can be understood in two or more conflicting ways. These mixups often happen by accident. You may turn out saying something ridiculous that you never meant, as in:

(96) Utah Girl Does Well in Dog Shows [*Salt Lake Tribune*, Dec. 30, 1981]

(97) Pullman Girl Tops Swine Division [*Spokane Daily Chronicle*, May 11, 1971]

Of course, people can probably figure out what you really wanted to say. But you'll look dumb anyway. So try to rule out the unintended meaning, for example:

(96a) Utah Girl's Dog Does Well in Shows

(97a) Pullman Girl's Swine Tops Division

Be careful about what you put together. If you say:

(98) Iraqi *Head Seeks Arms* [*El Centro* (Calif.) *Imperial Valley Press*, Nov. 11, 1980]

it sounds like the parts of a body are trying to find each other. Your choice of words has produced an odd coincidence, "head ↔ arms." You won't have that problem if you say:

(98a) Iraqi *Leader Seeks Weapons*

Be careful about putting common sayings where they would create weird mental pictures if taken literally. If you write:

(99) After I cut three fingers eating oysters, *I threw up my hands.*

the mention of "fingers" might carry over to give an odd image of literally "throwing up hands." You'll avoid the danger if you write:

(99a)   After I cut three fingers eating oysters, *I gave up.*

Play it safe and avoid bizarre meanings unless you want them for special effects.

■ 22. EXERCISE *on fixing doubtful statements*

Here are some more doubtful statements from newspapers. Find at least two meanings, and fix the passage so that only the intended meaning remains (make your best guess).

[1]   Officers Will Finally Get Shot at Promotion Exams [*Atlanta Constitution*, May 4, 1981]

[2]   19 Feet Broken in Pole Vault [*Wichita Eagle-Beacon*, June 6, 1981]

[3]   Albany Turns to Garbage [*New York Daily News*, Oct. 3, 1977]

[4]   Juvenile Court Tries Shooting Defendant [*Salt Lake City Desert News*, Oct. 24, 1975]

[5]   Pancakes Will Sell for Grave Flags [*Seattle University Herald*, Oct. 26, 1977]

[6]   Teachers Strike Annoying Students [*Palm Beach* (Fla.) *Post*, Nov. 21, 1979]

[7]   Teacher Wants to Be Unveiled at Meeting Tonight [*Springfield* (Mass.) *Daily News*, Aug. 17, 1970]

[8]   Kicking Baby Considered to Be Healthy [*Burlington* (Vt.) *Free Press*, Sept. 18, 1980]

[9]   Youngstown Police on Duty Are Getting Smaller [*Niles* (Ohio) *Daily Times*, Sept. 29, 1976]

[10] Missouri Deer Kill Nearly 50,000 [*Kansas City Star*, Nov. 19, 1975]

Sometimes, the doubtful statement comes from BAD PLACEMENT, a problem we just worked on for inconsistent statements (pp. 39–42). Bad placement makes things seem to go together when they shouldn't, as in:

(100)   It's Time for Football and Meatball Stew [*Detroit Free Press*, Oct. 19, 1977]

(101)   Student Struck by Bus; No Big Problems as Schools Start [*Richmond News Leader*, Aug. 29, 1977]

(102)   *PM Magazine* features restaurants that will bring you breakfast in bed and Lou Ferrigno, the Incredible Hulk. [*Atlanta Constitution*, Feb. 17, 1979]

Again, readers can tell what you meant to write, but the odd meaning distracts them from the statement you intended to make. To fix these doubts, you can ADD SOME WORDS to clear things up, as in (100a); you can ADD LINKING WORDS that show how things ought to go together, as in (101a); or you can REARRANGE things, as in (102a):

(100a)   It's Time to *Play* Football and *Cook* Meatball Stew

(101a)   Student Struck by Bus; *Otherwise*, No Big Problems as Schools Start

(102a)   *PM Magazine* features *Lou Ferrigno, the Incredible Hulk*, and restaurants that will bring you breakfast in bed.

23. EXERCISE *on doubtful statements with bad placement*

Here are some more doubtful statements due to bad placement. Figure out both the intended meaning and the unintended one. Then fix the passage until only the intended meaning remains (make your best guess). You can add words, insert linking words, or rearrange things.

[1]   Baseball Talks in Ninth Inning [*Philadelphia Daily News*, May 22, 1980]

[2]   State police charged Craft with firing several gunshots into a mobile home occupied by four persons and a pickup truck. [*Kittanning* (Pa.) *Leader-Times*, April 7, 1978]

[3]   The license fee for altered dogs with a certificate will be $3, and for pets owned by senior citizens who are altered the fee will be $1.50. [*Santa Barbara News-Press*, Jan. 13, 1975]

[4]   Doe Season Start Is Called Success; Four Hunters Are Stricken in Woods [*Williamsport* (Pa.) *Sun-Gazette*, Dec. 11, 1979]

[5]   Warranty Aids Home Owners with Defects [*Covington* (Ky.) *Virginian*, Jan. 24, 1980]

[6]   Bill to Help Poor Facing Early Death [*El Paso Herald-Post*, May 12, 1979]

[7]   Mayor Lorensen told aldermen that Smaha had received telephone death threats warning him that he and the mayor would be shot if he took the job. The council then approved the appointment of Smaha. [*Quad-City Times*, Aug. 14, 1979]

[8]   After the blast, Cooper said, his company was marched to the tower, then reduced to a pile of molten steel. [*New York Post*, April 6, 1977]

[9]   Milo and Pat Magnano are shown in the kitchen of their home, with Milo Jr. beating eggs and little brother Tony. [*Seattle Post-Intelligencer*, Sept. 27, 1980]

[10] Two men—one carrying a bomb and the other an officer of the New Jewish Defense League—were arrested today on charges of plotting to bomb the Egyptian government tourist office. [Associated Press wire, Dec. 18, 1978]

■ 24. QUIZ on doubtful statements

Fix these doubtful statements so that only the intended meaning is left. Use the methods discussed in this section.

[1] Stolen Painting Is Found by Tree [*Philadelphia Evening Bulletin*, Dec. 17, 1974]

[2] Mrs. Consigny was living alone in her home after her husband died in 1954 when the phone rang. [*This Is Madison*, July 8, 1978]

[3] City Will Add 12 Foot Cops [*The Trentonian*, March 24, 1977]

[4] Tuna Are Biting Off Washington Coast [*Seattle Post-Intelligencer*, Aug. 3, 1979]

[5] Jamaican Officials Are Considering Arson [*Eureka* (Calif.) *Times-Standard*, May 21, 1980]

[6] Shoot Kids to Halt Flu, Study Says [*Orlando* (Fla.) *Sentinel Star*, March 16, 1978]

[7] Dr. Tackett Gives Talk on the Moon [*Indiana Evening Gazette*, March 13, 1976]

[8] Nude Club Owner Is Going into Politics [*Burlington* (Vt.) *Free Press*, Dec. 14, 1979]

[9] FBI Is Needed for Bank Robberies [*News and Observer*, July 22, 1978]

[10] California Sheriff Wants Man Shot by Patrolman [*Cincinnati Post*, July 24, 1980]

■ 25. REVIEW QUIZ on doubtful statements

Same instructions as on the previous quiz.

[1] Reagan Visits Harrassed Blacks [*San Francisco Chronicle*, May 4, 1982]

[2] Drunk Gets Nine Months in Violin Case [*Lembridge Herald*, Oct. 30, 1976]

[3] If Kline's plan is to die, the legislature must act. [*Philadelphia Inquirer*, Nov. 25, 1976]

[4] Queen Ducks Ride to U.S. on Concorde [*Cleveland Plain Dealer*, May 21, 1976]

[5] Boy Scouts' Exploring Is Extended to Include Teenage Girls [*Today's Post*, March 15, 1971]

[6]   Distributor Finds Art of Producing Lies in Business [*New York Times*, Aug. 13, 1976]

[7]   Admitted Killer Gets 90 Years in Washington [*Detroit News*, Aug. 4, 1976]

[8]   Haig Insists Soviets Use Chemicals [*Sarasota* (Fla.) *Herald-Tribune*, Feb. 15, 1982]

[9]   Police Can't Stop Gambling [*Detroit Free Press*, July 1, 1975]

[10]   Reagan Raps Need to Prove Sanity [*The Oregonian*, July 7, 1982]

■   G.   INCONSISTENT AND DOUBTFUL STATEMENTS WITH PRONOUNS

PRONOUNS are short words that can stand in place of many things. The most common pronouns—"I," "you," "he," "she," "it," "we," "they," and their various forms ("my," "mine," "me," "your," "yours," "his," "her," and so forth)—can be very convenient. They can take the place of nouns, address people present or absent, and be adapted to fit all kinds of situations. They are really almost *too* versatile—they can lead you to make inconsistent or doubtful statements.

G.1   Pronoun Problems and Solutions

The use of pronouns in everyday talk is often vague. One student said on tape (talking about a Charlie Chaplin movie):

(103)   he gets intoxicated at the party....and her previous lover is on the side the whole time trying to reveal *his* true identity because *he* has been spying on *him he* knows that *he* really works in the bar

Unless you know the story already, you'll have trouble figuring out who is meant by "he," "him," and "his." Still, everyday talk can afford to be a little vague, because people are likely to give you the benefit of the doubt and try to make sense out of what you're saying.

But when you write, you should keep track of pronouns and prevent possible confusion. The danger comes from the fact that you, the writer, already have things sorted out in your mind, and you know what the pronouns are for. So you can easily overlook problems that could come up for readers who don't have your background knowledge. Small wonder that, according to a recent survey, composition teachers mark pronoun problems in student papers more often than any other slip-up except comma problems.

In extreme cases, it's impossible to tell what's meant, as in:

(104)   JoAnne told Sheila *she* couldn't come to *her* party.

If you don't already know all about it, you can't figure out who couldn't come to whose party.

Other times, you can get the message by picking what makes the most sense, as in:

(105)   Water pollution is one way people endanger alligators. I guess *they* aren't very smart, or else *they* just don't care what happens to *them*.

Here, "they" is probably for "people" and "them" is for "alligators." But even so, you shouldn't make readers work harder than necessary.

In particular, you should try to avoid doubtful statements with strange meanings. Students wrote:

(106)   I hate eggs, but these people were so hospitable I had to eat *them*.

(107)   I didn't really care for these grapes, but *they* went to all that trouble.

Let's hope nobody would believe that the writer ate people (106) or that grapes went to a lot of trouble (107). Still, you'll look better if you can avoid doubtful statements that distract attention from your message.

In everyday talk, people sometimes use a pronoun like "you," "they," or "it" for just about anything they have in mind. Many students write "they" to stand for whoever is involved (108) or for whoever is in charge (109):

(108)   Mexico's oil deposits may help strengthen *their* economy. [their = the Mexican people's]

(109)   The president wants to turn away the Haitian refugees, but how *they* are going to do it is not known. [they = U.S. officials, not Haitian refugees]

Students use "it" (110) or "this" (111) for the whole event or situation, rather than for any one item mentioned before:

(110)   The woman's citizenship in the town was recognized when she was too old to appreciate *it*. [it = recognition, not citizenship or town]

(111)   You can buy either the cable or the antenna. *This* will improve the reception. [this = buying one of the two, whether it's a cable or an antenna]

"You" is often written for people in general, rather than for someone the writer is specifically addressing. That use is all right for everyday writing (less suitable for formal writing), but should be done consistently. It's clumsy to shift around the way this student did:

(112)   *One* has a better chance of getting into upper-division courses when *you* begin with all the right prerequisites. What courses a *student* can take depends on what *they* have already taken.

Now let's look at some ways to clear up these pronoun problems. First, you can

REPLACE THE PRONOUN WITH THE NOUN
IT STANDS FOR

—as by changing (108) and (109) to (108a) and (109a):

(108) Mexico's oil deposits may help strengthen *their* economy.

(108a) Mexico's oil deposits may help strengthen *the nation's* economy.

(109) The president wants to turn away the Haitian refugees, but how *they* are going to do it is not known.

(109a) The president wants to turn away the Haitian refugees, but how *U.S. officials* are going to do it is not known.

But this tactic won't always work. It might give you something awkward or dumb, like (104a) or (104b):

(104) JoAnne told Sheila she couldn't come to her party.

(104a) JoAnne told Sheila that JoAnne couldn't come to Sheila's party.

(104b) JoAnne told Sheila that Sheila couldn't come to JoAnne's party.

depending on which you mean (let's ignore the prospect of telling someone she can't come to her own party). As we saw already (Section D.4), repeated words can be annoying. So putting in nouns for pronouns is frequently not the best way out. A better solution would be to

REARRANGE THE STATEMENT SO THAT THE
TROUBLESOME PRONOUNS CAN BE LEFT OUT

—for example:

(104c) JoAnne excused herself from coming to Sheila's party.

(104d) JoAnne was having a party and told Sheila not to come.

A vague "this" can be left out by making two statements into one (see also pp. 58, 182):

(111) You can buy either the cable or the antenna. *This* will improve the reception.

General quiz

15.

▼

on agreement

Circle the proper form for the agreeing verb in these samples.

[1] The woman on the sidewalk seems/seem upset.

[2] The best students in the whole class plans/plan to drop out.

[3] A talented foreman is/are very valuable.

[4] The editors of the paper wants/want a new contract.

[5] Technological advances changes/change society.

[6] The computers at the head office breaks/break down often.

[7] Robberies on the street makes/make you afraid to go for a walk.

[8] Students from every college attends/attend the meet.

[9] All the time in three years isn't/aren't going to be sufficient.

[10] Seven variables is/are a lot to handle.

[11] New developments in technology means/mean a new life style for everyone.

[12] *Eight and a Half* is/are a good film.

[13] The lakes in North County turns/turn warm enough for swimming after May.

[14] The Mexicans near the border migrates/migrate after the flooding of the Rio Grande.

[15] The relatives notifies/notify the church right away.

[16] Our local representative lives/live in town.

[17] The guard was/were risking a rifle shot.

[18] The jars behind the door needs/need new labels.

[19] The kids in the tenth grade hates/hate that class.

[20] Long ago, the world was/were not yet torn by the World Wars.

Back-up general quiz

16.
▼

on agreement

Same instructions as on the previous quiz.

[1]   A little understanding goes/go a long way.

[2]   Many times an officer of the law gets/get into an awkward position.

[3]   The truck from the station was/were a great help.

[4]   The problem is/are no cause for great alarm.

[5]   Thirty pieces of silver is/are not much of a bribe.

[6]   Those colors on a house constitutes/constitute a disgrace.

[7]   This total seems/seem outrageous.

[8]   Soon your sorrows becomes/become faded memories.

[9]   My sister comes/come home from college to monopolize the phone.

[10] My blood pressure rises/rise, but she doesn't/don't even notice.

[11] Many rocks in the desert doesn't/don't seem dense.

[12] "New microwave ovens has/have come out.

[13] The last day for late applications was/were March 4.

[14] Handguns with considerable power has/have appeared in the stores.

[15] Corvette owners has/have more fun, though not in the car, which doesn't/
      don't have much room.

[16] The old typewriter is/are going to be the cheapest.

[17] Math problems never gets/get any easier.

[18] You is/are responsible for the damage.

[19] A black and white cat comes/come here frequently.

[20] Your roommate always leaves/leave such a mess in here.

■ D. SPECIAL PROBLEMS WITH AGREEMENT

Several problems with agreement keep bothering people who write. In this section, we'll find out what to do about the main problems.

D.1 Having the Subject Far Away from the Agreeing Verb

Putting the subject far away from the verb can have drawbacks. By the time the verb comes along, you may have forgotten if you started out with a singular or with a plural. Students wrote:

(44) The *child* who doesn't learn to interact with other people *become* frustrated and angry.

(45) Three *tourist campgrounds* with electricity hookups and running water *is* located on the same lake.

You can easily check for this problem; just mentally

SHORTEN THE STATEMENT SO THAT
THE SUBJECT IS RIGHT NEXT TO
THE AGREEING VERB.

Then you can see a mistake much more easily:

(44a) The *child become* frustrated and angry.

(45a) Three *tourist campgrounds is* located on the same lake.

You can still keep all the materials in the long sentence; just use the short version as a mental check for subject-verb agreement.

A mistake is particularly likely if *the subject is followed by a noun with a different number before the verb comes along.* Writers accidentally make the verb agree with the *nearest* noun, not with the subject. Students wrote:

(46) The *proportion* of *divorces tend* to stabilize in the summer. [subject = *proportion*, but *divorces* nearer to the verb]

(47) One of those four *classes are* required. [subject = *one*, not *classes*]

They made the verb agree with a nearby noun. The mistake is hard to find because combinations like "divorces tend" (46) and "classes are" (47) sound and look all right by themselves. Here too, shortening the statement to get the subject next to the verb makes the slip-up more obvious. You won't be so likely to write:

(46a) The *proportion tend* to stabilize.

(47a) *One* are required.

It can also help if you find the subject by making up a "who/what" question; for instance:

(46b) The proportion of divorces tend to stabilize in the summer.
What tends to stabilize?
The proportion. [not: *divorces*]

(47b) One of those four classes are required.
What is required?
One class. [not: *four classes*]

If you shorten statements and make up "who/what" questions, you shouldn't have much trouble spotting the subject and telling if it is singular or plural. After that, you can check for agreement.

17. QUIZ *on sentences with the subject far from the agreeing verb*

Circle the subject and the right form for the agreeing verb. To find the subject, you can mentally shorten the sentence or make up a "who/what" question.

[1] A student taking twenty hours is/are working too hard.

[2] Two layers of steel is/are better than one.

[3] Surfing between the two piers goes/go against city regulations.

[4] Our three associates in the shop all says/say the same thing.

[5] One breed of musicians doesn't/don't read music.

[6] The number of townspeople in favor of busing is/are growing smaller.

[7] The stores in the downtown area has/have higher prices.

[8] The pains in the lower back starts/start in the early morning.

[9] The item shown in your new catalog is/are exactly the one we want.

[10] Several old men with the same shabby look always hangs/hang around the bus station.

Same instructions as on the previous quiz.

[1]   One out of a thousand tax returns gets/get audited.

[2]   The belt with the two marks go/goes over the camshaft pulley.

[3]   The loser in four primaries is/are contesting the election.

[4]   Just one among all her ideas has/have been widely accepted.

[5]   Anyone losing this ticket has/have to pay again.

[6]   Three mistakes in one program makes/make a big difference.

[7]   The garbage trucks belonging to the city has/have been inspected.

[8]   You residents in the industrial park don't/doesn't get to see a clear sky very often.

[9]   This set of numbers forms/form the second group.

[10] Four days in each month is/are set aside for inventory.

D.2 Having More Than One Subject or More Than One Verb

You can have more than one subject going with the same verb, or more than one verb going with the same subject. Here also, you may have problems.
We'll take the easier case first:

IF YOU HAVE MORE THAN ONE VERB GOING WITH THE SAME SUBJECT, THEN THE VERBS SHOULD BE EITHER ALL SINGULAR OR ALL PLURAL.

Since the subject stays the same, all the agreeing verbs should also be the same:

(48)   Heavy rains in a steep canyon *wash* away the topsoil, *erode* the cliffs, and *cause* mudslides.

Don't get confused if one of the verbs is placed far away from the subject. One student wrote:

(49)   His boss *reveals* the waiter's real identity and *cause* a huge commotion.

The student did okay on "boss reveals," but by the time she got to "cause," she didn't follow through with the singular, which would be "causes." You could make up two "who/what" questions, but they'd both have the same answer:

(49a)   Who reveals the waiter's real identity?
His boss.

(49b)   Who causes a huge commotion?
His boss.

The other case is a little more complicated. You'd think that a combination of more than one subject ought to make a plural; but actually, the issue depends on what kind of **LINKING WORD** is used. The most common situation would be:

SEVERAL SUBJECTS LINKED WITH "AND" CALL FOR A PLURAL VERB.

Since you have more than one thing, a plural is perfectly logical:

(50)   A *hamburger* and a *Coke cost* $1.19 with this coupon.

It makes no difference if any one of the subjects is singular or plural by itself. The combination linked with "and" still adds up to a plural verb:

(51)   *Two hamburgers* and a *Coke cost* $1.19 with this coupon.

(52)   A *hamburger* and *two Cokes cost* $1.19 with this coupon.

You still have a plural verb if the subjects linked with "and" are in DIFFERENT PERSONS, that is, first, second, or third person:

(53)   *You* and *I are* out of work.

(54)   *You* and *she are* out of work.

(55)   *She* and *they are* out of work.

But things are different if the subjects are linked with "or"—that is, if at least one "or" appears anywhere in the list of subjects.

WHEN SEVERAL SUBJECTS ARE LINKED WITH "OR," THE VERB AGREES WITH THE NEAREST SUBJECT.

"Or" means you have two or more choices, and the verb can apply to only one of the choices at a time. For instance, in (56) and (57), you get either "the doubleburger" or the "two hamburgers" with your coupon, but not both. The verb agrees with the nearer of the two subjects:

(56) Two hamburgers *or one doubleburger costs* $1.19 with this coupon.

(57) One doubleburger *or two hamburgers cost* $1.19 with this coupon.

The strategy is the same when you use "or" to link DIFFERENT PERSONS. The verb still agrees with the *nearest* subject:

(58) Either you *or I am* out of work.

(59) Either you *or she is* out of work.

(60) Either you, he, *or I am* out of work.

With the nearest subject being right next to the agreeing verb, you get a combination that sounds good, like "she is" in (59). Location works in your favor here, though it works against you when the real subject is far away from the verb (see Section D.1).

As you can see, the verb form depends on how the subjects are linked together:

(61) The bride *and* her mother *stand* on the groom's left.

(62) The bride *or* her mother *stands* on the groom's left.

(63) The bride *or* her parents *stand* on the groom's left.

(64) The bride, her parents, *or* the preacher *stands* on the groom's left.

However, be sure that all the verbs do go with the *same* subject. If you have several subjects and each one has its own verb, then each subject + verb combination needs to be matched up by itself for singular or plural:

(65) The *losers leave* the next day, but the *winner stays* for a two-week training course.

(66) One of us here is out of a job. Either *you are, he is, or I am.*

Each subject + verb unit has to be taken care of on its own.

🔲 **19. QUIZ on having more than one subject or more than one verb**

Circle the right verb forms.

[1] The usher takes/take the tickets and gives/give back the stubs.

[2] An accident or a disease puts/put you off the job.

[3] The secretaries and the accountants is/are very efficient and knows/know exactly what they is/are doing.

[4] My cousins from the big city is/are arriving this evening and doesn't/don't have hotel reservations.

[5] You or she has/have to call the hotel right away.

[6] The waiters takes/take your order and, when the meal is/are ready, brings/bring it to your table on a cart.

[7] You and he doesn't/don't see eye to eye.

[8] The motive for the series of attacks is/are still not clear and calls/call for further investigation.

[9] The tonsils or the throat becomes/become inflamed.

[10] My toolbox has/have fallen off the scaffolding and was/were smashed.

20. REVIEW QUIZ *on having more than one subject or more than one verb*

Circle the right verb forms.

[1] Either the injured parties or the court selects/select the date.

[2] The greatest general in the world and all his troops doesn't/don't matter if the winter is too severe.

[3] A movie by the Monty Python people is/are always hilarious.

[4] Either the pollution or the tourists spoils/spoil the beach and makes/make you want to stay home.

[5] Three dollars and one coupon buys/buy this colorful giant poster.

[6] One photo or the other needs/need to be retouched.

[7] Cinnamon and cloves tastes/taste good together and works/work for making hot wine.

[8] A hunter and a trained dog makes/make a good team.

[9] Mexico, Jamaica, or the Bahamas is/are a great place to go over Christmas.

[10] You and your bright ideas confuses/confuse everybody and throws/throw us off schedule.

D.3   Statements About Numbers

Statements about NUMBERS often mix people up. For instance, you might wonder which of these is right:

(67) Two dollars *is* a low price.

(68) Two and two *are* a low price.

(67) sounds all right with a singular verb, yet "two" certainly seems to be plural. The choice you should make actually depends on what you mean. Just use these strategies:

IF YOU CONSIDER THE NUMBER AS A UNIT, USE THE SINGULAR.

IF YOU CONSIDER THE NUMBER AS A COLLECTION OF INDIVIDUALS, USE THE PLURAL.

You might have:

(69) Twenty thousand *is* a huge total. [The number is just one sum, so you use the **singular**.]

(70) Twenty thousand voters *agree* with the mayor. [Each voter is an individual person, so you use the **plural** to include all of them.]

Statements about arithmetic usually treat numbers as units. The singular is therefore more common:

(71) Two and two *is* four.

(72) Seventeen times five *comes* to eighty-five.

A PERCENTAGE can go either way, too. You might be thinking of a unit (73), or of the individuals that make up the percentage (74):

(73) Seventy-eight percent of our business *is* done with the federal government. [*is* = singular]

(74) Seventy-eight percent of all businessmen *favor* the tax cut. [*favor* = plural]

A good strategy is:

THE EASIER IT IS TO COUNT THE THINGS, THE MORE LIKELY YOU ARE TO TREAT A PERCENTAGE AS A PLURAL.

You can count "businessmen" more easily than "business." The same strategy applies to these:

(75) Forty-three percent of our *water is* polluted with sulfates. [*is* = singular, because it's hard to count water]

(76) Forty-three percent of these *houses have* water purifiers. [*have* = plural, because it's easy to count houses]

A FRACTION is normally a UNIT, as in:

(77) Three-fourths of their income *goes* for rent. [*is* = singular]

You'd need the plural only in special situations where you'd want to count the pieces, as in:

(78) I just cut the pie into fourths a minute ago. Now *three fourths are* gone. [*are* = plural]

When you do calculations about arithmetic, you're usually just interested in units, so use the singular:

(79) Twenty-seven percent in taxes plus 12 percent in social security *means* a total of 39 percent gone from your paycheck.

(80) Three-fourths minus one-eighth *equals* five-eighths.

But you could use the plural instead if you're talking about individual parts you could easily count:

(81) Twenty-seven percent of the women plus 29 percent of the men *are* depending on social security. [*have* = plural, because it's easy to count women and men]

(82) Three-fourths of our company's shares, minus the eighth belonging to the trust fund, *are* being sold back to the corporation. [*are* = plural, because it's easy to count shares]

So if you're clear about what you mean, you can easily figure out whether you want singular or plural.

◻ **21. QUIZ on statements about numbers**

Decide whether you want the singular or plural and circle the right form. Be sure you know the reason for your choice.

[1] Only 19 percent of the congressman's constituents was/were able to recognize his photograph.

[2]   Nine-tenths of the island is/are covered with sea oats.

[3]   Three-fifths comes/come to less than five eighths.

[4]   Thirty-seven percent of the crop was/were destroyed by hail.

[5]   Six times 7 equals/equal 42.

[6]   A million Americans needs/need more food stamps for their families.

[7]   In this town, sixty people makes/make quite a crowd.

[8]   153 and 274 is/are 427.

[9]   Ten thousand dollars is/are too much for a used car.

[10] Nine-tenths of the oil comes/come from foreign import.

22. REVIEW QUIZ on statements about numbers

Same instructions as on the previous quiz.

[1]   Ten percent of the crop gets/get shipped out of the country.

[2]   According to the polls, 37 percent of the American people think/thinks the president is doing a good job.

[3]   The 3 percent increase plus the 4 percent inflation adjustment adds/add up to a 7 percent raise.

[4]   Seven-eighths is/are greater than three-fourths.

[5]   Ten dollars buys/buy a young person a ticket to the annual fair.

[6]   72 minus 19 come/comes to 53.

[7]   Almost 47 percent of the people interviewed believes/believe the future will be brighter.

[8]   57 take away 19 leaves/leave 38.

[9]   Two-thirds is/are the answer for the second problem on page 87.

[10] One-half of our students has/have considered financial aid.

D.4   Group Nouns as Subjects

Another special problem with agreement turns up when the subject of a sentence happens to be a **GROUP NOUN**, such as "group," "team," "family," "class," "committee," "club," "crowd," "mob"—any noun that indicates a group. These nouns follow strategies rather like the ones we used for numbers:

IF YOU'RE THINKING OF THE GROUP AS A UNIT, USE THE SINGULAR.

IF YOU'RE THINKING OF THE GROUP AS A COLLECTION OF INDIVIDUALS, USE THE PLURAL.

The people in a group might act the same, as in (83), or different, as in (84):

(83) The group is arriving on the 7:35 flight.

(84) The group were all going off by themselves.

If it sounds strange to say "the group were," you can change the subject to an obvious plural:

(84a) The *people* in the group were all going off by themselves.

Here's another good way to look at the problem:

IF YOU'RE INTERESTED IN HOW THE MEMBERS OF THE GROUP ARE ALIKE OR TOGETHER, USE THE SINGULAR.

IF YOU'RE INTERESTED IN HOW THE MEMBERS OF THE GROUP ARE DIFFERENT OR DIVIDED, USE THE PLURAL.

For instance, in (85), the "family" is acting all together, so the verb is in the singular ("takes"). In (86), the individual members of the "family" are "different," so the verb is in the plural ("are"):

(85) My family *takes* a trip to Maine every summer.

(86) My family *are* people of very different backgrounds.

Suppose you have:

(87) The team on the left side *doesn't/don't* play as well.

Since the whole team is being judged, you probably consider it a single unit, so you'll want the singular. But you could also view a team as a group of people with different assignments:

(88)   The football team *watch* each other closely so that each man gets the best results.

(89)   In the first half of the game, our football team *weren't* coordinating their moves very well.

Again, you could solve the problem by changing the subject:

(88a)   The *men* on the football team *watch* each other closely so that each man gets the best results.

Nouns like "class," "club," "family," "team," "committee," "tribe," "staff," and "personnel" work the same way.

23. QUIZ *on group nouns as subjects*

Decide what verb to pick. Use the singular when you're interested in how the members of the group are alike or together. Use the plural when you're interested in how the members of the group are different or divided.

[1]   Union leadership has/have still not agreed on what they want.

[2]   This senior class is/are the best in many years.

[3]   The committee is/are partly favorable and partly opposed.

[4]   The tribe belongs/belong to the New Guinea federation.

[5]   The population has/have gone to war among themselves.

[6]   The main group has/have changed its name.

[7]   The Lions Club holds/hold a picnic in the spring.

[8]   When the circus wears/wear their uniforms, you see a startling variety of colors.

[9]   The two groups is/are merging into one.

[10] The hospital staff doesn't/don't want to trade their offices.

24. REVIEW QUIZ *on group nouns as subjects*

Same instructions as on the previous quiz.

[1]   A street gang loses/lose its leader now and then.

[2]   A large crowd was/were booing the losing team.

[3] The most famous couple was/were Adam and Eve.

[4] The public views/view him as its worst enemy.

[5] The whole flock spreads/spread their wings and flies/fly away.

[6] This family is/are not going to give up their rooms.

[7] You and the executive board makes/make a dangerous combination.

[8] The whole army is/are considered one unit in wartime.

[9] The artist's club displays/display their latest paintings every Sunday.

[10] The group on the field is/are all trying to grab the ball away from one another.

D.5 "Everybody/Everyone," "Somebody/Someone," "Anybody/Anyone," and "Nobody/No One"

You also need to watch out with words like "everybody" (or "everyone"), "somebody" (or "someone"), "anybody" (or "anyone"), and "nobody" (or "no one"). Their form makes them look as though they ought to be singular, especially those ending in "-one." But their meaning is often plural. According to surveys, most people follow strategies like these:

THE CLOSER THE VERB OR PRONOUN IS TO THE WORD WITH "-BODY" OR "-ONE," THE MORE LIKELY YOU ARE TO USE THE SINGULAR.

THE FURTHER THE VERB OR PRONOUN IS FROM THE WORD WITH "-BODY" OR "-ONE," THE MORE LIKELY YOU ARE TO USE THE PLURAL.

You can stick with the singular all the way through:

(90) Everyone *is* bringing the food that *he or she likes* best.

But many people would say (91), where the singular gets used right after "everyone," but the plural gets used further on in the same sentence:

(91) Everyone *is* bringing the food that *they like* best.

A statement like (91a) just sounds wrong, because the plural verb "are" comes too soon after the subject:

(91a)   Everyone *are* bringing the food that *they like* best.

As you get further and further away from a word like "everyone," you'll feel more and more like switching to the plural. You could say (92) all right, but quite a few people would say (92a):

(92)   Somebody called late last night. But *he or she* didn't leave any message.

(92a)   Somebody called late last night. But *they* didn't leave any message.

And almost everyone would prefer the answer in (93) over the answer in (93a):

(93)   I'll bet everyone asks you that.
        Yes, *they certainly do.*

(93a)   I'll bet everyone asks you that.
        Yes, *he or she certainly does.*

In the same way, (94) is likely to be preferred:

(94)   Everybody knows about income taxes. But *they don't know* how many ways there are to save on taxes. [not: *he doesn't know*]

However, a few people might consider this somewhat informal.
   One way out is to fix the statement so that the problem doesn't even come up, as in:

(92b)   Somebody called late last night, but *didn't leave any message.*

(93b)   I'll bet everyone asks you that.
        Yes, *that is what happens.*

(94a)   Everybody knows about income taxes, but *not how to save on taxes.*

You play it safe and keep away from patterns that force you to choose between singular and plural.
   In informal writing, another way out is to follow up with the second person "you" or "your" wherever it works:

(95)   Anyone can enter the lottery. But *you* must be present at the drawing in order to win.

But don't jump around among "you," "he," and "they." Say (96), not (96a):

(96)   Nobody wants to lose a big game, but *you* can't always avoid it. Everyone has to take *your* turn as a loser. But *you* should always try *your* best.

(96a)   Nobody wants to lose a big game, but *you* can't always avoid it. Everyone has to take *his* turn as a loser. But *they* should always try *their best*.

Use your best judgment and try to steer away from combinations that don't sound natural. Using the plural is better than sounding forced or clumsy. At the very least, you should not use just a singular "he" for everybody, somebody, anybody, and so on, since women might be included. If you really want a third person singular, be sure to use "he or she" instead.

☐   **25. QUIZ** on *"everybody/everyone," "somebody/someone," "anybody/anyone," and "nobody/no one"*

Fix the statements that need fixing.

Example:
Everybody says he wants money. But he doesn't always know what to do with it.

You could fix it like this:
Everybody says they want money. But they don't always know what to do with it. [informal]
Everybody claims to want money, even without knowing what to do with it. [playing it safe]

[1]   Do anybody have a wrench?

[2]   We'll need someone to take over accounting. He should have a degree in business.

[3]   Everybody I know already lives out of town. That way, you don't get so much smog.

[4]   Anyone who commutes to your job should join a car pool. They can call this number for information.

[5]   Nobody wants a job that he or she can't do very well.

[6]   Somebody broke into our house and stole that old TV set. I'll bet they are still trying to get rid of it.

[7]   Anybody can learn to jog if you make the effort. They only need a little practice.

[8]   I asked everybody to write his name on a card. But they seem to have forgotten.

[9] The company is sending someone to fix the heater. Be sure you're home when he gets here.

[10] Everyone needs to be met at the door and shown to their seats. He doesn't know his way around.

▐ 26. REVIEW QUIZ on *"everybody/everyone," "somebody/someone," "anybody/anyone," and "nobody/no one"*

Same instructions as on the previous quiz.

[1] I see someone coming up the walk. I wonder what he or she wants.

[2] Anyone who get an "A" on their quizzes won't have to take your final exam.

[3] I suppose everyone will ask for a raise again. He all did last year.

[4] Nobody reads directions these days. They make a guess and try your best.

[5] Sooner or later, somebody is bound to slip up. Then the police will catch him.

[6] I thought everyone had the room he wanted. But someone always complains.

[7] After six hours, no one was left in the theater. I think they'd had enough by then.

[8] Everyone should vote, but they ought to know which candidates will really work for you.

[9] It would be best if everybody came right out and said what he thinks.

[10] If somebody acts like a child, they won't be treated like an adult.

D.6 "There Is" and "There Are"

"There is" and "there are" at the beginning of a statement can also cause trouble. In everyday talk, you hear "there is" or "there's" used almost all the time—as if "there" could be a singular subject of the sentence. In the transcript on page 2, the freshman says:

(97) there's three exits to Gainesville

This result is favored by the fact that the subject normally comes before the verb in a statement, though of course not if you start out with "there is" or "there are." Technically, "there" can't be the subject of the sentence, simply because "there" isn't a noun. The test for a **noun** doesn't work (see page 80): you can't say "the there." And "there" isn't on the list of subject **pronouns**: "I," "we," "you," "he," "she," "it," and "they."

Since "there" isn't the subject, the subject has to be the noun coming *after* "there is" or "there are"—as you'll see if you make up a "who/what" question, as we practised in Section B. Take (98). You'd use "there" in your question (98a), so "there" must belong to the *predicate*, not to the subject. You would hardly make up a question like (98b).

(98)   There is an exit on the right.

(98a)   What is there on the right? [normal]

(98b)   What is an exit on the right? [odd]

Since you'd say "an exit is" (not "an exit are"), you want a singular verb. In the same way, since you'd say "three exits are" (not "three exits is"), you'd want a plural verb:

(99)   There *are* three exits to Gainesville.

This point matters more when you write than when you talk.

If you have two or more subjects linked with "or," make the verb agree with the subject *nearest* to the verb—just what you'd expect from Section D.2.

(100)   There *is a rag* or some candy-bar wrappers on the floor over there.

Since the verb goes before, the nearest subject is the *first* one this time, not the last. But it's still the *nearest*, so the principle is the same.

■ 27. QUIZ on "there is" and "there are"

Underline the subjects in these sentences, and circle the verb form that you want. Make up a "who/what" question if you can't find the subject.

[1]   After the game, there was/were a bonfire at the stadium.

[2]   There's/there are a problem in the program.

[3]   There is/are, in every small town, several rich families.

[4]   Now that the war is over, there is/are a feeling of anxiety among our allies.

[5]   Sometimes there is/are only one way to go, and sometimes there is/are many ways.

[6]   There's/there are either a burnt circuit or a blown fuse in the switchboard.

[7]   There is/are a woman and a little dog out in the yard.

[8]   There is/are a wide range of sizes and colors on sale.

[9]   Between the fraternities and the sororities there is/are a strong competition.

[10] There is/are either two old editions or one new edition in each library.

▉ 28. REVIEW QUIZ on "there is" and "there are"

Same instructions as on the previous quiz.

[1]   At night, there is/are sometimes a crowd of tourists gathered at the harbor.

[2]   Before the overhaul there was/were only three-fourths of the circuits in operation.

[3]   There is/are one loss and five wins on her record.

[4]   At the lake itself, there is/are either a campground or two motels to stay at.

[5]   There is/are no major party supporting any candidate in the runoff.

[6]   Then too, there is/are 35 percent of the voters who wrote in their own candidates.

[7]   Every June, there is/are a festival with three bands at the stadium.

[8]   In addition, there is/are a boat trip and a bicycle tour to go on.

[9]   After all, there is/are only two weeks between sessions.

[10] There is/are one big town and three little ones along that highway.

D.7   Subject Versus Object Pronouns

"There" isn't the only word that gets mistaken for the subject of a verb. **PRO-NOUNS** have **OBJECT** forms—"me," "us," "him," "her," and "them"—that sometimes get used as subjects instead of the real **SUBJECT** forms—"I," "we," "he," "she," and "they." You might find:

(101)   That's *him* in his brand-new car.

(102)   There's *me* in the picture.

(103)   It was *him* that forgot to shut off the lights.

(104)   It must be *them* coming along the road.

(105)   *Her* and her friends came late.

(106)   *Us* janitors are all through for the day.

Some of the patterns, such as (101), (102), and (103), are influenced by the fact that the *subject* normally comes *before* the verb in a statement, so that you'd expect to have an *object* coming *after* the verb. People might think the subject is "there" (102) or "it" (103). However, you can tell what the real subject is by making up a "who/what" question, such as:

(103)   It was *him* that forgot to shut off the lights.

(103a) *Who was it* that forgot to shut off the lights? [Everything used again except *him*, so *him* was supposed to be the subject]

You wouldn't make the "who/what" question like this:

(103b) *Who was him* that forgot to shut off the lights? [odd]

so "it" can't be the subject.

You could fix the problem by replacing the object pronouns with subject pronouns. But you'd get technically correct versions that sound a little strange or formal:

(101a) That's *he* in his brand-new car.

(102a) There am *I* in the picture.

(103b) It was *he* that forgot to shut off the lights.

(104a) It must be *they* coming along the road.

(105a) *She* and her friends came late.

(106a) *We* janitors are all through for the day.

If you want to be safe, change the sentence around so you can start with the subject pronoun. That order sounds more natural:

(101b) *He* is the one driving his brand-new car over there.

(102b) There *I* am in the picture.

(103b) *He* is the person that forgot to shut off the lights.

(104b) *They* must be coming along the road.

(105b) *She* came late with her friends.

Or you can make the pronoun into something besides the subject, as in:

(106b) The day is all over for *us* janitors.

Either way, you've solved the problem without resorting to strange-sounding constructions of the "It is I" type.

29. QUIZ *on subject versus object pronouns*

Find another way to say the following statements, where object forms have been mistaken for subjects. Either make the pronoun be the subject at the start of the sentence, or make the pronoun be a real object later on in the sentence.

[1] It's me you want to ask.

[2] It seems to be her winning first prize.

[3] That was them back there waving at us.

[4] Us night clerks are paid by the parent company.

[5] Me and my roommates will get diplomas from the same college.

[6] That's him knocking at the door now.

[7] Here's us having to pay a fine again.

[8] It might be him that wants an extra copy.

[9] After all the trouble, it was her who complained.

[10] It doesn't have to be me taking out your garbage all the time.

30. REVIEW QUIZ *on subject versus object pronouns*

Same instructions as on the previous quiz.

[1] Nowadays, us college students can hardly get good jobs.

[2] That was me ringing the doorbell.

[3] It should have been her taking tickets that night.

[4] All winter, it was us who got in the firewood.

[5] That ought to be him going to jail, not his wife.

[6] There's them coming in the gate now.

[7] It wasn't me that lost the certificate.

[8] This was him shown here as a little boy.

[9] So that was her wanting a different schedule.

[10] Next it could be me who gets fired.

General quiz

31.

on mistakes in agreement

▼

Fix the samples that have mistakes in agreement. One sample may have *more than one mistake! Some samples are fine as they stand.*

[1] Our club meet in the community center.

[2] Three waiters and a cook was hired this week.

[3] The public was making their opinions known.

[4] The good guy always rides across wild landscapes and pursue the bad guys.

[5] My family belong to several religions, and really try to follow the Bible.

[6] Nobody watches their machines every minute. But you should make regular checks.

[7] Two-twelfths multiplied by five equals five-sixths.

[8] The whole crowd is going to raise their hands.

[9] It was her that signed the contract.

[10] Fourteen percent of the students doesn't have parking spaces.

[11] Anyone who wants their numbers changed should bring his old license plates.

[12] Three hundred pounds of sugar is rotting in those sacks.

[13] Of all the people I know, there's only two who have asked me that.

[14] In this country, either the insiders group or the outsiders group oppose every public project.

[15] Besides, the insiders group is always fighting among themselves.

[16] 17 and 28 make 45.

[17] The boss or the workers will have to propose a new plan.

[18] My friends and I were all talking at once and nobody was listening to his own words.

[19] On the road to Ocala, there's a park and three nice lakes.

[20] The drawback with computers are the danger to low-skilled jobs.

Back-up general quiz

32.

on mistakes in agreement

▼

Same instructions as on the previous quiz.

[1]   A small part of our basketball team are really sure of themselves.

[2]   Thirty-five thousand dollars was an attractive offer.

[3]   Three-fourths of the total are more than enough.

[4]   Everyone has a secret dream. They may not admit it, but you just can't

help it.

[5]   Two and a half hours allows for time spent on the road.

[6]   About 10 percent of the packages has defective wrappers.

[7]   She and I are in full cooperation.

[8]   Either the resident or the neighbors has to adjust.

[9]   We saw someone near the door, but they didn't come in.

[10] After forming a Little League, there's more for the children in the commu-

nity to do.

[11] In boxing, the goal of the boxers are to score points.

[12] There's several categories of points, depending on whether the boxers in

each match hits their opponents in the face or in the stomach.

[13] At the end, the fighter still standing with the most points win the match.

[14] Sometimes, there are a long series of matches needed to decide a championship.

[15] The number of rounds in a fight depend on the conditions that the promoter and the trainer sets up.

[16] Our group need a more experienced leader.

[17] 24 times 5 equal 120.

[18] Either you or she have to give in.

[19] The main symptom of adenoids are disturbed breathing.

[20] Everybody in the audience is a local citizen. He knows how to vote.

■ E. FINDING INDEPENDENT CLAUSES

Some problems with writing come from not paying attention to how clauses get put together. In this section, you'll learn to recognize when you have an "independent clause."

In Section B, we had some basic definitions:

A SENTENCE MUST HAVE AT LEAST ONE
INDEPENDENT CLAUSE.

A CLAUSE MUST HAVE A SUBJECT
AND A PREDICATE.

So a real **SENTENCE** must have at least one **SUBJECT** and one **PREDICATE** in an **INDEPENDENT CLAUSE**. Clauses are building blocks for sentences, not the other way around.

As you might expect from the name, an "independent" clause can stand by itself as a sentence, because it doesn't "depend" on anything else to help it seem complete. When you write, you need to make sure that what you're marking off as a sentence has at least one independent clause. This matter isn't so important when you're talking.

Here's one easy way you can often tell if you have an independent clause. Try to make up a *"yes/no" question*—that is, a question whose answer would be either "yes" or "no"—about your statement.

IF YOU CAN ASK A SENSIBLE "YES/NO"
QUESTION ABOUT YOUR STATEMENT, YOU
HAVE AN INDEPENDENT CLAUSE.

To make a "yes/no" question, start with a **helping verb**—a word that you can put "not" right after (unless the word already ends in "-n't") (page 80), such as "does/do/did," "is/are," "was/were," or "will." You might get:

(107)   He looks exhausted.

(107a)   Does he look exhausted? [can be answered with: Yes.]

Be careful not to overlook a **linking word** at the start of the clause. Suppose you had:

(108)   Just because you work too hard.

(108a)   Just because do you work too hard? [not a sensible question]

The linking word is the main signal that (108) is not an independent clause, so it can't be a complete sentence. Be sure to make only a *"yes/no" question*. Don't use "who," "what," "when," "where," "why," or anything else—you'd spoil the technique. For instance, (109) could be made into a "when" question:

(109)   When the mail arrives.

(109a)   When does the mail arrive?

But since it wouldn't make sense to answer the question with "yes" or "no," (109) can't be an independent clause or a complete sentence.

We can see that the type of clause you have depends mainly on whether or not it starts with a **linking word**—that is, with a word that can link two clauses, such as "and," "but," "because," "while," "which." Some linking words have several parts, such as "so that," "as soon as," "in order that." The whole thing counts as one link.

We can use linking words as the surest way to tell if we have an independent clause. Our first condition is plain enough:

A CLAUSE NOT STARTING WITH ANY LINKING WORD IS INDEPENDENT.

You'd expect that a clause standing by itself with *no linking word* would naturally count as "independent." We could have:

(110)   Government offices take their time.

(111)   Five senators wanted the nomination.

Since each of these has one independent clause, each is a real sentence.

A sentence may have *more than one clause*. Then, the independent clause might not be the *first* one in the sentence. But you can still recognize it when there's no linking word at the start:

(112)   Although you may be in a hurry, ↓ government offices take their time.

(113)   Before the primaries began, ↓ five senators wanted the nomination.

The first clause starts with a linking word ("Although," "Before"), but the second one doesn't, so each statement is a full sentence with one independent clause.

Now suppose your clause *does* start with a linking word. In that case, you need to find out *what kind* of a linking word you have. You should learn one short list:

AND   BUT   OR   SO

If you use **YET** and **FOR**, put them in the list too, though they are less commonly found nowadays. **EITHER** can also be used, but only with **OR** shortly after it in the sentence. **NEITHER** and **NOR** are negative forms for **OR**, but are rather special, and we won't deal with them here.*

This list is important because

AT THE BEGINNING OF A SENTENCE, THE LINKING WORDS ON THIS LIST START AN INDEPENDENT CLAUSE.

So when a clause starts with any other linking word *not on the list*—"before," "after," "although," "if," "as," "since," "until," "because," "when," "while," "which," "that," "in order that," "due to the fact that," and so on—you know right away that the clause *can't* be independent. The same goes for a *combination* including any linking word not on the list: "and when," "but if," "or whether," "so that," and so forth. No such combination can start an independent clause.

If you have *only one clause*, and the linking word from the list really is at the *start* of the clause—that is, before the subject—then the clause must be independent:

(114)   *And* that was the whole secret of their fabulous discovery.

(115)   *But* the world was not yet ready for it.

(116)   *Or* the necessary technology was not available.

(117)   *So* we had to wait a hundred years before the machine was actually built.

But don't be fooled if the linking word is *not at the start* of your clause before the subject, as in:

(118)   Politicians *and* reporters often disagree. [*and* links two subjects]

(119)   Seeing that the circuit is overloaded *or* defective. [*or* links two modifiers]

---

*A clause beginning with "neither" and not having "nor" later on would be rare, and probably couldn't stand alone as a sentence anyway. You can have a sentence beginning with "Nor," but the order of the words is unusual, as in: "Nor did they realize the extent of the disaster."

Both (118) and (119) contain linking words from the list of four, but we are only interested in what's at the start. (118) is an independent clause because it starts with no linking word. (119) is not independent because it starts with linking words that are not on the list ("Seeing that").

If you have more clauses *after* the independent clause, they don't change it from being independent. You might have:

(120)   *And* that was the whole secret of their fabulous discovery, *which* stunned all of science.

(121)   *But* the world was not yet ready for it, *because* technology was not advanced enough.

The second clauses can't be independent, because they start with linking words that aren't on the list: "which" and "because." However, the first clauses are still independent, because they do start with linking words from the list: "And" and "But." So (120) and (121) are still real sentences.

We can see that in order to have a real sentence, you need to check for three possibilities:

1.   You can make up a sensible "*yes/no*" *question* (a question whose answer would be "yes" or "no") about your statement.
2.   You can have a clause that starts with *no* linking word at all.
3.   You can have a clause that starts with a linking word from the *list of four*, but that clause has to be at the *start of the sentence*.

If any one of these three conditions is met, you have at least one independent clause. It's important that you can tell when you do have at least one. Otherwise, you might punctuate as sentences some things that don't qualify, such as:

(122)   Which seemed like a good solution at the time.

(123)   Whenever the weather is right, and we're in the mood.

(124)   But if they are still expecting to win the election.

You can't make sensible "yes/no" questions here. You could hardly say, for instance:

(124a)   But if are they still expecting to win the election?

Besides, these clauses start with linking words that are not on the list of four: "Which" in (122), "Whenever" in (123), and "if" in (124). We do have a clause starting with "and" in (123), but it's not the first one in the sentence. The combination "But if" in (124) is disqualified because "if" is not on the list of four, although "But" is.

Of course, a sentence can have a number of clauses, including several independent clauses. The main thing is to make sure you have *at least one*. Suppose you have:

(125)   We visited the fort where they imprisoned the Seminole Indians, and then we saw the Old Spanish Town.

(126)   But the guard resigned after the bank was robbed, and they had to look for a replacement.

(127)   Whenever a building is renovated, the city offers important benefits, but only if certain conditions are met.

You don't need to worry about finding and identifying every clause. Just be sure you have one that counts as independent. In (125), the first clause qualifies because it starts without any linking word. In (126), the first clause qualifies because it starts with a linking word from the list of four. In (127), the second clause qualifies because it starts without any linking word. After you've found one independent clause, you know you have a real sentence, and you don't need to look any further.

33. EXERCISE *on finding independent clauses*

Check these samples and put *Yes* if the sample has at least one independent clause to make it a real sentence. Put *No* if it doesn't.

[1]   They complain, and we have to listen.

[2]   Although their wealth will be greater, part of their income will come from social security.

[3]   As soon as population goes into a steep decline.

[4]   Public services will be reorganized, so new funds are needed.

[5]   In order that computers can be made useful in today's society.

[6]   But we tried all night, and we couldn't reach them.

[7]   The programmer programs it such that the computer gets the first move.

[8]   And after the computer makes its move and its opponent replies.

[9]   The lesions should be treated as soon as the shots are given, but you should use mild disinfectants.

[10] Since riots are sure to follow whenever those two parties clash.

34. QUIZ on finding independent clauses

Check these samples and put *Yes* if the sample has at least one independent clause to make it a real sentence. Put *No* if it doesn't. Watch for a clause that starts with no linking word or for a clause that comes at the beginning of the sentence and that starts with a linking word from the list of four. Also, try making up a "yes/no" question.

[1] One side defeats the other, or the authorities break it up.

[2] Just because these centers are the only place where a veterinary student can go.

[3] Religions that have many believers are an important part of the social order.

[4] After a religion is established, and it loses its strangeness.

[5] As soon as the store opened, we went in, changed clothes, and got to work.

[6] Because of the fact that the minimum conditions are not satisfied.

[7] You'll believe it when you see it, so you shouldn't make up your mind yet.

[8] They were very hopeful and their work improved when the new company took over.

[9] Where they ever managed to get all that information so fast.

[10] We'll graduate soon, when this semester ends, and a whole new life will begin.

[11] So it wasn't the course that held my interest, it was the teacher.

[12] Since the storms came, and the future looks dark.

[13] In view of the fact that they had an inspiration that changed the whole method.

[14] Whereas we are very much in agreement with the chairperson.

[15] Either the phone is ringing or the neighbors are yelling whenever I want to meditate.

[16] Customers get angry after the company overcharges them.

[17] They wrote back, but it didn't do any good.

[18] As the planes came closer, the army ran down the hill, and the battle began.

[19] The guns were out of ammunition, since supplies couldn't get through.

[20] Even though the public soon forgot the man that had caused the sensation.

35. REVIEW QUIZ *on finding independent clauses*

Same instructions as on the previous quiz.

[1]   When winter comes and the temperature falls.

[2]   The conditions which they were demanding were unacceptable.

[3]   The court fined her because she ran three stop signs, and she lost her license.

[4]   As I remember, the club was more dignified before they joined it.

[5]   They gave the loan to another bank, which seemed unfair.

[6]   Keeping in mind that their wages are higher than average, and their work is excellent.

[7]   After the sudden return of the missing commander.

[8]   The time was right and the chances were very good.

[9]   You sign up by mail, or you pay at the door.

[10] We'll come to the picnic if the weather stays good.

[11] When we were on vacation in Hawaii all that winter.

[12] Painting woodwork is a bad job when you'd rather be sailing.

[13] We'd better hurry, or we'll miss the train, because it's leaving in ten minutes.

[14] If I do the cooking and you wash the dishes.

[15] But if you don't like washing dishes of course.

[16] We waited three days and gave up.

[17] We ought to hurry because it's after midnight.

[18] If you don't fall down on these waxed hardwood floors.

[19] So the real inventor never knew what became of it all.

[20] Seeing that his mind is made up, and I can't change it.

■ F.   COMMON SENTENCE PROBLEMS

In everyday talk, people don't worry much about where one sentence ends and the next one begins. Talkers are mainly concerned with making STATEMENTS and asking QUESTIONS. There is usually no reason to make sure that every statement or question has the form of a real and complete SENTENCE. In writing, however, the form of your sentences is much more important. Readers need a way to see how things are put together. The sentence marks off a unit very clearly and deserves to be handled carefully. Especially if your experience with language has been mainly with talking, you need to watch out for problems with sentences.

F.1   Splices and Comma Splices

When you make spoken statements, you don't have to put marks between them. You just make a pause and go on. For example, here's part of a recording spoken by a student who painted his roof.

(128)   I steam-cleaned the roof..by attaching a hose..and plugging the machine into the wall..the machine is light enough that you can put it up on the roof

In writing, you need to mark the boundaries of statements. A SENTENCE needs at least one INDEPENDENT CLAUSE (see Section E). If you put two independent clauses together with *nothing* between them, you get a **SPLICE**:

(129)   I steam-cleaned the roof by attaching a hose and plugging the machine into the wall ↓ the machine is light enough that you can put it up on the roof.

The result looks confusing, because you have to stop and figure out where one clause ends and the next one begins.

   A plain splice with nothing between the two clauses is not terribly common in the writing of college students. Most writers want at least some mark at the point where the first statement ends and the second one begins. The comma is often used here. But if you put two independent clauses together with *only a comma* between them, you get a **COMMA SPLICE**:

(130)   I steam-cleaned the roof by attaching a hose and plugging the machine into the wall, the machine is light enough that you can put it up on the roof.

Now, at least, the boundary between the two clauses is marked. However, readers normally expect *just one* independent clause in a sentence, so you need to give them some clear signal if you've got *more than one*. A comma has so many possible uses that it's not really enough of a signal. You should use a *period*, a *semicolon*, or a *comma plus linking word*.

F.1.1   *Finding Splices*

Being able to find splices and comma splices is important when you're doing formal writing. After going through Section E, you should know how to locate independent clauses. You tend to splice together two statements about the same thing, because you feel you want to keep them in one sentence. In this splice, the student followed up one statement about John Steinbeck's novel *Of Mice and Men* by telling what consequences resulted:

> (131)   Lennie has killed a girl up at the ranch in Weeds that's why they left and came to the barley ranch.

In the following comma splices, the second statement backs up the first—that is, it offers a reason to believe the first statement (132), tells what the cause was (133), or gives more details (134):

> (132)   The months of waiting paid off, I was accepted.
>
> (133)   Melvin couldn't get in, he didn't look old enough.
>
> (134)   There are many kinds of shoes, each one is cut and designed its own way.

Comma splices are pretty common in the writing of college students. So it pays to be able to tell a comma splice apart from a real sentence.

The main thing is to pay attention to where you put clauses. You can get a real sentence by putting two clauses together with nothing between them (135), or with only a comma between them (136), *provided the first one is not an independent clause*. As you remember from Section E, a clause can't be independent if it starts with any *linking word* that is *not on the list of four*: "*and*," "*but*," "*or*," and "*so*" (see page 125). You could use linking words like "because," "since," "when," "while," "as," "which," "that," and so on. You might have:

> (135)   *When* the air comes in off the ocean, their weather gets better.
>
> (136)   *As* they were arriving, the owner came to the door.

In each of these sentences, the first clause is not independent, so you don't have a splice.

Here's an easy way to find a splice. Since a splice contains two independent clauses, it gives you two "yes/no" questions, like the ones we made up in Section E. You could get:

> (132)   The months of waiting paid off, I was accepted.
>
> (132a)   Did the months of waiting pay off? Was I accepted?
>
> (133)   Melvin couldn't get in, he didn't look old enough.
>
> (133a)   Couldn't Melvin get in? Didn't he look old enough?
>
> (134)   There are many kinds of shoes, each one is cut and designed its own way.
>
> (134a)   Are there are many kinds of shoes? Is each one cut and designed its own way?

It wouldn't work to make just one question. You would hardly say:

(132b)   Did the months of waiting pay off I was accepted?

If you do get just one sensible "yes/no" question, then you have only one independent clause. You could have:

(136)   As they were arriving, the owner came to the door.

(136a)   As they were arriving, did the owner come to the door?

Making up "yes/no" questions also keeps you from getting fooled by a sentence where you have *one subject with two verbs*. You get only one question, as in (137a); or if you get two questions, as in (137b), you have to *supply a subject for the second question*:

(137)   The insulation caught fire and burned at an extremely high temperature.

(137a)   Did the insulation catch fire and burn at an extremely high temperature?

(137b)   Did the insulation catch fire? And did *the insulation* burn at an extremely high temperature? [or: And did *it* burn at an extremely high temperature?]

You can't have a splice unless you have two full independent clauses—two full units each containing a subject with its agreeing verb.

As we see, a sentence with nothing or only a comma between two independent clauses counts as a splice. You can tell a splice because it makes two "yes/no" questions.

▢   **36. QUIZ** *on telling splices from real sentences*

Put *SPL* next to the splices and *OK* next to the real sentences.

[1]   When the lights went out, the dancers came on stage.

[2]   There is something wrong, the crowd looks angry.

[3]   It's not important, nobody will notice them.

[4]   Their team is in bad shape and is bowing out of the tournament.

[5]   As soon as the alarm goes off, the watchmen throw the switch.

[6]   These plants are huge, it is hard to believe.

[7]   You aren't going it's too far.

[8]   The tenants should be careful, the paint isn't dry.

[9]   It's the last copy, the library wants to buy it.

[10] Wherever she goes, the same rumors get started.

37. REVIEW QUIZ *on telling splices from real sentences*

Same instructions as on the previous quiz.

[1]   He forgot his own address, he was terribly absent-minded.

[2]   Since she had a headache she left very soon.

[3]   It's too dry here, we haven't had any rain for a month.

[4]   It won't make any difference it's too late now to save the crop.

[5]   The accident was so serious that the airline had to close down.

[6]   A fire would be nice we should get in some logs.

[7]   It's not worth it, the chimney is plugged.

[8]   When the substance is that powerful, one dose is already too much.

[9]   Nobody could even speak, the sight was too terrifying.

[10] The newspaper made a big fuss, and published the report on page one.

F.1.2   *Fixing Splices*

Once you are able to find splices, you can use some simple techniques for fixing them. First, you can put a PERIOD between the clauses, taking out the comma if you have one:

(134)   There are many kinds of shoes, each is cut and designed its own way.

(134b)   There are many kinds of shoes. Each is cut and designed its own way.

Of course, you capitalize the first letter of the second clause in order to begin a new sentence.

However, the period breaks your two statements apart, and after all, you probably spliced them in the first place because you thought they should go together. For that reason, simply putting in a period is not usually the best solution, especially not when the two clauses are short. You could end up with two tiny sentences, as in (138a):

(138)   I just walked out, I got so furious.

(138a)   I just walked out. I got so furious.

You might do better to put a SEMICOLON between the clauses, taking out the comma if you have one:

(132)   The months of waiting paid off, I was accepted.

(132c)   The months of waiting paid off; I was accepted.

The semicolon is a signal that the materials before and after it are closely related and belong together in one sentence (see also page 311). So when you put a semi-colon, you make it clear that you do want the two statements together, instead of breaking them apart with a period.

However, the semicolon doesn't tell *how or why* the two statements go to-gether. So the best cure for a splice is to

---

PUT IN A LINKING WORD THAT SHOWS HOW OR WHY THE TWO STATEMENTS ARE RELATED.

You might keep the comma and use it with a linking word from our list: "and," "but," "or," "so." Then you'll still have two independent clauses, but they'll be linked up the right way:

(132)   The months of waiting paid off, I was accepted.

(132d)   The months of waiting paid off, *and* I was accepted.

(134)   There are many kinds of shoes, each is cut and designed its own way.

(134c)   There are many kinds of shoes, *but* each is cut and designed its own way.

Or you can use a linking word that's not on our list. Then, one of the clauses is *not independent*:

(133)   Melvin couldn't get in, he didn't look old enough.

(133b)   Melvin couldn't get in, *since* he didn't look old enough.

(138)   I just walked out, I got so furious.

(138b)   I just walked out *when* I got so furious.

If you fix a splice this way, the linking word doesn't have to go *between* the clauses. You can also *start* the sentence with the linking word, so that the *first* clause is no longer independent. The independent one then follows without any linking word. As we saw for (135) and (136) in Section F.1.1, this pattern makes a real sentence. For instance, the comma splice in (139) is cured by starting with the linking word in (139a) as well as by putting the linking word between the two clauses in (139b):

(139)   There isn't much time left, we need to mail the entry today.

(139a)   *Since* there isn't much time left, we need to mail the entry today.

(139b)   There isn't much time left, *so* we need to mail the entry today.

Remember, whichever clause gets the linking word in front of it is not independent any more.

Linking words work just as well if you've spliced *three* clauses. You could fix this sample by putting one linking word at each point where splicing had happened:

(140)   I can't go; I'm not finished here; you should come back late this afternoon.

(140a)   I can't go, *because* I'm not finished here, *so* you should come back late this afternoon.

You might even use linking words when you've spliced more than three clauses. But splices this big hardly ever happen.

38. QUIZ *on fixing splices*

Use linking words to fix these splices.

[1]   It's getting colder, you'll need your winter clothes.

[2]   There is going to be a delay, the parts haven't been delivered yet.

[3]   I called the manager, he said to be patient, the repair truck is on its way.

[4]   I knew how to repair the motor, I read the directions carefully, I am trained as a mechanic.

[5]   We'll drive out to the woods, we can pick some mushrooms to eat, it's just the right time for them.

[6]   The costs won't be too high, we're fully insured.

[7]   The roads aren't very good, tire pressure is important.

[8]   My term paper's due, I need to run to the library.

[9]   Heart operations are difficult, the heart is a complex organ, it must be handled with the greatest care.

[10]   We'll leave the door unlocked, they can get in this evening.

39. REVIEW QUIZ *on fixing splices*

Go back to Quiz 36, on telling splices from real sentences, and use linking words to fix the splices you marked. Do the same for the splices you found on Review Quiz 37.

F.1.3 *Creating Comma Splices by Confusing Linking Words with Non-linking Words of Similar Meaning*

Comma splices are sometimes formed when students confuse LINKING WORDS with NON-LINKING WORDS OF SIMILAR MEANING. "And" gets confused with "also," "moreover," "in addition," and "besides." "But" gets confused with "however," "still," "nevertheless," "nonetheless," and "all the same." "Or" gets confused with "otherwise." "So" gets confused with "therefore," "thus," "in that case," and "that's why."

Because of this confusion, some students use these non-linking words to join independent clauses the same way they'd use the real linking words. For example, students wrote these comma splices:

(141)   The newspaper wanted a sports editor, *besides*, I was an expert on sports.

(142)   We weren't there, *however*, we read the reports afterward.

(143)   The letter said to enroll the next week, *otherwise*, enrollment would be closed.

(144)   The stadium wasn't filled up yet, *that's why* the show started pretty late.

To fix these comma splices, you could put in a **period** and make two sentences out of the clauses. You'd take out the comma if you have one.

(141a) The newspaper wanted a sports editor. Besides, I was an expert on sports.

(142a) We weren't there. However, we read the reports afterward.

But the period breaks your two statements apart, and since you spliced them, you probably wanted them to go together. So instead of putting in a period, you might do better to put a **semicolon** between the clauses and take out the comma if you have one:

(143a) The letter said to enroll the next week; otherwise, enrollment would be closed.

(144a) The stadium wasn't filled up yet; that's why the show started pretty late.

Another method is to put in a *real* linking word:

(141b) The newspaper wanted a sports editor, *and* I was an expert on sports.

(142b) We weren't there, *but* we read the reports afterward.

(143b) The letter said to enroll the next week, *or* enrollment would be closed.

(144b) The stadium wasn't filled up yet, *so* the show started pretty late.

Switching to a real linking word keeps the statements together. If the result sounds good, you can use the real linking word *in addition to* the word you already had:

(141c)   The newspaper wanted a sports editor, *and besides*, I was an expert on sports.

(144c)   The stadium wasn't filled up yet, *so that's why* the show started pretty late.

This method doesn't work all the time, but there's nothing much wrong with it. Just be sure that you do have *at least one real linking word.*

40. QUIZ *on fixing splices caused by confusing linking words*

Fix these comma splices. You can put in a semicolon or a real linking word. Or you can replace the non-linking word between the clauses with a real linking word.

[1]   We're leaving early, otherwise we'll get caught in traffic.

[2]   Three witnesses identified the suspect, all the same, it was hard to convict him.

[3]   The wedding date was already set, besides, her gown had been delivered.

[4]   The guarantee had expired, nevertheless, the company repaired it for free.

[5]   The expenses were high, still, it was well worth the money.

[6]   We had to hand in two take-home quizzes, in addition, the term project was very complicated.

[7]   Last week was too busy, moreover, several of our best people were out with the flu.

[8]   The contest wasn't to begin for two days, nonetheless, the cars were already coming into town.

[9]   It was his birthday, therefore everyone was very kind.

[10] The track may be very rough, in that case the race is a high risk.

41. REVIEW QUIZ *on fixing splices caused by a confusion of linking words*

Same instructions as on the previous quiz.

[1]   I made a deposit, nevertheless, the bank bounced the check.

[2]   The publicity had better be good, otherwise, our company will get into difficulties.

[3] The costs were ruinous, moreover, the deadlines were not met.

[4] It seemed like a high rent, still, the location was excellent.

[5] The report came late, in addition, it was full of mistakes.

[6] The figures seemed right, all the same, I had them checked.

[7] The service wasn't the best, however, we had to be content.

[8] All the doors were locked, also, there was a guard at the gate.

[9] There was some decline, all the same, the quality was fairly good.

[10] We were tired, nevertheless, we decided to try it.

General quiz

42.
▼

on splices

You should now be able to find and fix splices. You have a splice whenever you put two independent clauses together in one sentence with nothing or only a comma between them. You can fix the splice with a semicolon, but your best bet is usually to put in a real linking word that shows how the clauses fit together. Fix the splices in the following statements. Watch out for the ones that have three clauses spliced together.

[1] Life moves quickly today, in addition, fashions change.

[2] Field goals are dramatic the guy sets up the ball and kicks it over the goal posts.

[3] I was nervous and excited, I forgot my lines, it was horribly embarrassing.

[4] She wore the same outfit as yesterday, however, she changed her hair style.

[5] The situation is more relaxed, the customers feel at ease.

[6] We can't drive my car it doesn't have a tag we ought to use yours.

[7] The weather gets below freezing, we lose our orange harvest.

[8] I can't work very fast, besides, the phone rings constantly.

[9] The circus is coming next week, in that case we should get tickets.

[10] The storm subsided, we stopped worrying about the ship sinking.

[11] The lion escaped, everybody was in a panic.

[12] My game is getting better, therefore, I'll enter the tournament.

[13] You shouldn't read it, it's such a dull book.

[14] The birds eat from your hand they're extremely tame.

[15] We don't feel like having breakfast, we'll wait for lunch instead.

[16] Nobody came, it was too dark by that time, besides, it was raining.

[17] She made a big fuss, the trip had to be canceled.

[18] They bought a hundred shares, the price was low it was a great opportunity.

[19] I'm surprised you accepted, the job has heavy responsibilities.

[20] Gasoline got very expensive we switched to roller skates.

[21] The crowd didn't even protest, they were so frightened.

[22] The bar was shut down, it got to be a public nuisance.

[23] You keep a book too long, the library forgets you have it.

[24] Students drop calculus, they can't get into computer programming.

[25] The children are home they'll be screaming for dinner.

Back-up general quiz

on splices

43.

▼

Same instructions as on the previous quiz.

[1] My cousins are coming I haven't seen them for years.

[2] They're down at the bus station, we'd bettery hurry.

[3] I couldn't leave yet, I'm on the job, however, I'm free after 6 o'clock.

[4] They won't mind they know how busy we are.

[5] I don't even read the newspaper, I'm so tied up.

[6] You've done it now, the roof you built is collapsing.

[7] It's not my fault, it's the weight of all that snow.

[8] The manufacturers shouldn't worry about it, nobody is blaming them, still, the product will have to be recalled.

[9] We had a fine dinner we want to go back soon.

[10] The job is improving, in addition, a new office building is opening.

[11] It's much nicer, it has air conditioning, also, the view is spectacular.

[12] I'm not complaining, anyway, it's time for a change.

[13] We've redecorated, you should come over.

[14] I decided on a pet turtle, it's very tame.

[15] It's easy to feed, after all, it eats lettuce.

[16] It got out of the cage once, we looked everywhere.

[17] We finally found it, it was down behind the dresser, it couldn't get out by itself.

[18] It's getting warmer the dogwood trees are blooming spring must be here.

[19] I went to campus, I needed to ask about the notice.

[20] It took a long time to clear up, nobody knew anything about it, moreover, the supervisor wasn't in.

[21] I had to stand in line it was infuriating.

[22] I felt like moving to some other college they wouldn't treat students like that.

[23] The situation is always that way at registration, they blame it on the computer.

[24] It's no minor matter, they inconvenience such a lot of students.

[25] The procedures will get better soon they'll figure out a new way I hope so anyway.

w let's look at some ways to clear up these pronoun problems. First, you can

---

REPLACE THE PRONOUN WITH THE NOUN
IT STANDS FOR

—as by changing (108) and (109) to (108a) and (109a):

(108)   Mexico's oil deposits may help strengthen *their* economy.

(108a) Mexico's oil deposits may help strengthen *the nation's* economy.

(109)   The president wants to turn away the Haitian refugees, but how *they* are going to do it is not known.

(109a) The president wants to turn away the Haitian refugees, but how *U.S. officials* are going to do it is not known.

But this tactic won't always work. It might give you something awkward or dumb, like (104a) or (104b):

(104)   JoAnne told Sheila she couldn't come to her party.

(104a) JoAnne told Sheila that JoAnne couldn't come to Sheila's party.

(104b) JoAnne told Sheila that Sheila couldn't come to JoAnne's party.

depending on which you mean (let's ignore the prospect of telling someone she can't come to her own party). As we saw already (Section D.4), repeated words can be annoying. So putting in nouns for pronouns is frequently not the best way out. A better solution would be to

---

REARRANGE THE STATEMENT SO THAT THE
TROUBLESOME PRONOUNS CAN BE LEFT OUT

—for example:

(104c) JoAnne excused herself from coming to Sheila's party.

(104d) JoAnne was having a party and told Sheila not to come.

A vague "this" can be left out by making two statements into one (see also pp. 58, 182):

(111)   You can buy either the cable or the antenna. *This* will improve the reception.

---

[10] Two men—one carrying a bomb and the other an officer of the New Jewish Defense League—were arrested today on charges of plotting to bomb the Egyptian government tourist office. [Associated Press wire, Dec. 18, 1978]

24. QUIZ *on doubtful statements*

Fix these doubtful statements so that only the intended meaning is left. Use the methods discussed in this section.

[1]   Stolen Painting Is Found by Tree [*Philadelphia Evening Bulletin*, Dec. 17, 1974]

[2]   Mrs. Consigny was living alone in her home after her husband died in 1954 when the phone rang. [*This Is Madison*, July 8, 1978]

[3]   City Will Add 12 Foot Cops [*The Trentonian*, March 24, 1977]

[4]   Tuna Are Biting Off Washington Coast [*Seattle Post-Intelligencer*, Aug. 3, 1979]

[5]   Jamaican Officials Are Considering Arson [*Eureka* (Calif.) *Times-Standard*, May 21, 1980]

[6]   Shoot Kids to Halt Flu, Study Says [*Orlando* (Fla.) *Sentinel Star*, March 16, 1978]

[7]   Dr. Tackett Gives Talk on the Moon [*Indiana Evening Gazette*, March 13, 1976]

[8]   Nude Club Owner Is Going into Politics [*Burlington* (Vt.) *Free Press*, Dec. 14, 1979]

[9]   FBI Is Needed for Bank Robberies [*News and Observer*, July 22, 1978]

[10] California Sheriff Wants Man Shot by Patrolman [*Cincinnati Post*, July 24, 1980]

25. REVIEW QUIZ *on doubtful statements*

Same instructions as on the previous quiz.

[1]   Reagan Visits Harrassed Blacks [*San Francisco Chronicle*, May 4, 1982]

[2]   Drunk Gets Nine Months in Violin Case [*Lembridge Herald*, Oct. 30, 1976]

[3]   If Kline's plan is to die, the legislature must act. [*Philadelphia Inquirer*, Nov. 25, 1976]

[4]   Queen Ducks Ride to U.S. on Concorde [*Cleveland Plain Dealer*, May 21, 1976]

[5]   Boy Scouts' Exploring Is Extended to Include Teenage Girls [*Today's Post*, March 15, 1971]

[6] Distributor Finds Art of Producing Lies in Business [*New York Times*, Aug. 13, 1976]

[7] Admitted Killer Gets 90 Years in Washington [*Detroit News*, Aug. 4, 1976]

[8] Haig Insists Soviets Use Chemicals [*Sarasota (Fla.) Herald-Tribune*, Feb. 15, 1982]

[9] Police Can't Stop Gambling [*Detroit Free Press*, July 1, 1975]

[10] Reagan Raps Need to Prove Sanity [*The Oregonian*, July 7, 1982]

■ G. INCONSISTENT AND DOUBTFUL STATEMENTS WITH PRONOUNS

PRONOUNS are short words that can stand in place of many things. The most common pronouns—"I," "you," "he," "she," "it," "we," "they," and their various forms ("my," "mine," "me," "your," "yours," "his," "her," and so forth)—can be very convenient. They can take the place of nouns, address people present or absent, and be adapted to fit all kinds of situations. They are really almost *too* versatile—they can lead you to make inconsistent or doubtful statements.

G.1 Pronoun Problems and Solutions

The use of pronouns in everyday talk is often vague. One student said on tape (talking about a Charlie Chaplin movie):

(103)   he gets intoxicated at the party....and her previous lover is on the side the whole time trying to reveal *his* true identity because *he* has been spying on *him he* knows that *he* really works in the bar

Unless you know the story already, you'll have trouble figuring out who is meant by "he," "him," and "his." Still, everyday talk can afford to be a little vague, because people are likely to give you the benefit of the doubt and try to make sense out of what you're saying.

But when you write, you should keep track of pronouns and prevent possible confusion. The danger comes from the fact that you, the writer, already have things sorted out in your mind, and you know what the pronouns are for. So you can easily overlook problems that could come up for readers who don't have your background knowledge. Small wonder that, according to a recent survey, composition teachers mark pronoun problems in student papers more often than any other slip-up except comma problems.

In extreme cases, it's impossible to tell what's meant, as in:

(104)   JoAnne told Sheila *she* couldn't come to *her* party.

If you don't already know all about it, you can't figure out whose party.

Other times, you can get the message by picking what m as in:

(105)   Water pollution is one way people endanger alligators. very smart, or else *they* just don't care what happens to

Here, "they" is probably for "people" and "them" is for "alligat you shouldn't make readers work harder than necessary.

In particular, you should try to avoid doubtful statements wit ings. Students wrote:

(106)   I hate eggs, but these people were so hospitable I had to eat

(107)   I didn't really care for these grapes, but *they* went to all that

Let's hope nobody would believe that the writer ate people (106) o went to a lot of trouble (107). Still, you'll look better if you can av statements that distract attention from your message.

In everyday talk, people sometimes use a pronoun like "you," "they, just about anything they have in mind. Many students write "they" t whoever is involved (108) or for whoever is in charge (109):

(108)   Mexico's oil deposits may help strengthen *their* economy. [their = Mexican people's]

(109)   The president wants to turn away the Haitian refugees, but how *they* going to do it is not known. [they = U.S. officials, not Haitian refuge

Students use "it" (110) or "this" (111) for the whole event or situation, than for any one item mentioned before:

(110)   The woman's citizenship in the town was recognized when she was too old to appreciate *it*. [it = recognition, not citizenship or town]

(111)   You can buy either the cable or the antenna. *This* will improve the re- ception. [this = buying one of the two, whether it's a cable or an antenna]

"You" is often written for people in general, rather than for someone the writer is specifically addressing. That use is all right for everyday writing (less suitable for formal writing), but should be done consistently. It's clumsy to shift around the way this student did:

(112)   *One* has a better chance of getting into upper-division courses when *you* begin with all the right prerequisites. What courses a *student* can take depends on what *they* have already taken.

(111a)   Buying either the cable or the antenna will improve the reception.

Rearranging is particularly useful when the statement has more than one part. Take this famous example:*

(113)   If your baby doesn't thrive on raw milk, you ought to boil *it*.

One part of the statement ("if your baby doesn't thrive on raw milk") has two nouns ("baby," "milk"), and the other part ("you ought to boil it") has a pronoun ("it"). You want to make sure that the pronoun can only go with one noun ("milk") and not with the other ("baby"). So you

---

MOVE THE PRONOUN INTO THE SAME PART OF THE STATEMENT WITH THE NOUN YOU WANT TO RULE OUT.

In this case, you want to move the "it" into the same part of the statement as the "baby" you want to keep from getting "boiled." Watch what happens:

(113a)   If your *baby* doesn't thrive on *it*, you ought to boil the raw milk.

(113b)   You ought to boil the raw milk if your *baby* doesn't thrive on *it*.

As you can see, two versions are possible. Since pronouns normally *look back*, as in (113b), you'll usually want to put the part of the statement containing the pronoun *after* the other part. Still, putting it *before*, as in (113a), sometimes works, provided you don't have too many words between the pronoun and its noun. If you're not sure how many is too many, play it safe and put the pronoun after the noun.

You can also clear things up if you

CHANGE THE NOUN YOU WANT TO RULE OUT SO THAT IT NO LONGER FITS THE PRONOUN

—as in this version of (113):

(113c)   If *babies* don't thrive on raw milk, you ought to boil *it*.

The singular "it" that gets boiled can no longer fit the plural "babies."
Let's try fixing another example:

* Invented by Otto Jespersen, a famous grammarian.

(114)   If your shoes hurt your feet, you should have *them* reshaped on a machine.

Again, a problem arises because you have two nouns ("shoes," "feet") in one part of the statement and the pronoun ("them") in another. Once you get the "them" into the same part with the thing you don't want to "reshape" ("feet"), the problem is gone. As we saw for (113b), in order to place the pronoun *after* the noun it points to, you need to reverse the parts of the statement. This time, you get:

> (114a)   You should have your shoes reshaped on a machine if *they* hurt your feet.

If you leave the two parts in the same order, the pronoun has to look ahead rather than back:

> (114b)   If *they* hurt your feet, you should have your shoes reshaped on a machine.

Or you can apply the tactic of leaving out one of the nouns:

> (114c)   You should have your shoes reshaped on a machine if they hurt *you.*

since you can safely assume that the "feet" are the obvious part of "you" that shoes would "hurt."

Now, suppose you have *three or more* nouns in one statement, and all of them could fit the same pronoun. In

> (115)   The *frat guys* leave their *bottles* on the *steps* until *people* trip over *them.* *They* ought to be more considerate. [them = bottles; They = guys]

you have four plural nouns ("guys," "bottles," "steps," "people") and two pronouns ("them," "they") to sort out. If you try putting in even more nouns or moving the parts of the statement around, you're likely to make a big mess. So your best solution is to streamline the statement and leave out the pronouns. You could have:

> (115a)   The frat guys who leave bottles on the steps for people to trip over ought to be more considerate.

The more nouns and pronouns you have floating around, the better it is to streamline and leave things out.

◻ 26. QUIZ *on pronoun problems*

Try clearing up the pronoun problems in these statements.

Example:
    He Found God at the End of His Rope [*Fort Worth Tribune,* Feb. 3, 1978]

You could fix it like this:
He Was at the End of His Rope When He Found God

[1]   The wedding guests brought so many cuckoo clocks that we had to hide most of them in the closet.

[2]   Before you take the driver's test, you should study the booklet of questions they hand out.

[3]   Laurie asked Rhonda if she would be able to enroll in her class.

[4]   France's inflation is so bad I don't know how they stand it themselves.

[5]   The Treasury Department wants to shut down the money market, but we don't believe they'll really do it.

[6]   A sales clerk should not make too many mistakes or they'll get fired.

[7]   The citizen always has to pay out more of their income in taxes than you expected.

[8]   Police said they had to bring the suspect to the ground twice before they confiscated the pistol from a pants leg. "I would describe it as hairy," said Sgt. Lou Daliso. [*White Plains* (N.Y.) *Reporter Dispatch*, March 15, 1981]

[9]   We wrote the school and told them to send our transcripts.

[10] After such a spectacular failure, our team ran into a string of successes. This was inspiring.

[11] When the junk overflowed our garage, we stored it up in the attic.

[12] A runny nose can annoy the whole class. You should always blow it.

[13] The wasp wouldn't leave my car, so I had to smash it.

[14] The children fought over the ice cream cones until they started to melt all over the sidewalk.

[15] The earplugs are in the drawer with your pills. Be careful when you stick them in your ears.

▪ 27. REVIEW QUIZ *on pronoun problems*

Same instructions as on the previous quiz.

[1]   The horses don't have their blankets because we sent them all to the laundry.

[2]   News came down from the budget department on the top floor that it still wouldn't balance.

[3]   That cold front might spoil our picnic. Maybe we ought to save it for tomorrow.

[4]   When traffic is heavy, you shouldn't ride your bicycle. It might not pay any attention to you.

[5]   The sun isn't good for that plant. You should put it on top of the refrigerator.

[6]   He has just the sense of humor to appreciate a team like that. It's pretty sick.

[7]   The spark plugs in our cars are so dirty that I don't see how they can go racing down the road so fast.

[8]   I have her name on the tip of my tongue, but I can't get hold of it right now.

[9]   After a thundershower ruined my jacket, I stuffed it in the trash dumpster.

[10] Both my sisters got new sundresses. People really stare when they go out walking all by themselves.

G.2   Pronouns and Possessives

Pronouns for POSSESSIVES can be troublesome too. Technically, a pronoun is not supposed to refer to the POSSESSOR, but rather to the THING POS-SESSED. If you write:

(116)   Every time I forget the *dog's dinner, it* barks furiously.

you have the dinner barking instead of the dog. We saw before that you can fix a vague pronoun if you

---

MOVE THE PRONOUN INTO THE SAME PART OF THE STATEMENT WITH THE NOUN YOU WANT TO RULE OUT.

For possessives, you can do the same thing if you

MAKE THE PRONOUN BE THE POSSESSIVE.

The pronoun gets moved into the possessor slot; for example:

(116a)   Every time I forget *its* dinner, the dog barks furiously.

The pronoun can't point to the noun that's right next to it ("its dinner"). If you want to keep the pronoun *after* the noun—usually a good idea, as we saw be-fore—switch the parts of the statement around as well:

(116b)   The dog barks furiously every time I forget *its* dinner.

If the vague pronoun is in a *separate sentence* from its noun (if there's a period in between), the pronoun really should look back, not ahead. Take a passage like:

(117)   We should clean the bird's cage. *It* is looking unhappy. [It = bird, not cage]

Your best bet is to exchange the position of the two sentences when you move the pronoun:

(117a)   The bird is looking unhappy. You should clean *its* cage.

The other way around—

(117b)   You should clean *its* cage. The bird is looking unhappy.

—doesn't work so well because there's too much of a wait between seeing the pronoun and finding out what's meant.

☐ 28. QUIZ *on pronouns and possessives*

Fix the pronoun and possessive problems in these statements.

Example:
   After consulting with the sailboats' captains, we decided to repaint them.

You could fix it like this:
   We decided to repaint the sailboats after consulting with their captains.

[1]   When we came too close to the alligator's pond, it swam away.

[2]   The moon's shape has changed. It has a darker color, too.

[3]   That dog's owner should be jailed. He howls all night long.

[4]   The senators' rooms here aren't ready. They can take a taxi to our down-town hotel.

[5]   After all he's done to reform the state's tax laws, you'd think they would give him some recognition.

[6]   The sailing club's reputation is terrible. It should kick the troublemakers out.

[7]   Last year's production declined because it was a period of political unrest.

[8]   The miners' picks and hammers are back in the tool shed. They must have knocked off work early.

[9]   At my sister's house, the parrot's vocabulary has some obscene words. We'll have to rap her on the beak with a stick.

[10] You'd better distribute the players' bowling shoes immediately. They're getting impatient and might walk out in a huff.

☐ 29. REVIEW QUIZ *on pronouns and possessives*

Same instructions as on the previous quiz.

[1]   Don't be afraid of the dogs' teeth. We sent them all to obedience school to sharpen their training.

[2]   His children's glasses are really thick. They must not see very well with unaided eyes.

[3]   I'm going to check out the horses' hooves. They've been kicking up a fuss lately.

[4]   The club's new yacht is so fancy that it's been acting very snobbish.

[5]   We always appreciate a day's pay when it's been long and tiring.

[6]   I told the cat's owner she shouldn't try to sit on my lap all the time.

[7]   When a gust of wind caught the sheet music for the brass band, it blew all over the football field.

[8]   It's time to set up the ladies' chairs. I see them walking in the door right now.

[9]   My brothers' hands are terribly dirty. They must have been slapping together another Volkswagen engine.

[10] Why should we clean the cat's litter box when it's always running away?

G.3   Pronouns for Missing Nouns

Another problem comes up when you MAKE A PRONOUN STAND FOR A MISSING NOUN—that is, for something you have in mind, but didn't mention. The student who wrote:

(118)   I was having engine trouble, so I parked *it* and hitched a ride.

wanted the "it" to stand for the "car" she never mentioned, though "engine" suggests there was one; she seems to be saying she "parked" the "engine trouble." This time, the best remedy is to

---

REPLACE THE PRONOUN WITH THE NOUN
IT STANDS FOR

—for instance:

> (118a)   I was having engine trouble, so I parked *the car* and hitched a ride.

Here, the replacement can't lead to repeated words since the noun was totally missing before—not like the awkward samples (104a) and (104b) on page 50, with too many repeats.

30. QUIZ *on pronouns for missing nouns*

Clear up the following. Use your imagination to supply missing nouns.

Example:
I hear noises in the printing room. We must have forgotten to switch it off.

You could fix it like this:
I hear noises in the printing room. We must have forgotten to switch the printer off.

[1]   The umpire had better watch out for the next two batters. When they get a hit, they don't watch where they throw it.

[2]   We heard the fire siren as it screeched to a halt outside our house.

[3]   If you don't measure the salt and baking powder right, it will taste awful when it's baked.

[4]   Leave the air conditioning on and lower the awning. That way, it will stay cool until we get back.

[5]   The tourists saw the big waves hitting the pier and decided it was too rough to swim in.

[6]   If I really work on my baseball, I'll be one someday in the major leagues.

[7]   Don't be too slow when you put in the birdseed. It might peck at your hand.

[8]   That's the main expense with being a taxi driver. You have to fill it with gas all the time.

[9]   The mailman is getting careless. He lost one yesterday.

[10]   We'll have to return the books and magazines now. They close at five o'clock.

31. REVIEW QUIZ *on pronouns for missing nouns*

Same instructions as on the previous quiz.

[1]   I'm not going to that butcher shop any more. It had too much bone and fat on it last time.

[2]	The question on the board was so tricky that I threw it in the wastebasket and started over three times.

[3]	Fighting fires is a hard job. I've never known one myself, but I suppose it really interferes with your personal life.

[4]	Cooking in a microwave oven can be very frustrating. Mine turned out awful last week.

[5]	Get on the phone and send for a plumber before it runs all over the kitchen floor.

[6]	When we heard the hurricane was approaching, we ran to nail it up with boards.

[7]	The barking at the door frightened our baby. We had to chain it to the doghouse.

[8]	That whine in your car is going to be expensive to fix. You will not be happy when you have to pay it.

[9]	The furniture repairers haven't gotten to the dining room yet, so you'd better sit on it carefully.

[10]	I've been dreading that class all week. Have you handed yours in already?

G.4 Vague Pronouns for Whole Events or Situations

Pronouns that POINT TO A WHOLE EVENT OR SITUATION may have no noun to go with (see also page 56). The pronouns most often used this way are "this," "that," "which," and "it." Students wrote:

(119)	The American colonists wished to escape involvement in the war in Europe. *This* was one cause of the American Revolution. [This = the wish to escape involvement]

(120)	My apartment was separated from campus by a freeway and a ditch. *It* prevented me from getting to class in a hurry. [It = the whole location]

Here, the same tactic can be used that works for missing nouns:

REPLACE THE PRONOUN WITH A NOUN

—as in:

(119a)	The American colonists wished to escape involvement in the war in Europe. *This wish* was one cause of the American Revolution.

(120a) My apartment was separated from campus by a freeway and a ditch. *That location* prevented me from getting to class in a hurry.

A more economical solution is to

STREAMLINE THE STATEMENTS
AND GET RID OF THE PRONOUN

—as in:

(119b) The American colonists' wish to escape involvement in the war in Europe was one cause of the American Revolution.

(120b) Having an apartment separated from campus by a freeway and a ditch prevented me from getting to class in a hurry.

This way, the event or situation is clearly the main thing in your total statement.

32. QUIZ *on vague pronouns for whole events or situations*

Try both ways, inserting a noun and streamlining statements, for clearing up these pronoun problems. Sometimes, one way is obviously better than the other.

Example:
> The neighbors bought a new car with a turbo charger. This was terribly extravagant.

You could fix it like this:
> The neighbors bought a new car with a turbo charger. This purchase was terribly extravagant. [noun inserted]
> The neighbors were terribly extravagant to buy a new car with a turbo charger. [streamlined]

[1] The first race set a new record. I heard about it that evening.

[2] The club was opposed to such a strong measure. This was very unusual.

[3] Reading his handwriting is a terrific strain. It's really annoying.

[4] We might live on campus. That would be more expensive.

[5] The musical had a fine cast last night. Did you see it?

[6] Although some students sell their tickets, and some even make a profit, others can't do this.

[7] They have to pay over twelve dollars, which is unreasonable. This is due to a scarcity of tickets.

[8] We turned off the air conditioning, which makes small rooms unpleasant.

[9] He is phasing out the social program. This is because of budget problems.

[10] The White House wanted to censor that newspaper for reporting the Watergate scandal. The public thought it was outrageous.

☐ 33. REVIEW QUIZ *on vague pronouns for whole events or situations*

Same instructions as on the previous quiz.

[1] The detective saw the scar on her foot and knew this was something big.

[2] When I saw my face in the mirror, it was shattering.

[3] The pitcher got mad and threw the ball right at the heckler's head. This was really stupid.

[4] The whole crowd at the disco was drunk. It was staggering.

[5] She wasn't too upset at the noise of her baby. It's something she's been expecting for months.

[6] The experts were not impressed by my best swarm of honey bees. This really hurt.

[7] I received the bill for the plastic surgery on my nose. It was huge.

[8] I couldn't help noticing that the blacksmith was using a special hammer. In fact, it struck me the minute I entered the shop.

[9] The press did a full-page story on the starlet's background. This was way out of proportion to everything else.

[10] My friends found out the ammunition would not fit our new rifle. This shot the hunting trip all to pieces.

General quiz

34.
▼

on pronoun problems of all kinds

The following statements contain all the pronoun problems we have been looking into. Circle the troublesome pronouns, and fix things up. Make your best
guess about what was meant.

[1]   Ted saw Harry on Monday. He said he missed an important meeting.

[2]   His personality offended the whole town, so he put it under psychiatric

      treatment. This is still going on now.

[3]   The bowling ball's cover is too loose. It almost fell out on my foot.

[4]   The big difference between the sandbagger and the avid golfer is that he

      never practices.

[5]   My brother got in a fight last Saturday with another guy from our school.

      He asked him if he thought he looked like a real football hero.

[6]   The bugs were biting our ankles, which made us spray them with poison.

[7]   The conductor was late for the opening concert. This was a memorable

      occasion.

[8]   I wish I had her phone number. It would be a real asset, even if it didn't

      work out.

[9]   When the pie hit his face, it really flew apart.

[10] Basketball players learn to be good at making a foul shot. This comes from

      illegal body contact.

[11] We made sure to lock the lion's cage. It's feeling very hungry today.

[12] I never used to think about reporting for a newspaper, but now I am one.

[13] The kids' voices hurt my ears. I should stick plugs in them.

[14] After writing for two hours, she handed it in and ran home to the dorm. It was an ungodly mess.

[15] When we line the doorway with rubber, it won't slam so loudly.

[16] The ship's radio room was a madhouse. Everybody thought it was sinking.

[17] In high school they didn't have us write long papers.

[18] When Chuck's partner died, he felt very depressed.

[19] Although humans have partly overcome nature, they are helpless against old age and death. They are ominous and overwhelming.

[20] Their original plan was to cover the whole floor with shag carpet. But it fell through.

Back-up general quiz

35.

▼

on pronoun problems of all kinds

Same instructions as on the previous quiz.

[1]   A soccer player is not like a football player, because he uses his feet more.

[2]   He didn't even warn me about sitting on the hot upholstery. This made my blood boil.

[3]   If you carry the sack on your head, it might split open and spill beans all over the ground.

[4]   We put on the camel's saddle very carefully. We were afraid it would spit on us.

[5]   When the Fire Department came out, they saw nothing more could be done for the house. It was all over.

[6]   Her head was still sticking up out of the water. But it looked pretty turbulent.

[7]   The wind knocked over that screen, so we gave it to the Salvation Army. I don't know if they ever managed to sell it.

[8]   Racing cars was an attractive profession, and I soon became one.

[9]   There's a storm brewing. I can see it in her eyes.

[10] The snake's owner didn't have many neighbors over until his fangs were removed. They must have been relieved.

[11] The challenger tired out in the eighth round. This was what the crowd had been waiting for.

[12] Those kids spilled a Slurpy on your artwork. It was disgusting.

[13] I only opened the birdcage one second and it flew to the top of the flagpole. This was going too far.

[14] Cheryl thought LuAnne was using her credit cards.

[15] After the last sudden attack, the army kept an eye on it.

[16] Those bottles were thrown from a carful of drunken rowdies. They woke up in a jail cell the next morning, filled with confused memories.

[17] Once the brakes are fixed, it will be much safer to drive.

[18] Salesmanship is important to me. My uncle is one.

[19] I have a lot of patience with the puppy she smuggled into our dorm, but yesterday it ran out.

[20] The commission wanted to audit the dealers' books, but they closed up, jumped on a plane, and left the country.

General quiz

36.

▼

on inconsistent and doubtful statements

The following items from newspapers and student papers contain the kinds of inconsistent and doubtful statements we've been working on in this section. Please fix them up.

[1]   Fried Chicken Cooked in Microwave Wins Vacation Trip [*Portland Oregonian*, July 8, 1981]

[2]   Speaking with a distinct accent, René Jules Dubos was born in Saint Brice, France, on February 20, 1901. [*Today's Health*, Sept. 1969]

[3]   Child Teaching Expert to Speak [*Birmingham* (Ala.) *Post-Herald*, March 28, 1977]

[4]   Teachers' Head Goes Off to Jail [*Sarasota* (Fla.) *Herald-Tribune*, April 20, 1974]

[5]   Dear Readers: We invent your comments and criticisms. [*Worcester* (Mass.) *Recorder and Labor News*, Dec. 12, 1973]

[6]   The main doors at the dorm are encouraged to stay locked at all times.

[7]   Cabell Democrats Have Two Heads [*Huntington* (W.Va.) *Herald Dispatch*, July 6, 1978]

[8]   Shouting Match Ends Teachers' Hearing [*Long Island* (N.Y.) *Newsday*, July 13, 1977]

[9]   Deadline Passes for Striking Police [*Indianapolis News*, Aug. 20, 1975]

[10] Navy Finds Dead Pilots Flying with Hangovers [*Washington Post*, Sept. 18, 1981]

[11] Left all alone, the TV set becomes your friend.

[12] Mauling by Bear Leaves Woman Grateful for Life (*Huntington* (W.Va.) *Herald-Dispatch*, Sept. 8, 1977]

[13] Inside the sun, California scientists observed a major disturbance.

[14] Defective show unofficially starts new TV season [*Toronto Star*, Aug. 24, 1979]

[15] Genetic Engineering Splits Scientists [*Washington Post*, Nov. 29, 1975]

[16] Daphne Hamilton, co-president of the North Country Bird Club, is recuperating from surgery. All bird calls are being taken by Peggy Coe. [*Watertown* (N.Y.) *Daily Times*, April 21, 1980]

[17] While paging through my old photo album, my decision to turn over a new leaf was finally made.

[18] Local Charity Group Helps Disable Man [*Clayton* (Ga.) *News Daily*, Sept. 14, 1981]

[19] The bathtub is not advised to use steel wool for cleaning.

[20] Two innings later, Jefferson was beaned in the back of the head by a line drive. Jefferson was not injured in the play; the baseball, which ricocheted all the way to right field, was taken to the hospital for X-rays. [*Toronto Globe and Mail*, Aug. 21, 1979]

NAME _____ CLASS _____ DATE _____

Back-up general quiz
37.
▼ on inconsistent and doubtful statements

Same instructions as on the previous quiz.

[1] The low quality of the steel in the metalworkers' tools is shocking. They would file a suit if they thought they could nail it down.

[2] The pets' new collars repel fleas. Now they won't be scratching themselves all day.

[3] Weighing three hundred pounds, the janitor was afraid to move the machine.

[4] There are good reasons why we shouldn't sign up for modern fiction. It just doesn't make sense.

[5] No judge was about to listen to such foul language from their mouths. They were slapped with a heavy fine.

[6] That dog reaches the size of a teddy bear when it's all grown up.

[7] The garbage is overflowing the can. It's too gross for words.

[8] We thought the kids would be safe using wooden spoons for toys. But they're stirring up trouble already.

[9] The second model's evening gown received great applause and took several bows.

[10] There was a remarkable wart on his chin until he had it removed.

[11] The guest made a remark toward the end of her speech that nobody wanted to hear.

[12] The weatherman predicts two inches of participation for tomorrow.

[13] Built of solid steel, she felt her new door was much safer.

[14] The landlord is still trying to find out who made the noise. He must be very nervous about it.

[15] Her eyesight is getting worse and should go see the eye doctor.

[16] Until the test is finished, you should remain in your seat. Then you may hand it to the teacher and go home.

[17] After jumping the last hurdle with astonishing ease, the trophy was sure to be mine.

[18] Panhandlers have been offending people at suburban bus stations. They may have to shut up soon.

[19] String the guests along until I get there with my special spaghetti. That will wrap up the feast.

[20] His family are desperate about the cockroaches. They might survive the pesticide again. This would be an outrage.

Review quiz
on talking versus writing

38.
▼

The following passage contains the various problems we have looked at in Chapter 1: fillers, hedges, repeated words, repeated content, and inconsistent or doubtful statements. Mark the problems you find and then write a complete new version.

Frequently, it often happens that I tend to go on long shopping trips. But unfortunately, these shopping trips bring home a difficulty that can be a problem, namely money. So what it turns out that I end up doing when I shop is shopping in a lot of different shops. The selection is huge and has a hard time deciding on anything.

Shoes is an example of the kind of thing that demonstrates what I'm trying to say. Looking at one pair after another, my feet get confused about sizes and styles. At one store, a shoe I slipped on told me something was wrong with my foot. Well, I was so hopping mad I put my foot down and hopped on a bus to another shopping center across town. Anyway, it closed up just as I got off.

Another thing that worries a lot are bikinis. I try on every store to find one that's open to my particular assets. My tastes are well-rounded, but won't fit just any old bikini that happens to walk in, you know. I tan easily, so I try to get a really tan tan when I can. Well, many colors don't appreciate this fact. Another thing is that, in addition, I also have to watch my financial foundations in order to support a stylish bikini.

In conclusion let me finish up by saying that when my tastes collide against my finances, they have a hard time getting dressed.

Back-up review quiz
on talking versus writing

39.
▼

Same instructions as on the previous quiz.

One of the many things that are hard to get used to when you leave high school and go to college is those kind of changes you'll have to be making when you get into college. The whole problem begins even before you start leaving high school.

I remember high school graduation. The ceremony ended up lasting so long it began to get dark before it ended. When the diplomas were all handed out, it seemed strange to watch them march out with total confidence as if they could breeze through life. This ended sooner than expected, namely as soon as the time came for them to enter college.

You also have to adjust to dorm life. It has many rooms whose occupants' tastes are very strange. They run through the halls at all hours. You hear doors slamming and cars starting, but they never say why. Sleeping near the main entrance, my ears suffer a lot of abuse and can't fight back. Some students keep dogs and cats, and bark or meow for hours. The toilets, showers, and sinks are in great demand in the morning, often being in a bad mood because of partying all night. They may say kind of mean things as they push you around the halls which I'd rather not mention, if you know what I mean.

Anyway, college is a whole new world compared to high school. If I can only survive it I'll end up coming out as a new person. This will be stiff, but all hope is not entirely and completely lost yet—it's looking up, in fact.

2.
Putting Clauses Together

Preview

In this chapter, we'll be working on some problems in grammar—that is, in the way people put words together. Since you've been putting words together in your talk for a long time, you obviously know a lot of grammar already. So we'll work only on the problems that come up when you go from talking to writing. We'll learn how to find the parts of a clause and how to tell when a clause is independent. We'll discuss some problems with the agreement of singular versus plural. Finally, we'll take a look at two main worries with the sentence: splices and fragments; these two can easily be handled once you know how to deal with clauses.

■ A. CLAUSES AND SENTENCES IN TALKING VERSUS WRITING

Talk is composed mainly of STATEMENTS. Writing is composed mainly of CLAUSES and SENTENCES that aren't always the same size and shape as the statements of talk. Compare what one student said with what she wrote:[*]

(1) *Spoken version*: you..TAKE the INterstate north..from where—to GAINESVILLE....and..you'll see TWO..a SIGN telling you that there's three exits to Gainesville..aaannnd..you'll get off at the EXIT that.... um..that's the HOSPITAL exit..aand you turn RIGHT onto ARCHER Road

[*] Two dots are for a short pause, and four dots for a long pause. Stressed items are in capitals.

(2) *Written version:*   You take the Interstate north to Gainesville. You'll see a sign telling you that there are three exits to Gainesville. Get off at the Hospital Exit. Turn right onto Archer Road.

The spoken version has stretches of talk broken by pauses (shown with dots) and loosely hooked together with linking words like "and" and "that." The written version has sentences plainly marked with periods, and has no linking words between sentences.

Students who rely too much on their talking habits are liable to have problems with writing clauses and sentences. Pauses aren't very reliable, because they can fall in the middle of a statement, not just at the beginning or at the end. Student writers typically make two kinds of errors when putting clauses together into sentences (see Section F). The statement may not contain enough parts to be a real sentence, or the statement may contain parts not put together well enough to make a real sentence.

All the same, your skill in talking can help you put together clauses and sentences in your writing. This chapter will show you how.

To get started, we'll need to think about **GRAMMAR**. Now, when I say "grammar," I don't mean a big book of complicated rules—I mean the way people put words together. You've been putting words together for a long time when you talk, so you obviously know a lot of grammar already. For instance, knowing grammar makes you say things like (3) rather than (4):

(3)   You take the Interstate north to Gainesville.

(4)   North you to Interstate take the Gainesville.

If it's true you already know grammar, the trick is to *make yourself aware* of what you know and to *put it to use* when you write. You don't need to know all the terms and charts a grammarian uses. After all, those terms and charts aren't *grammar*—they're just *one way of talking about grammar*. In this chapter, you'll learn about a different way many students have found pretty easy. We'll need only a few terms that are helpful for what we want to do. To keep things simple, we'll focus on sentences that convey STATEMENTS. Questions, exclamations, and commands are not usually difficult; we'll have a look at them in Section E of Chapter 5.

■   B.   THE PARTS OF A CLAUSE: SUBJECTS AND PREDICATES

A few basic terms are enough to get us going. The first one is the SENTENCE:

A SENTENCE MUST HAVE
AT LEAST ONE INDEPENDENT CLAUSE.

Since the sentence contains a clause, we need to define the CLAUSE next:

A CLAUSE MUST HAVE
A SUBJECT AND A PREDICATE.

In general, the SUBJECT is the take-off point for your statement, while the PREDICATE tells something about the subject—who or what it is, what it does, and so forth. But there's a simple way to find them, as we'll see in a moment.

This chapter should help you to recognize clauses, sentences, subjects, and predicates. You must already know what these things are, because you use them when you talk. So you won't really be learning anything new—you'll only be learning new ways to make use of what you've known all along.

A pair of "before and after" tests should prove my point. Below are five simple sentences. Take a pencil and, in each sentence, underline all parts of the subject *once*, and underline all parts of the predicate *twice*.

(5) Her father owns the store.

(6) Every morning I oversleep.

(7) Sometimes one of my dogs runs away.

(8) The girls in the freshman class missed my party.

(9) Once upon a time a king had three daughters.

Did you have trouble? Did you feel like you were guessing? There's no need for any doubt if you attack the issue the right way.

Your first step is:

MAKE UP A "WHO/WHAT" QUESTION ABOUT
YOUR STATEMENT

—that is, a question asking *who or what does or did something* (or is or was something) according to your statement. The "who" or "what" must be at the *start* of the question—don't say "the what" or "he does what," or anything that puts the "who" or "what" away from the start. Let's take sentence (5), where you get:

(5) Her father owns the store.

(5a) *Who* owns the store?

The rest is simple:

THE PREDICATE OF THE ORIGINAL SENTENCE IS ALL THE WORDS YOU USED AGAIN IN THE "WHO/WHAT" QUESTION.

THE SUBJECT IS THE REST.

So you should have underlined "owns the store" twice as the predicate, leaving "her father" to be underlined once as the subject.

If you have a choice of "who/what" questions, for instance, if you thought of saying:

(5b) *What* does her father own?

then ask the question word "who" or "what" about the *earlier* part of the statement—here, "her father" comes earlier than "the store," so you want (5a), not (5b). Of course, you have to base your question on "who" or "what" *only*— "when," "where," "how," "why," "which," "what kind of," and the like, will *not* work.

Does it seem easy so far? Let's try number (6):

(6) Every morning I oversleep.

(6a) *Who* oversleeps every morning?

Since "oversleeps every morning" got used in the "who/what" question, these words must make up the predicate. "I" must be your whole subject. This time, the question *moved* some words away from the start of the sentence, namely, "every morning." So you can tell that those words weren't part of the subject of (6). Don't be fooled just because they happened to go at the front of the sentence. The subject *usually* comes before the predicate, but *by no means always*. If you use a "who/what" question instead of guessing, you can't miss. Again, be sure to use *only* "who" or "what" in the question—don't say something like "When do you oversleep?"

Now, let's make a "who/what" question out of (7). You could have two possible results:

(7) Sometimes one of my dogs runs away.

(7a) *What* sometimes runs away?

(7b) *What* runs away sometimes?

Either way, the predicate includes the same three words, though in different order: "sometimes runs away" (7a) or "runs away sometimes" (7b). The subject must be "one of my dogs." Like (6), statement (7) had a part of the predicate at the start ("Sometimes"), but making the question moved it.

Now let's make questions for the statements in (8) and (9), and find the predicate and subject of each:

(8) The girls in the freshman class missed my party.

(8a) Who missed your party?

(9) Once upon a time a king had three daughters.

(9a) Who had three daughters once upon a time?

In (8), you get "missed my party" as predicate, and "the girls in the freshman class" as subject. In (9), you get "once upon a time" plus "had three daughters" as predicate, and "a king" as subject. (9) also had part of the predicate at the start, just like (6) and (7) did.

This method will work for most sentences in statement form. But you really have to make up a "who/what" question if you want to be certain to get it right. DON'T GUESS! Guessing only works for some people some of the time—it's too easy to get fouled up, so it's not worth the risk.

Now go back to the "before" test, where you underlined subjects and predicates in (5) through (9) before trying it with "who/what" questions. Did you get them all right before? Were you just guessing? If you're like most of the students who took the test, you'll see that the question method is a safer bet.

Now let's try the "after" test. Here are five more examples. Underline all parts of the subject once, and all parts of the predicate twice. Use the question method—don't guess!

(10) The man on the street doesn't know about this.

(11) Last night, the baseball season officially ended.

(12) A woman he knew wrote him a letter.

(13) The next day, she got a phone call.

(14) Quite a few of those students know how to roller-skate.

If you made up a short, simple "who/what" question for each statement, you came up with the right solutions. My point should now be clear: you can *do* grammar, though you may not be able to *talk about* grammar like a grammarian. You know what "subjects" and "predicates" are because you can make statements into questions. So use that knowledge and don't worry about memorizing complicated technical definitions or drawing big diagrams.

Let's run back over what we've had. Here are some sentences written by students. Underline the *subject once*, and the *predicate twice*. Use the "who/what" question method.

Example:

<u>That day</u>, <u>several salesmen from the same company</u> <u>came to the door</u>.
Who came to the door that day? [predicate = <u>that day</u> + <u>came to the door</u>; subject = <u>several salesmen from the same company</u>]

[1] A home near the water helps you learn windsurfing.

[2] On the first try, your experiment turned into a disaster.

[3] Cancer is the most feared of all known diseases.

[4] Every year new wonder drugs such as interferon come out.

[5] In combating leukemia, chemotherapy is used.

[6] A mail-program can be bought at a computer store.

[7] The business world demands new software.

[8] Business has a special interest in accounting programs.

[9] The first steps in writing a program are time-consuming.

[10] A day spent at the lake inspires good feelings.

[11] The whole family stays home to watch TV.

[12] After the debate, the delegate from Africa was at a loss for words.

[13] Part of the student body has realized the danger.

[14] Single rooms are available at the motel next door.

[15] Her answer is correct after all.

[16] A few of my relatives are from Philadelphia.

[17] New students should proceed to counseling.

[18] A small lake is usually calm enough for water-skiing.

[19] On Friday the circus will be in town.

[20] After three years a diploma will be awarded.

2. REVIEW QUIZ *on subjects and predicates*

Same instructions as on the previous quiz.

[1] The woman in the car is my cousin.

[2] Yesterday, more than a hundred people staged a protest march.

[3] Columbus, Ohio, is the state capital.

[4] At the fair, the younger artists displayed some new paintings.

[5] Soon the luncheon guests will arrive.

[6] Eighty percent of the people attending came from Georgia.

[7] Cleaning can be a terrible chore.

[8] Three of the films won a prize.

[9] At the conference, the Japanese received the most applause.

[10] The typewriter from the office broke down.

[11] Everybody in my family is going to Virginia.

[12] The chemistry professor is the nicest person around.

[13] Students must be careful about giving their opinions.

[14] The man you saw is suspected of the robbery.

[15] Once a week I eat at a local restaurant.

[16] The locusts were making all that noise.

[17] On weekends, the new watchman is on duty.

[18] Someone from the phone company is working behind the house.

[19] In a dusty area, the carburetor should be checked often.

[20] Two dogs and a cat live in that garage.

■ C. AGREEMENT

AGREEMENT is the requirement that

THE SUBJECT AND VERB MUST BOTH BE EITHER IN THE SINGULAR OR IN THE PLURAL.

Normally, the SINGULAR is used if *just one* thing is involved in the subject, and the PLURAL is used if *more than one* thing is involved. Though it's usually clear enough from your statement which of these two possibilities is meant, readers expect you to keep track of agreement. It's a traditional problem, partly because everyday talk doesn't always show agreement, at least in some dialects. There are some other stumbling blocks in subject-verb agreement; see Section D.

C.1 Nouns and Verbs

Suppose you had a list of words and you were told to find which ones could be NOUNS or VERBS. You might consult the *meaning* of each word: nouns are usually for *objects* (people, places, things, and the like) and verbs are usually for *events* (actions, happenings, situations). But meaning isn't a very reliable guide. A safer test is to try to put something in front of the word:

**A NOUN IS A WORD YOU CAN PUT "THE"
IN FRONT OF.**

**A VERB IS A WORD YOU CAN PUT "DIDN'T"
IN FRONT OF, OR "NOT" RIGHT AFTER.**

Most verbs take "didn't" in front of them, so try that first: "go" → "didn't go," "find" → "didn't find," and so on.* But *helping verbs* take "not" right after them, as in "can" → "can not," "must" → "must not," and so on. A word that already ends in "-n't" must be a helping verb anyway: "can't" is the same as "cannot," "don't" is the same as "does not," and so on.

Some words can be used *either as nouns or as verbs*. But our test picks out those words just as easily. For instance, you can say "the wreck" as well as "didn't wreck." Some words can't be either nouns or verbs, such as "under"—neither "the under" nor "didn't under" sounds right.

⬜ **3. QUIZ** *on finding nouns and verbs*

Here is a list of words. Mark nouns with N, verbs with V, and words that can be either nouns or verbs with N + V; leave the others blank. *Use only "the," "didn't," or "not" to check whether a word is a noun or a verb. Don't add anything except one of these three words!*

maintenance	of
glass	waste
through	response
possibility	happen

---

* We're dealing with the *basic form* of the verb here, such as "steal" rather than "steals" or "stolen," "say" rather than "says" or "said," "go" rather than "goes," "went," or "gone." The verb "be" and its various forms ("is," "are," "was," "were," and so on) slips through this test, but it's an exception in almost every situation, including this one.

move	sky
might	rob
puppy	will
cherry	decide
relate	help
nearby	secretary
assistant	furthermore
when	tackle
sit	every
sail	salt
knowledge	gas tank
insult	could
trend	commit

4. REVIEW QUIZ *on finding nouns and verbs*

Same instructions as on the previous quiz.

over	tell
darkness	that
enter	apartment
rain	the
personnel	at
phone	inform
should	paint
teacher	would
population	discover
fish	whether
extremely	lamp
evening	eraser
society	light
lose	reminder

may	weather
work	terribly
won't	explore

C.2 Past, Present, and Future Tense

Agreement makes a difference only for the PRESENT TENSE of verbs. So we'll need an easy way to tell which tense you're dealing with.

English verbs have three "simple" tenses: PAST TENSE, PRESENT TENSE, and FUTURE TENSE. These tenses generally indicate what *time* your statement is talking about, as compared to what time you're making the statement; but time isn't always a reliable guide. You also can't rely every time on the *form* of the verb. Many verbs—but not all—change their forms according to tense.

So let's try a more dependable way to recognize the tense. We'll make a DENIAL of the statement (unless the statement already *is* a denial)—that is, we'll say that whatever's involved *doesn't*, *didn't*, or *won't* happen as stated. (Never mind if you end up denying obvious facts!) Let's use only four DENIAL WORDS: "DOESN'T," "DON'T," "DIDN'T," and "WON'T." Here's the strategy:

INSERT A DENIAL WORD
INTO YOUR STATEMENT.
IF YOU USED "DOESN'T," OR "DON'T,"
YOU HAVE THE PRESENT TENSE.
IF YOU USED "DIDN'T,"
YOU HAVE THE PAST TENSE.
IF YOU USED "WON'T,"
YOU HAVE THE FUTURE TENSE.

Take these examples:

(15) The children set the table every day.

(15a) The children *don't* set the table every day. [tense: present]

(16) Our team set a new record last week.

(16a) Our team *didn't* set a new record last week. [tense: past]

(17) The sun will set before 7:00 tonight.

(17a) The sun *won't* set before 7:00 tonight. [tense: future]

You see right away that the first statement (15) is in the present, the second (16) is in the past, and the third (17) is in the future—even though the verb "set" looks the same in all three statements.

☐ 5. QUIZ on past, present, and future tense

Indicate which tense each of the following statements has. Mark the present with PR, the past with PA, and the future with FUT. Use the denial words "don't/doesn't," "didn't," and "won't" to determine which tense a statement has.

[1] Last year's awards included a cash prize.

[2] Once in a while, one of our projects works out as planned.

[3] After New Year's, my family will be going to Sea World.

[4] The storm tore up all the trees long ago.

[5] The clerk will stamp the receipts "paid."

[6] Only two people in the whole class dropped out before the end of the term.

[7] Some citizens vote in every community election.

[8] The ambassador sent them an invitation in June of 1982.

[9] The new honors class will be for freshmen.

[10] The authorities had the suspects in custody until last Monday.

☐ 6. REVIEW QUIZ on past, present, and future tense

Same instructions as on the previous quiz.

[1] At most stores, cigarettes cost less than a dollar a pack.

[2] In my early childhood, I learned to manage for myself.

[3] The American colonies waited for the British to lower taxes.

[4] In the twenty-first century, the world will look very different from the world of today.

[5] Ten dollars buys you a very good meal.

[6] Students live in dorms to save on rent.

[7] The Romans conquered every country they invaded.

[8] Trees provide the raw materials for paper.

[9] Our sun will go dark within the next few million years.

[10] Every winter, the rains come in January.

C.3 Telling Singular from Plural

It's usually pretty obvious whether you have singular or plural, but not always. One easy way to tell the difference is a question method a little like the one you learned in Section C.1 for finding subjects and predicates (pages 75–77). This time, when you make up a question about your statement, you use "which one" or "which ones" instead of "who" or "what." Here's the strategy:

MAKE UP A QUESTION ABOUT THE STATEMENT, USING EITHER "WHICH ONE" OR "WHICH ONES."

IF YOU USED "WHICH ONE," YOU HAVE A SINGULAR SUBJECT.
IF YOU USED "WHICH ONES," YOU HAVE A PLURAL SUBJECT.

For instance, you could have:

(18)   The new guidebooks are the most helpful.

(18a)   *Which ones* are the most helpful? [subject: plural]

(19)   That week, my oldest brother moved out.

(19a)   *Which one* moved out that week? [subject: singular]

Be sure to apply the "which one" or "which ones" test to the *subject* of the sentence, which, as we saw for "who/what" questions, is usually *early* in the sentence (see page 76). Use only "which," not "in which," "with which," "for which," and so forth.

The words "each" and "every" are special. Technically, they always make the subject *singular*, even though, if each one or every one does something, a large number is likely to be involved. If you had:

(20)   *Each* of the thirty contestants made the finals.

(21)   *Every one* of the thirty contestants made the finals.

you could ask "which *ones*?" But the subject is still singular, since you're thinking of each or every single "contestant." Just remember that *"each" and "every" always go with the singular.*

7. QUIZ *on telling singular from plural*

Here are ten statements. Mark each singular subject with *SI* and each plural subject with *PL*. Use the question strategy with "which one" or "which ones."

[1]   Three million women with a higher income joined the movement.

[2]   Public services will shift soon.

[3]   A huge fish swam into the net.

[4]   The worker's wages are going down.

[5]   Florida is a state with a rapidly growing population.

[6]   Each of your problems calls for a different approach.

[7]   The main wave length determines the frequency.

[8]   The simpler setting impresses the viewer more.

[9]   Her first successes at a track meet set a new record.

[10] The slalom races are closed to beginners.

□ **8. REVIEW QUIZ** *on telling singular from plural*

Same instructions as on the previous quiz.

[1]   Three contestants didn't finish.

[2]   Shorter surfboards are better for doing stunts.

[3]   The chemistry lab was the hardest course.

[4]   The right-hand road goes to the farmhouse.

[5]   Her best friends were out of town at the time.

[6]   The really hot sauce is ideal for this recipe.

[7]   Every new student has to report for registration early.

[8]   A fierce watch dog would be the best dog to have on an isolated ranch.

[9]   These new plans will bring a substantial profit.

[10] Last year, each of the residence halls got a new manager.

C.4   Telling When Agreement Matters

Often, agreement doesn't matter much because the singular and the plural forms of the verb are *exactly the same*. Sometimes, though, there's a big difference:

(22)   Which one *is* missing?

(23)   Which ones *are* missing?

We need to figure out under which conditions agreement does matter. There are three conditions involved:

1.   The statement must be in the **PRESENT TENSE**.
2.   The statement must be able to accept a **DENIAL WORD**.
3.   The subject must be in the **THIRD PERSON**.

We'll take a closer look at each of these three conditions.

We saw how to check for the present tense in Section C.2. The **future tense** looks just the same for singular and plural. The **past tense** also looks the same for singular and plural, except for "was" versus "were." That leaves us the **present tense**, which you'd probably guess has two different forms because it needs two different denial words—"doesn't" for singular and "don't" for plural.

However, some statements will not accept a denial word. One case is when the statement *already is* a denial. If you have something like:

(24)   The telegram *didn't* arrive on time.

you can't fit in another denial word. However, this situation doesn't create any big agreement problems. Except for "doesn't" (or "does not") versus "don't" (or "do not"), "isn't" (or "is not") versus "aren't" (or "are not"), and "wasn't" (or "was not") versus "weren't" (or "were not"),

---

DENIALS DON'T CHANGE VERB FORMS
FOR SINGULAR VERSUS PLURAL.

For example, you can have:

(25)   The *three telegrams didn't* arrive on time.

and the verb form is just the same as it was in (24). So you don't have to worry about agreement if your statement is a denial—aside from the exceptions listed here.

Not being able to insert a denial word is a clue to other cases that don't change for singular versus plural. One of these cases includes statements containing HELPING VERBS, such as "can," "could," "should," "must," "may," "might," and so forth. As we saw in Section C.1, a helping verb takes "not" right after it, so you wouldn't want another denial word in front of it. Noting this inability to take the denial word is a good way to remember that

HELPING VERBS DON'T CHANGE THEIR FORMS FOR SINGULAR VERSUS PLURAL.

Compare:

(26)   A new business *should* expand.

(27)   All new businesses *should* expand.

The verb is still "should." You can see there's no place to put the denial words "doesn't" or "don't" in statements like these.

Again, we have just a few exceptional helping verbs that *do* change for singular versus plural. Most of them we've run into already. They are: "does" versus "do," "is" versus "are," "was" versus "were," and "has" versus "have." For these helping verbs, the singulars end with an "-s"—the usual ending for a singular verb. Compare:

(28)   The bus *is leaving.*

(29)   Two buses *are leaving.*

Remember, these are the *only* helping verbs for which agreement matters.

Our third condition for agreement has to do with **PERSON**. "Person" depends on who's making the statement to whom. Person is distinguished in English only through **PRONOUNS**:

1.   If the subject is "*I*" or "*we,*" you have the **FIRST PERSON**.
2.   If the subject is "*you,*" you have the **SECOND PERSON**.
3.   If the subject is *anything besides "I," "we," or "you,"* you have the **THIRD PERSON**.

The **first person** is normally for the speaker or writer, and the **second person** is normally for whomever you're speaking to or writing to. The **third person** is for everything else. In the present tense, the third person is usually different for singular versus plural:

(30)   *He wants* the yellow papers.

(31)   *They want* the yellow papers.

However, singular and plural are usually the same verb forms when you have the first or the second person:

(32)   *I want* the yellow papers.

(33)   *We want* the same yellow papers that *you want.*

The verb is "want" in both cases. Again, we have a couple exceptions. These first-person forms do change: "I am" versus "we are," and "I was" versus "we were." Compare:

(34) Now *I am* in charge.

(35) Now *we are* in charge.

But aside from these few exceptions, your main concern is with the third person—that is, whenever the subject of the sentence is anything besides "I," "we," or "you."

9. QUIZ *on telling when agreement matters*

Put *Yes* beside the statements where agreement does matter and *No* beside the statements where agreement does not matter. Remember, three conditions must be met if agreement is going to matter:

1. The statement must be in the present tense.
2. The statement must be able to accept a denial word.
3. The subject must be in the third person.

[1] The sun gets hot in the afternoon.

[2] Our government works in secrecy.

[3] The total adds up to exactly 100.

[4] The delivery didn't make it before five o'clock.

[5] Exercises increase flexibility.

[6] People don't want to be confined to a wheelchair.

[7] Higher fees mean fewer enrollments.

[8] Whirlpool baths help to improve muscle tone.

[9] You have to be present every day.

[10] To produce a play, a person should know a great deal about the theater.

10. REVIEW QUIZ *on telling when agreement matters*

Same instructions as on the previous quiz.

[1] Ten years went by with no improvement in the crops.

[2] Most people don't support high taxes.

[3] My roommate always stays out late.

[4] People didn't act so rude in the old days.

[5] Many TV viewers see the same things every day.

[6] The mail comes at noon on Saturdays.

[7] Before the storm, the dunes stretched all along the beach.

[8] Each student is responsible for keeping registration appointments.

[9] I don't know any reason for the delay.

[10] The neighbors moved out last winter.

C.5 Forming Singular and Plural Verbs

You should now be able to tell when agreement does or does not matter for the form of the verb. Knowing that, you shouldn't have much trouble putting down the right verb form. When agreement does matter, the major strategy is:

ADD "-S" TO THE VERB FOR THE SINGULAR.

DO NOT ADD "-S" TO THE VERB FOR THE PLURAL.

One reason why the "-s" might be confusing is that it also is a sign of the **PLURAL** on most **NOUNS**. Some people think that if the noun adds an "-s," then the verb should too. That idea might be reasonable, but the English language doesn't work that way. Maybe it would help to remember this guide:

DON'T ADD "-S" TO THE NOUN IF YOU ADD "-S" TO THE VERB.

A few verb forms make *minor changes* when the "-s" is put on (see also pages 371–72):

1. "have" → "has"
2. verbs ending in **-o** like "go" → "goes"
3. verbs ending in **-s** like "miss" → "misses"
4. verbs ending in **-sh** like "wash" → "washes"
5. verbs ending in **-z** like "buzz" → "buzzes"
6. verbs ending in **-y** like "fly" → "flies"

As you can see, these minor changes nearly always involve putting in the letter "e" before the "-s" at the end.

11. QUIZ *on forming singular and plural verbs*

In the following statements, add "-s" to make the verb agree only where necessary. Use the steps you've been learning. Find the statements that are in the present tense. Be sure you could put in a denial word; otherwise, the verb stays the same for singular and plural. And be sure you have the third person—that is, be sure that the subject is not "I," "we," or "you." Then add the "-s" to the singular verbs. Watch for verbs ending in "-o," "-s," "-sh," "-z," or "-y," and make the minor changes they need.

[1]   Every woman complete the race.

[2]   This office always try to reply right away.

[3]   One day at the beach pass sooner than you'd ever think.

[4]   The dollar will rise next year.

[5]   Every good actor know his lines perfectly.

[6]   The public favored another attempt.

[7]   The officer at headquarters reply by walkie-talkie.

[8]   An egg make the pancakes lighter.

[9]   Patience go a long way toward helping families live in peace.

[10] I know the missing answer.

12. REVIEW QUIZ *on forming singular and plural verbs*

Same instructions as on the previous quiz.

[1]   The team rally its supporters before each game.

[2]   Our tires need more pressure.

[3]   The light flash every ten seconds.

[4]   I can't leave right now.

[5]   This test quiz you on organic compounds.

[6]   Our list contain four items.

[7]   Most Latin American countries rejected the proposal.

[8]   You see the problem now.

[9]   A house need a lot of upkeep.

[10] We didn't go after all.

C.6   Finding the Agreeing Verb That Takes the "-s" at the End

People sometimes get confused about *which* verb is the **agreeing verb** that should get the "-s" added on. A predicate can contain verbs that don't have to agree with the subject, such as "call" in

(36)   Our boss wants to call a meeting.

Here, too, putting in a denial word helps:

INSERT A DENIAL WORD.
THE VERB RIGHT AFTER THE DENIAL WORD
WAS YOUR AGREEING VERB IN THE ORIGINAL.

If you take (36), you get:

(36a)   Our boss *doesn't want* to call a meeting.

You see at once that "wants" was the agreeing verb of the original in (36), and not "call." Now try this:

(37)   The tourists intend to move on.

(37a) The tourists *don't intend* to move on.

So "intend," rather than "move," must have been the agreeing verb in (37).

  Your statement might have a HELPING VERB, such as "can," "could," "should," "must," "might," or a verb that is sometimes a helping verb, such as "am/is/are," "has/have/had," and "do/does/did." (A helping verb takes "not" right after it, as we saw in Section C.1.) If so,

---

THE HELPING VERB IS THE AGREEING VERB.

You could have:

(38) The doctor *can* see you now.

(39) He *is* leaving very soon.

(40) They *had* called in sick.

The agreeing verbs are "can," "is," and "had," rather than "see," "leaving," and "called." The same applies if these helping verbs have a denial signal like "-n't" tacked on the end:

(41) The doctor *can't* see you now.

(42) He *isn't* leaving very soon.

(43) They *hadn't* called in sick.

The agreeing verbs are "can't," "isn't," and "hadn't."

13. QUIZ *on finding the agreeing verb*

Circle the agreeing verb in each of the following statements. It's either the verb that you could put a denial word in front of or a helping verb that you could put "not" after or that already ends in "-n't."

[1]   Children like to hear stories.

[2]   They begin reading in first grade.

[3]   We can leave at five o'clock.

[4]   He plans to make a deal soon.

[5]   Prices are rising this month.

[6]   Surfers enjoy going out in this weather.

[7]   The winner might refuse the prizes.

[8]   On Mondays, the mailman has to hurry.

[9]   Some companies stop sending catalogs through the mail.

[10] Offers weren't easy to come by back then.

14. REVIEW QUIZ *on finding the agreeing verb*

Same instructions as on the previous quiz.

[1]   They try to keep customers informed.

[2]   The boss tells us exactly what to do every time.

[3]   Insects could destroy the crop overnight.

[4]   I know how to figure averages.

[5]   A small delay matters very much.

[6]   The jurors have heard all the evidence.

[7]   That soap comes packed in a red wrapper.

[8]   The officials counted the votes fairly.

[9]   The strikers expect to get a very large raise.

[10] Cold days don't happen here often.

F.2 Sentence Fragments

Everyday talk often has units that don't contain an independent clause. For example, here's more from the recording of a freshman telling how he painted his roof.

(145) first I went and I bought all the materials....bought two five-gallon containers of paint....a roller....a roller handle attachment that you put the roller on....and....went home..with the materials....

Making pauses while talking does not divide up the message the same way as marking off sentences with periods while writing. You'd get a strange-looking paper if you matched up periods with pauses:

(146) First I went and I bought all the materials. Bought two five-gallon containers of paint. A roller. A roller handle attachment that you put the roller on. And. Went home. With the materials.

The paper looks strange because it's hard to see a reason for having so many fragments marked off as sentences. You'd expect the sentences to form sensible units, like the ones the same student marked off in his *written version*:

(147) First I went and bought all the materials. I bought two five-gallon containers of paint, a roller, and a roller handle attachment that you put the roller on. Then I went home with the materials.

This way, each sentence puts together the things that go together.

The point is that if you mark off as a sentence something that doesn't have at least one **INDEPENDENT CLAUSE**, you get a **SENTENCE FRAGMENT**. Either you have a clause that is *not independent*, or you don't have a clause at all because the **SUBJECT** or the **AGREEING VERB** is missing, or both. Fragments do turn up in informal writing because it's usually easy to guess what the missing parts should be, but you ought to watch out for them in more formal writing.

F.2.1 *What Causes Sentence Fragments and What They Look Like*

A fragment sometimes gets used to *answer a question*. When you have the question right there, you tend not to repeat the entire question in the answer. Take this stage routine that George Burns and Gracie Allen used to do:

(148) GRACIE: My poor brother Willie, he was held up last night.
GEORGE: Your brother was held up?
GRACIE: Yeah, by two men.
GEORGE: Where?
GRACIE: All the way home.

Gracie's short answers may be fragments, but they're vital for the pace of a comedy routine. The dialogue would be wrecked if we insisted on complete sentences:

> (148a) GRACIE: My poor brother Willie, he was held up last night.
> GEORGE: Your brother was held up?
> GRACIE: Yeah, my brother was held up by two men.
> GEORGE: Where was he held up by two men?
> GRACIE: He was held up by two men all the way home.

The audience would get restless pretty soon. On stage, every word counts, and you want to keep moving along.

Sentence fragments can also happen when you *make a pause during a statement and then continue.* The place where you paused can get marked with a period, cutting off two parts of the sentence from each other. This mistake is especially likely if you make your statement *long and complicated.* The second part of (149), for example, has no independent clause, since it starts with "Because," a linking word not on that list of four: "and," "but," "or," "so" (see page 125). The clause "depends" on the one in the sentence just before it.

> (149) Every year, senseless accidents occur on our highways. Because people don't keep their cars in good running condition.

Or, the fragment may be a clause that "depends" on the sentence right after it, as in:

> (150) Until my father happened to look out the back window. He didn't see our car smoking heavily from the rear.

Finally, there's the danger of accidentally marking off a *long modifier* as a sentence—for example, in the second part of (151):

> (151) Coming off the bench, Junior Mickey Mastics performed superbly. Averaging in the double figures with consistent outside shooting.

The length of the modifier probably fooled the student into thinking it was a sentence.

Some modifiers are easy to mistake for clauses. The freshman who wrote:

> (152) North Carolina has some of the nation's most beautiful objects. These objects being the mountains.

said she thought the fragment was a sentence because it looks so similar to:

> (152a) These objects *are* the mountains.

Besides, the fragment sounds like a good continuation of the sentence just in front of it. Still, *an "-ing" form can't be an agreeing verb.* So if it's the only verb in your sentence, you must have a fragment.

In Section E (page 123), we saw how to make up *"yes/no" questions* in order to find independent clauses. The same method can help you spot fragments. Most sentence fragments won't yield a sensible "yes/no" question, because something's missing.

A *clause that is not independent* makes a silly "yes/no" question. For the second part of (149), it makes no sense to say (149a):

(149)   Every year, senseless accidents occur on our highways. Because people don't keep their cars in good running condition.

(149a)   Because don't people keep their cars in good running condition?

A question for the first part of (150) sounds just as odd:

(150)   Until my father happened to look out the back window. He didn't see our car smoking heavily from the rear.

(150a)   Until did your father happen to look out the back window?

Trying to make a "yes/no" question tells you whether or not you really have an independent clause.

Modifiers are easiest to spot as sentence fragments when some major part is entirely missing. For instance, some modifiers with an "-ing" verb have nothing you could use as the subject, as in the second part of (153):

(153)   The Lady Gators scampered to a five-and-two start. *Building high their faithful fans' hopes.*

By itself, the fragment doesn't say who was doing the "building." In order to make up a "yes/no" question, you'd have to supply a subject as well as get rid of the "-ing":

(153a)   Did *they build* high their faithful fans' hopes?

So you have two clues that (153) must be a sentence fragment.

Modifiers with no "-ing" verb can also be missing either the subject or the agreeing verb. Here's one student's fragment with both missing:

(154)   Carried away by her appearance and lost in new thoughts.

To get a "yes/no" question, you'd have to furnish a subject and a verb, such as:

(154a)   *Was he* carried away by her appearance and lost in new thoughts?

So if you find something you suspect of being a fragment, try making a "yes/no" question and noticing if any of the important parts you need are missing.

44. QUIZ on spotting sentence fragments

Underline the fragments in these ten items. One item may have more than one fragment.

[1] The voters will find out his real view. After he is elected.

[2] Why they had to do that. Releasing the news before we were ready. It's a mystery to me.

[3] When the moon rises and the clouds gather. The dogs begin to howl.

[4] After night fell, they closed the stores. Even though the danger was over.

[5] The tenants demand a new lease. From time to time. Maybe every five years or so. Sometimes more often.

[6] It's really more than I can stand. Being in a place like this. When you consider where I'm from.

[7] That's the whole idea. To keep a step ahead of inflation.

[8] So when did we get our bill? After they'd already cut off the power. Which made no sense at all.

[9] I'm writing them a letter for the last time. Absolutely the last. No more Mr. Nice Guy.

[10] His family came from a long line of Irish nobles. His father being the last to hold the title.

45. REVIEW QUIZ on spotting sentence fragments

Same instructions as on the previous quiz.

[1] This is it. The last race of the day. The big moment.

[2] They were absolutely stunned. All that money gone. And for nothing.

[3] She lost her hat. The big red one. It was her favorite.

[4] We always use the recipe. But with honey instead of sugar. Which is much healthier.

[5] Any minute now. The finalists will be announced. I can hardly wait.

[6] Three years in jail. A cruel sentence for simple possession.

[7] Why should we go there now? After all the rooms are taken.

[8] Two jars with lids. A large pot. That's what we'll need for the jelly.

[9] This is an outrage. Waking us at six in the morning. The telephone crew.

[10] Classes start next week. On Wednesday. Or Thursday. At the latest.

F.2.2 *Fixing Sentence Fragments*

Sentence fragments might be included as one kind of the BAD PLACEMENTS
we worked on in Chapter 1, Section D.2. The fragment is left floating around,
rather than being firmly attached to a person or an action. The same techniques
we used for fixing bad placement are also helpful for dealing with sentence
fragments.

FIRST, READ BACK OVER YOUR WRITING TO
CHECK FOR FRAGMENTS.

Watch for unattached modifiers, especially modifiers with an "-ing" form where
you should have an agreeing verb. Also, check to see if each sentence has at least
one independent clause.

SECOND, ORGANIZE SCENES AND EVENTS
AROUND THE PEOPLE DOING THE ACTIONS.

That way, you can easily see that fragments like (153) and (154) don't say *who*
was "building" or *who* was "carried away":

(153) Building high their faithful fans' hopes.

(154) Carried away by her appearance and lost in new thoughts.

THIRD, PUT TOGETHER WHAT GOES
TOGETHER.

The fragment should often be made a part of a nearby sentence. For example, a
clause that is not independent can be hooked onto a clause that is:

(149) Every year, senseless accidents occur on our highways. *Because people
don't keep their cars in good running condition.*

(149b)   Every year, senseless accidents occur on our highways ; because people
don't keep their cars in good running condition.

FINALLY, DON'T MAKE THINGS TOO COMPLICATED.

If you let your statements get too long and involved, you're more likely to overlook a fragment such as this one:

(155)   The entire population suffering great distress over the loss of their
leader, who was assassinated while leaving a train station.

There are several ways to fix fragments. The easiest way can be used when there's
a real sentence nearby to hook the fragment onto. Your strategy is simple:

ATTACH THE FRAGMENT TO A NEARBY SENTENCE.

You might do the job just by changing a period to a comma and making the capital letter after it into a small letter; for instance:

(153)   The Lady Gators scampered to a five-and-two start. Building high their
faithful fans' hopes.

(153b)   The Lady Gators scampered to a five-and-two start , building high their
faithful fans' hopes.

You put the action of "building" into one sentence together with the people who
did it ("Lady Gators"). Now everything fits into one picture.

If there's no real sentence nearby that looks like a good place to hook onto,
you can

SUPPLY THE PARTS THE FRAGMENT DOESN'T HAVE: A SUBJECT, AN AGREEING VERB, OR BOTH.

You could have:

(156)   The election was a mistake. *Should have known about the scandal sooner.*

(156a)   *The voters* should have known about the scandal sooner. [subject
supplied]

(157)   Too hard, this job.

(157a)   This job *is* too hard. [verb supplied, the rest rearranged]

(154)   Carried away by her appearance and lost in new thoughts.

(154b)   *He was* carried away by her appearance and lost in new thoughts. [subject and verb supplied]

Still another strategy—a good one for short fragments—is like one we already used for cutting down on restatements in Chapter 1 (see page 22):

PUT THE KEY WORDS FROM THE FRAGMENT SOMEWHERE INSIDE A NEARBY SENTENCE.

The KEY WORDS are the ones that add something new or important to the message. Here's how you might get them into a nearby sentence:

(158)   Last night I heard an album by Grover Washington. Fantastic.

(158a)   Last night I heard a *fantastic* album by Grover Washington.

(159)   The test was bad. Far too difficult for me.

(159a)   The test was *far too difficult for me.*

(160)   At the end of the semester, this always happens. A sudden mob at the library. Camping there all night.

(160a)   At the end of the semester, *a sudden mob* always *camps all night at the library.*

As you see from that last one (160a), some unimportant words drop out to make a good fit, such as the vague "this" and "happens." The new statement is compact, and the fragment has been fixed.

For *question plus fragment answer*, you have two options. First, you can drop the question/answer pattern altogether and just make a statement. This tactic means combining the fragment with the nearby question, such as:

(161)   How did we finish the season? By winning the conference title.

(161a)   We finished the season by winning the conference title.

But if you like the pattern, then keep it; add just enough to make the answer a real sentence:

(161b)   How did we finish the season? We won the conference title.

You don't have to make the answer repeat all the words from the question. The result would be boring:

(161c)   How did we finish the season? We finished the season by winning the
         conference title.

We already put a lot of effort into getting away from repeats like this in Chapter 1.

46. QUIZ *on fixing sentence fragments*

You have seen three basic ways to fix a fragment: (1) hook it onto a nearby sentence; (2) add enough to make the fragment into a real sentence; (3) put the key words from the fragment inside a nearby sentence. Use those strategies to fix the following items.

Example:
   A sudden change. Used to be open farmland, this whole county. Now shopping malls and condominiums. Ugly ones. Very depressing to look at, too.

You could fix it this way:
   This whole county has suddenly changed from open farmland over to ugly shopping malls and condominiums. They are very depressing to look at, too.

[1]   Right before the big game. The weather gets like this. Awful.

[2]   The neighbors are too loud. Far too loud. Particularly when they have their friends over.

[3]   A terrible racket. But I did get some sleep in spite of it. How did I do that? By taking two sleeping pills.

[4]   During the big storm, when the trees fell down. We were out of town. Luckily.

[5]   Just what I would have done. Back when I was in high school. Trying out for every team.

[6]   The first person on the plane. And the last one off. My little sister loves to fly.

[7]   Every year you see the same thing. When they start to run out of funds. Dorm food getting worse and worse. Disgusting in fact.

[8]   Said he'd bring the money. But he didn't. After all the trouble we went to. Just to get here.

[9]   The best way to cure a cold? Drinking hot red wine with sugar and rum in it. Although you may get a hangover.

[10] All the same to me. They can do whatever they want. Whenever they're ready.

[11] Never goes out any more. A real hermit. Old Mr. Daniels.

[12] Lost in the crowd of nameless faces. Just another student. Me off at college.

[13] Who could do that physics assignment? Only a genius.

[14] Ten bottles taken from the cellar. And emptied to the last drop. And who was it? Our famous friends.

[15] This could only happen to us. Running out of money the second week of school. Completely out.

[16] The defeat of the Equal Rights Amendment? A scandal! Florida voting it down. At the very end.

[17] In the next important experiment with organic substances. Just a few common chemicals needed. But a very uncommon result.

[18] Usually a pants outfit. Maybe slacks, a silk shirt, and matching jacket. That's what she likes to wear.

[19] Iran was the second time the United States was humbled by another country. The first time occurring in Vietnam.

[20] Their children are enrolling next fall. A new school. Just opened on the northwest side.

47. REVIEW QUIZ on fixing sentence fragments

Same instructions as on the previous quiz.

[1] We're leaving. Going out of town. To avoid any more trouble. Today.

[2] They are going to clean the house. The whole house. Thoroughly. From the basement to the attic.

[3] The horse is doing fine. Green grass in the pasture. And plenty of room to run around.

[4] My mother calling from Detroit all the time. At least once a week. There's no reason.

[5] The cup and saucer were dropped. Broken of course. Into a thousand pieces. It was your careless cousin.

[6] When is the appointment? Today or yesterday? Let us know. And do it soon.

[7] There's a monument. Really impressive. Over on the left. We should watch for it.

[8] She has a genuine show horse. Clipped mane. Glossy coat. Shiny hooves.

[9] The letters must be postmarked. Very important. Before midnight.

[10] All candidates having to declare their assets. Personal fortune, contributions, everything. No exceptions.

[11] How did the committee vote? Against the proposal. By a margin of seven to one.

[12] Comes of living in the South. Relatives from up north coming to visit. Hordes of them.

[13] The tournament will be held in Savannah this year. The sailing tournament. An annual event.

[14] Not much time left before the deadline. Filing for bankruptcy. In district court.

[15] She plays the guitar. The piano. The musical talent she's got.

[16] Too late. No more cars entered in the race. Closed at noon today.

[17] We play tennis every day. Why? To get the exercise. And to be outdoors.

[18] After all their service. First-rate bookkeepers. And now unemployed.

[19] A little more paint. In the corner. Under the sink. All we need.

[20] Not being one of our buildings. A public project. Community-owned. The apartment houses by the river.

☐ 48. FURTHER REVIEW QUIZ *on fixing sentence fragments*

Go back to Quizzes 44 and 45, on spotting sentence fragments, and fix the fragments you found there.

General quiz

49.

▼

on splices and fragments

In the following items, label all the fragments with *FR* and all splices with *SPL*. Then fix the samples to make real sentences out of them. *Warning*: a single item may contain more than one sentence problem.

Example:

          FR   *FR*   *SPL*

More dents in the shield. Twelve more. It must be repaired, the spacecraft is taking off in three days.

You could fix it this way:

Twelve more dents in the shield must be repaired, because the spacecraft is taking off in three days.

[1]   Their demands are unreasonable. Far too expensive. We think so.

[2]   It's hard to say yet, they'll be announcing the winner in a minute. A little patience.

[3]   How she can admit it. In public. I'll never know. That we lost last year's files.

[4]   My next course was chemistry, it was difficult, nevertheless, I eventually passed it.

[5]   I chose engineering for a major. Why? It's a good profession to be in, moreover, I already have some job experience.

[6]   Although you never know. Because things might change. Without warning. Computers still seem to be on the increase.

[7]   Nothing to worry about we'll run your program again in the morning. First thing.

[8]   I was just imagining how we would live without electricity. Without all the things we take for granted. Stereos. Micro-wave ovens. And so on.

[9]   We need new energy sources, otherwise, our civilization is moving into a crisis.

[10] If taxes are raised, they'll only build more bombs besides, they're building too many already.

[11] Veterinary medicine is a good field. Hard to get into, though. Very competitive.

[12] I like animals, I would enjoy working with them. All day long.

[13] If you own a horse, for example. It might get colic. Or become lame. Should know how to cure it.

[14] Animals aren't like human beings. Doing things on purpose to damage their health. Like smoking cigarettes.

[15] I don't understand people, they seem in a hurry to get out of life, they do so many unhealthy things.

[16] Your body is like your house you have to live in it, moreover, you can't move out. A permanent house.

[17] Children in particular. Television teaches them violence. That it's the way people get what they want.

[18] Satellite TV will change the whole scene, we'll finally see some real variety, commercial TV always offers the same things. Every season.

[19] Society is changing. New professions opening up. Old ones disappearing. Nobody's future very secure.

[20] What's the answer? Flexibility. Being able to retrain when your field becomes obsolete.

[21] Some skills are always in demand, you should concentrate on those.

[22] Analyzing a task. Setting up operations. Finding and solving problems. All skills that go with any job.

[23] The commission filed its report, nothing has been done about it yet.

[24] Colder winters. Wetter summers. Climate seems to be shifting. On a large scale.

[25] Canada has a lot to offer, however, you mustn't expect it to be like the United States.

Back-up general quiz

50.

on splices and fragments

Same instructions as on the previous exercise.

[1]   They didn't even put on the brakes, they didn't see the train in time.

[2]   We climbed Mount Washington. A nice day. The nicest that spring.

[3]   The telegram was delayed, it took four days, that's why the contract was not signed.

[4]   We saw her at the beach, her face was sunburned. Totally. A television actress.

[5]   We couldn't buy the machine. The reason being that we wouldn't get paid for another week. Because our boss is out of town.

[6]   The races are fun, they give you some intense moments of excitement.

[7]   We're changing things all around. Since she went away. Our place not being the way it used to.

[8]   The town has only one church, that's a Catholic one, the priest comes from out of town.

[9]   Whenever an emergency happens. The trip can be made in a short time, however, it's very expensive.

[10] She said a strange thing. It was extremely strange. Said the forest should be cleared.

[11] Pocket calculators are a great help they're fast and accurate. Extremely.

[12] The journalism class was a good one, we all worked together. Even when the sports season was a bad one. Which often happened.

[13] The supplies are gone. Down to the last nail. We'd better restock, otherwise, the garage won't get built this year.

[14] Your question is a hard one, it really is, you'd better come back later. For example, next week.

[15] Because there we were busy all week. I couldn't attend, all the same, I didn't just forget about it.

[16] It's still unknown, science hasn't found an answer yet. The true cause of cancer. The most dreaded disease.

[17] Whether the game is canceled, or the teams decide on a draw. Hardly matters now.

[18] We suspected there was something wrong, they looked very annoyed.

[19] The members of the panel sat down. Seeing the interview would take time. A long time.

[20] The reporters decided to leave. Before the soldiers arrived. And surrounded the palace. The soldiers from the Civil Guard.

[21] Simply not knowing what your employer wants. It's very frustrating. For everybody.

[22] It was getting pitch dark, we didn't know the swamp, therefore, our situation looked pretty desperate.

[23] The man that came to dinner. Stayed too long. Far too long. I'll never forget him.

[24] The crowd was mainly from my home town, however, a few were just here for the game.

[25] The speech he made this morning. The windiest one I've heard in years. Without question.

3.

Putting
Sentences
Together

Preview

In Chapter 2, we saw how to build *individual clauses and sentences*. Now we want to find out how to build *groups of sentences inside paragraphs*. We'll need to work on three questions in particular:

A. How LONG AND COMPLICATED should your sentences be?
B. How SIMILAR should your sentences be?
C. What ORDER should your sentences be in?

The answers to these questions depend on what you're saying in your paper and who's going to be reading it. We'll be practicing some ways to work on length, similarity, and order. We won't worry about the length and arrangement of whole paragraphs or papers until Chapter 4. Instead, we'll focus here on the size, shape, and order of sentences that go together inside one paragraph. Still, the strategies we'll be practicing on a smaller scale work on a larger scale for the things we'll want to do in Chapter 4.

■ A. HOW LONG AND COMPLICATED SHOULD YOUR SENTENCES BE?

There are no rules that force you to write sentences with a certain number of words. Nor are there rules for telling whether all your sentences should be simple or complicated. In fact, in most writing, you find a mixture of sentences ranging from short to long, and from simple to complicated. This variety has a good reason: not all the materials in a piece of writing are equally *hard to understand*. Your strategy should be:

USE SHORTER, SIMPLER SENTENCES
FOR HARD MATERIALS;
USE LONGER, MORE COMPLICATED
SENTENCES FOR EASY MATERIALS.

Materials are HARD to understand if they are *unfamiliar, unexpected, complicated,* or *technical*. Materials are EASY to understand if they are *familiar, predictable, simple,* or *everyday*. Here are some illustrations from *Science Digest* (June 1983). Sentence (1) is easy to read, even though it's a pretty long and complicated sentence (32 words). Sentence (2) is hard to read, even though it's a little shorter (29 words).

(1) That bright light you see in the western sky right after sunset, long before any stars are visible, is Venus—not a plane, a balloon, or a UFO, as is often thought.

(2) An advanced air-to-air missile has intercepted a high-speed target, showing its ability to find low-flying targets amid high clutter caused by the missile's own radar returns reflecting from the ground.

Probably, you're familiar with "seeing a bright light in the western sky right after sunset," and you've "often thought" it might be "a plane, a balloon, or a UFO." You may have already heard somewhere that the light is "Venus," though you may have forgotten it. This background knowledge makes it easy for you to read a long, complicated sentence like (1).

In contrast, you aren't so likely to know about missile interception and radar clutter. We could make (2) easier by breaking it up into shorter, simpler sentences:

(2a) An advanced air-to-air missile has intercepted a high-speed target. The missile showed its ability to find low-flying targets amid high clutter. This clutter is caused by the missile's own radar returns reflecting from the ground.

This pattern gives you the material a bit at a time, so that you're not trying to figure it all out at once.

In contrast, we don't gain much by breaking up (1) into shorter, simpler sentences. The result would be pretty boring:

(1a) You see a bright light in the western sky. You see it right after sunset. You see it long before any stars are visible. That light is Venus. It is not a plane, a balloon, or a UFO. People have often thought so, though.

If the material is easy, you have no reason to dole it out in so many small pieces.

To get the right length for your sentences, you'll need some techniques for making them shorter or longer, depending on how hard or easy your materials will be for readers to understand. Let's work on making sentences shorter and simpler first.

A.1 Making Sentences Shorter

One type of sentence that needs shortening might be called a "run-on": a long string of clauses that "runs on and on." A run-on is most noticeable if it has a lot of **independent clauses**, either with no linking word or with a linking word from this list: "and," "but," "or," and "so" (with "yet" and "for" used much less often) (see Chapter 2, Section E). When you reach three independent clauses, your sentence is likely to be a bit long and awkward. These sentences came from student papers about a lifeguard job (3) and about an argument with the power company (4):

(3) I'm on the university swim team and I can swim well, but I'm not one to get involved, so I hope I don't have an emergency situation, or I won't know what to do.

(4) I went to City Hall, and the clerk checked my bill, but there was no record of payment, so I had to pay again.

Once you notice a run-on, the simplest remedy is to

BREAK UP A RUN-ON INTO MORE THAN ONE SENTENCE.

You might just put in a period and a capital letter. You could get:

(3a) I'm on the university swim team and I can swim well. But I'm not one to get involved. So I hope I don't have an emergency situation, or I won't know what to do.

(4a) I went to City Hall, and the clerk checked my bill. But there was no record of payment, so I had to pay again.

However, it is often better to

STREAMLINE THE STATEMENT TO GET FEWER CLAUSES.

That way, you can still have just one sentence, but not such a long, complicated one. The usual way is to

---

TAKE THE KEY WORDS OUT OF ONE CLAUSE AND PUT THEM INSIDE ANOTHER CLAUSE.

We already concentrated on key words in Chapters 1 and 2 (see pages 22 and 149). **Key words** are the ones that add something new to what was said already. You can get rid of unimportant words that don't tell us much. Our two examples might then look like this:

(3b) Although I swim well and belong to the university team, I wouldn't know what to do if I needed to get involved in an emergency. [25 words instead of the original 35]

(4b) Since the clerk at City Hall couldn't find a record of payment, I had to pay my bill again. [19 words instead of the original 24]

To get (3b), we took the key words "university" and "team" and put them in the clause with "I can swim well"; and we took "get involved" and "emergency" and put them together with "I won't know what to do." Unimportant words like "I'm not one" and "situation" dropped out. To get (4b), we took "City Hall" plus "rec-ord" and made up one clause telling what "the clerk" did. We got rid of unimpor-tant words like "there was," "I went," and "checked"—the main point is not that you went there and the clerk checked, but rather that you had to pay your bill again because the clerk found no record. These shorter versions still give the essentials.

Even so, you would not want to crowd everything inside one sentence if the result would be hard to read or understand. You could overdo your struggle for shortness:

(3c) A good team swimmer, I'm not emergency-oriented. [7 words]

(4c) I repaid my bill the City Hall clerk found no payment record for. [12 words]

So much got left out this time that the statements are confusing and hard to make sense of. Readers have to work harder, and there's no saving on effort.

☐ 1. EXERCISE *on shortening run-ons*

Put a period where the following run-ons might be broken up. Then streamline them into just one or two sentences, but don't crowd things too drastically. Save the key words and drop out the unimportant words.

Example:
> Exercises increase flexibility of the muscles, so they should be done, because unless patients get exercise, they will be confined to a wheelchair sooner than is necessary.

You could fix it this way:
> Exercises to increase flexibility of the muscles help keep patients from being confined to a wheelchair sooner than necessary.

[1]   In a sleazy punk dress, you can put on leather from head to toe, or you can choose leopard skin, or you may just wear a ripped-up T-shirt and black pants, but you should always look tough and messy.

[2]   The software is complicated, and the average programmer finds it difficult, but the programmer eventually learns to handle the software, and the game is ready to run.

[3]   There may be an infection, so I carry out a blood count, and it's called a white-blood-cell count.

[4]   There are mountains in the north, and you find lakes in the south, and all this scenery is very beautiful, so you should visit it.

[5]   The first batter struck out, but the second one hit a single, and the third one hit a double, so the coach sent out their best home-run hitter.

[6]   Society will be made up of older people, and when that happens, government services will change and public needs will be shifted toward the needs of the older people.

[7]   A tax lawyer may work for a private firm, or he or she may go to a corporation, or he or she may be employed by the government.

[8]   The program accepts the input data, and then it processes the data, and finally it is ready to output the results, so the program has three parts.

[9]   The Vietnam war confused the country, and the hawks were for it, but the doves were against it, so the groups clashed and rioted.

[10] Lake Tahoe is scenic, but it is also exciting, so you can go there to get away from the city and yet you will not be bored.

A sentence with a number of clauses is less likely to seem like a run-on if most of the clauses are *not independent*. However, the sentences may still be too long. A student wrote this one:

> (5) There are also parts of the body, of which the appendix is a good example, which are supposed to be remnants of organs that were useful to our ancestors, and which although no longer any use to us have not yet disappeared. [1 sentence, 40 words]

Many writers, let alone readers, get mixed up themselves with writing like that. Although this student didn't make any mistakes, the sentence is not easy to read. We ought to break it up and streamline it:

> (5a) Some body parts, such as the appendix, are supposed to be remnants of ancestral organs. Although no longer any use to us, these parts have not yet disappeared. [2 sentences, 28 words]

We took "parts" and "body" and put them together in a clause with "are supposed to be remnants"; in between, we shortened "of which the appendix is a good example" down to "such as the appendix" and put it in the middle of that same clause. We made the last part of the statement into a separate sentence, so that it's easier to figure out what goes with what. This method works better than just chopping the sentence up into many:

> (5b) There are also certain parts of the body. The appendix is a good example. They are supposed to be remnants of organs. Those organs were useful to our ancestors. They are no longer any use to us. But they have not yet disappeared. [6 sentences, 43 words]

Now we're crawling along. A bunch of very short sentences can be just as tiresome as one very long one. Find a compromise between long and short, so that you don't confuse readers but don't bore them either.

☐ 2. EXERCISE *on streamlining complicated sentences*

Streamline and break up the following sentences, but not too drastically.

Example:
> It's hard to raise a child, because nobody knows everything you need to know about how to raise a child when there are many pressures from outside the home and the parent can't control all those pressures.

You could fix it this way:
> Raising a child is hard, because the parent can't control all the pressures from outside the home.

[1] After you open the lid of the washing machine and find the slot for the soap, put in your laundry and put in the soap and close the lid again before you switch the machine on.

[2] Darth Vader wants to capture Luke Skywalker, who is off somewhere, so Vader plans to capture Luke's friends and torture them so Luke will come to the rescue and get caught too.

[3] The Christmas season wasn't very prosperous in 1982, because money was scarce because many people were out of work, and besides, the government was taking away its support programs for low-income families.

[4] When the old part of town needed to be restored, the city council got together, and they asked for subscriptions, after which they collected a lot of money from the townspeople for the restoration.

[5] If you want good stereo sound, you should get a high-quality turntable, and when you get a powerful amplifier, and when you find speakers to match, you should be sure to connect all the wires correctly.

[6] It's easy to keep in touch if you use long distance, because you get low rates on weekends when you dial direct, and the rates are also low late in the evening, and you reach your friends immediately and they can reply immediately.

[7] There was this magazine I subscribed to and it had an article about the nutritional value of fast food where it said how bad for you it is to eat fast food because the nutritional value is low and starch and cholesterol content is high, so I decided to change my diet.

[8] A palm tree that is growing in a pot needs water, but if you give it too much water, the branches start turning brown on the tips and the roots get weak.

[9] I don't know, since I'm just a visitor, but if you'll ask the receptionist, she'll tell you whatever you want to know.

[10] Photography is an enjoyable hobby, though a good camera costs a lot of money, and the attachments such as flash, lenses, and light meter, are expensive, and after you buy all that you still have a lot of things to set just right, and you make a lot of mistakes until you get to be an expert.

3. QUIZ on shortening and streamlining sentences

Shorten and streamline the following sentences, but not too drastically.

Example:
> The voice must be practiced and blocking must be learned, and sound and lighting effects must be created, and everything must be carefully rehearsed.

You could fix it this way:
> Rehearse everything carefully, including voice, blocking, and sound and lighting effects.

[1] My next course was chemistry, and it was difficult, but I stayed with it, and eventually I passed after I took it three times.

[2] We thought it would be fun to drive from Miami to San Francisco, but we didn't know how far it was until we tried it, and it took us six days of driving all day, and the Interstate Highway wasn't finished in Texas or Arizona.

[3] The town has only one hospital and that's a general one, and the chief doctor comes from out of town, and he has patients in five other towns.

[4] Things looked pretty depressing because we couldn't find an apartment and it was snowing at a time when we didn't have an apartment and couldn't get in out of the snow.

[5] Once the computer is switched on and the screen goes on and asks whether you want to edit, you can load the file that you want to work on, and you can edit it.

[6] The high diving board is being repaired next week when the tournament is over so that the repair of the diving board won't interfere with the tournament, but I hope the board won't cause any trouble while the tournament is going on.

[7] It is a street bike so I use it for pleasure because I like the feeling of the wind blowing against my body, and besides, I like to see the expressions on people's faces when they see a female cruising on a motorcycle when I'm out riding.

[8] The best time to find good waves for surfing is after a storm, but it's a good thing if you wait a while until the waves have had time to smoothe out and become glassy, because they're choppy at first and that makes them hard to ride when they're choppy.

[9] The shape of the beach is very important because the shape of the beach can cause a current that carries the surfer down the beach to where he will have to keep walking back up the beach to get to the best place.

[10] A board can have anywhere from one to four fins, and most surfers agree that the boards with more fins give you more mobility to produce the more radical stunts, but the board with one fin gives you more stability, so it's a good board to learn on.

4. REVIEW QUIZ on shortening and streamlining sentences

Same instructions as on the previous quiz.

[1] Actors have a big job that they need to be able to do well, so that they will convince the audience, and they need to make the whole play hang together in the way it should.

[2] Pronunciation is critical and you must face downstage, because if the audience can't hear what you're saying they'll wonder what's going on.

[3] Community theaters are less fortunate, and the actors won't be experts, but you can work very hard and you can produce a great show when you're all done.

[4] I was so nervous during the first performance that I fell off the stage, but since nobody paid much attention it wasn't too terribly bad because it hardly got noticed.

[5] I was supposed to enter on my cue, but I missed the cue, so the director gave me a big shove, and I flew out like a rocket.

[6] When I finally got a job I went to work at a shoe store where I waited on customers who came in, even though they often didn't buy any shoes.

[7] Although I didn't know it, many people won't admit their real shoe size because they're embarrassed because they think their feet are too big, so they ask for shoes that are so much too small that they can't even get them on.

[8] When things go wrong, the customers always blame the salesman, or they say the shoes are defective, or they do anything to keep from admitting that their feet are really bigger than they claim.

[9] Then one day a woman demanded tiny boots and even though I thought for sure she couldn't get them on, she did get them on, but nobody could get them off again after that, so she bought them and left, though she had some difficulty walking.

[10] I stayed at that job as long as I could stand it, but it didn't seem to have much future and it didn't lead anywhere, so I eventually left and got a job in an office instead.

A.2 Making Sentences Simpler

A.2.1 *Useless Hard Words*

So far, we've been working on fixing sentences that were hard to understand because their form was *too long and complicated*. Now we're going to try fixing some sentences that suffer from having *useless hard words*. Hard words are "useless" when you could easily say the same thing in ordinary words. Writers don't gain much by racking their brains and hunting around in dictionaries for long, unusual words to show off with.

You may be able to impress some people with a display of useless hard words, but there are some serious risks involved. The harder you work at piling up hard words, the more people will suspect that you don't have much of anything worth saying. You can take the most trivial, obvious statements, such as (6) and (7), and try to make them appear deep and new by decorating them with hard words, as in (6a) and (7a):

(6) Two plus two equals four.

(6a) The *numerical quantity* of two placed in *mathematical union* with an *equivalent quantity* of two brings into *existence* the *numerical quantity* of four.

(7) As time goes by, people get older.

(7a) An *accumulation* of time periods has as its *consequence* an *increase* in the *human age factor*.

Once your readers see through this act, they won't take you seriously at all. They'll probably be mad because you made them work so hard just to get a dumb message.

Worse yet, useless hard words are often chosen to deliberately mislead and conceal. A Watergate conspirator is reported to have said (8), because a simpler version like (8a) would have sounded too incriminating:

(8) We conducted a *vulnerability and feasibility study* of the *premises*.

(8a) We looked for ways to *break in and burglarize* the *place*.

On another occasion, a military officer is reported to have said (9), because a simpler statement like (9a) would have shocked people:

(9) Our *pacification initiative adversely affected* civilian *female and juvenile segments of the population*.

(9a) Our *bombing killed* civilian *women and children*.

Many military people seem to think that they can convert horrible things into neutral ones by talking about them with fancy words.

We all know what the language of bureaucrats looks like. It's heavy, complicated, and difficult to understand—often on purpose. Many politicians, lawyers, business people, administrators, and many others like to show their power by inflicting complicated language on ordinary people. They'll say "it is incumbent upon you" when they mean "you should"; or they'll say they "attempted to secure pertinent information" when they mean they "tried to find out what happened."

Fixing sentences to get rid of useless hard words is fairly easy once you manage to figure out what they're talking about. You just throw out the complicated language and say the statement simply. For instance, when you've understood a statement like (10), saying it in an easy way like (10a) is no great problem:

(10) My work superior inquired about the nature of the problem.

(10a) My boss asked what was wrong.

Sometimes you can get several different versions, depending on what matters and what doesn't. If you have a statement like (11), you can replace the hard words here and there and get (11a), or you can use an entirely different pattern and get (11b):

(11)   The college *dispatched* an *administrative memorandum stating* its *affirmative response* to my request for financial aid.

(11a)   The college *sent a memo giving* its *decision to grant* my request for financial aid.

(11b)   The college *said yes* to my request for financial aid.

depending on whether the actual sending of the memo makes enough difference to be worth mentioning. You don't want to simplify so much that you lose anything you consider important.

5. EXERCISE *on getting rid of useless hard words*

Here are some complicated statements from students' papers. Find simpler words to say the same thing. Use your own judgment about how many details you want.

Example:
The agent representing the interests of our real estate agency made a declaration of her intention to advertise immediately the availability of the property for sale.

You could fix it like this:
Our real estate agent said she would advertise the property for sale right away.

[1]   The residents of the home located directly next to our own have formed a decision to transfer their place of residence to a different location.

[2]   The purchasers communicated their interest in becoming participants in another project devoted to the construction of housing.

[3]   The government obtained knowledge regarding the activities of the intelligence agent during the time span of the preceding year.

[4]   The war resulted in the termination of the existence of three million members of the population.

[5]   It was my approximate estimation that the accident was of serious character.

[6]   Informed sources transferred to the board of supervisors pertinent information about the recent misplacement of significant quantities of legal tender.

[7]   Acute financial embarrassment compelled me to refrain from offering a contribution.

[8]   I trust you will permit me to make a communication to you of my sincerest apologies.

[9]   The unfavorable weather has created an undesirable situation involving the economic status of the agricultural community.

[10] It was the inclination of the judge to impose a more prolonged penalty of institutional incarceration upon the perpetrators of the larceny.

A.2.2   *Special Terms Versus Useless Hard Words*

In **scientific and technical writing**, you do need to use the **special terms** of the field you're writing about (see Chapter 1, Section C.4). Since these terms are well established, trained readers will know and understand them. But be careful of assuming too much. If you aren't *really sure* your readers will know the terms, then *briefly explain* them. You could put in a brief explanation, as in (12a), or you could give more detailed information, as in (13a).

(12)   There is a major increase in the number of *actuarians*.

(12a) There is a major increase in the number of *actuarians, that is, special insurance agents who use probabilities to figure risks.*

(13)   *Electrophoretic separation* techniques are hindered by *gravity-induced convection mixing.* [*Science Digest*, June 1983]

(13a) *Electrophoresis is a means of using electrical fields to separate a mixture of molecules.* Gravity can hinder this electrophoretic separation *by making some molecules flow other ways besides those in the electric field, so that mixing occurs.*

Readers who don't already know the special words will appreciate your courtesy. Readers who do know them can just skim past the explanations.

But remember: use *only the special terms you really need.* It's much too popular these days to clutter up scientific and technical writing with useless hard words just to be snobbish toward the general public. For instance, one student wrote (14) to explain the social worker's term "resettlement." Most of the other hard words aren't needed for the explanation—(14a) does the job just as well with a lot less effort required of readers:

(14)   Resettlement is essentially a procedure designed to achieve the greatest use of patients' abilities in their work and self-care.

(14a) Resettlement helps patients to work and care for themselves as best they can.

To fix such sentences, get rid of the useless hard words and keep only the useful ones. In (15), "behavior," "disturbances," and "communication" are the main points of the message. So you can keep those words and simplify the rest, getting (15a).

(15) Various forms of behavioral disturbance result from a child's inability to participate in communication.

(15a) A child's behavior becomes disturbed if he or she can't communicate.

Some special terms you really can't get away from, because there is no good way to replace them. In a case like (16), you have to keep "intravenous injection," because no other words mean exactly the same thing. But the rest of the statement could certainly be simplified, as you can see from (16a):

(16) Following the lapse of a substantial period of time, an intravenous injection was administered.

(16a) After a long time, an intravenous injection was given.

So the point is not to get rid of *all* hard words, but to get rid of *useless* hard words you don't need in order to make yourself clear.

6. EXERCISE *on telling special terms from useless hard words*

Here are some complicated statements. Keep only the special terms and get rid of the useless hard words.

Example:
An individual employed in the profession of inorganic chemistry must be conversant with the operation of a spectroscope.

You could fix it like this:
An inorganic chemist must know how to operate a spectroscope.

[1] His spouse was placed in receipt of a subpoena.

[2] Among schizophrenics, an inability to employ difficult vocabulary items is not infrequent.

[3] Last year I became the occupant of an employment position as a systems analyst.

[4] Satellite communications are currently undergoing a particularly sizeable increase.

[5] Dot-matrix printers result in a type output the appearance of which is distinctly less satisfactory than the type obtainable through utilization of daisy-wheel printers.

[6] The damaged analog board in the computer's disk drive was the component responsible for the repeated presentation of incomprehensible messages.

[7] Subsequent to the occurrence of significant peculiarities, the rocket proto-type was removed to a withdrawal condition.

[8] The calculation of the rapidity of the retro-rockets entailed extensive difficulties.

[9] Life spans of short duration can be considered to be a frequently appearing characteristic trait of microorganisms.

[10] The city commissioner brought under consideration an intensification of the police investigation.

General quiz
on hard words

7.
▼

Fix these complicated statements. Keep the necessary special terms, but get rid of useless hard words.

[1] The owners in possession of our condominiums are afforded great satisfaction.

[2] The inquiry submitted by yourself regarding software updates possesses a potentially problematic character.

[3] The large square notification device posted by the intersection insisted on a maximum vehicle velocity of 35 mph.

[4] The committee observed a lack of inclination on the part of the populace in regard to the attendance of the convention.

[5] Substantial pay raises have brought our employees into a state identical to that enjoyed by persons under the employment of our competitors.

[6] The corporate representative discharged an instruction to us that the mislaid merchandise should be restored into the possession of its proprietors.

[7] Previous to that particular point in time, I had not undergone any encounter with an influenza virus.

[8] We determined that the probability was not inconsiderable that a computer malfunction would endanger the operation of the turbine.

[9] Our obsolescent catamaran's stability displayed a noteworthy tendency to diminish on days characterized by the presence of high winds.

[10] Inexact financial calculations from my direction resulted in a circumstance of insufficient funds in my bank account.

Back-up general quiz
on hard words

8.

▼

Same instructions as on the previous quiz.

[1]   The negative reaction of the American populace toward the destruction of our natural environment has intensified in recent time intervals.

[2]   To terminate the practice of late registration, a monetary addition to student fees will be implemented.

[3]   The residence of domesticated pet animals in university domiciles is a target of administrational disapproval.

[4]   The department instituted precautionary measures to ensure a maximum of ease in the installation of refrigeration units.

[5]   It is my confident expectation that my proposal will encounter complete acceptance from the executive commission.

[6]   The inconsiderate conduct of intoxicated fraternity members reveals the usefulness of the establishment of a committee assigned to investigation.

[7]   The problematic nature of an unemployed situation has occasioned some nervous tension among workers in low-technology fields.

[8]   Two officers of the law proceeded to the apprehension of a gentleman under suspicion in connection with the illegal appropriation of monetary funds from a gasoline-selling establishment.

[9] Upon receiving this information pertaining to the maintenance of the generator, our team was placed in a position to eliminate future blackouts.

[10] Despite a substantial expansion in the quantity of unemployed workers in the construction and automotive industries, the economic situation was not unstable.

A.2.3   *Getting Rid of Excess Nouns*

Another common problem that makes sentences hard to understand comes up when the writer puts too much into NOUNS instead of VERBS. (As we saw in Chapter 2, Section C.1, a **noun** is a word you can put "the" in front of, and a **verb** is a word you can put "didn't" in front of.) When you use too many nouns, the world seems to be made up of *things*. You tend to lose track of the *events* that you could emphasize better by using more verbs. Compare these two versions:

(17)   There was *annoyance* on our part because of their *arrival* in town after midnight and their *appearance* at our front door.

(17a)   We *were annoyed* when they *arrived* in town after midnight and *appeared* at our front door.

The first version, with so many nouns (and a pretty empty verb like "was"), is harder to follow than the second version, where the action is expressed with verbs: "were annoyed," "arrived," and "appeared." Using too many nouns just like using useless hard words, is common among bureaucrats. Company memos come out looking like (18), when you'd do better to say (18a):

(18)   There was a *communication* from management with a *request* for our *participation*.

(18a)   Management *wrote* us and *asked* whether we would *participate*.

Students sometimes pile up nouns too, probably because so many other people do it. But it's still showing off, and it makes your writing harder to read. So why not fix up statements like (19) to make something plain and direct, like (19a)?

(19)   Confrontation *resolution* has a helpful *effect* on student *maturity*.

(19a)   It *helps* students *to mature* when they *resolve* confrontations.

The technique is perfectly simple. Sometimes you can keep the same basic word, but change it from a noun to a verb, as in (20): "consideration" → "considered" and "replacement" → "replace."

(20)   The city council took under *consideration* the *replacement* of the chief of police.

(20a)   The city council *considered* whether they should *replace* the chief of police.

Other times, you'll do better to use a completely different word, as in (21): "occurrence" → "made," and "removal" → "take off."

(21)   After the *occurrence* of many errors in the computer, the company decided on its *removal* from the market.

(21a)   After the computer *made* many errors, the company decided they would *take it off* the market.

You can do it either way, as long as you make the statement clear and direct.

9. EXERCISE *on getting rid of excess nouns*

Fix these statements with too many nouns. Use verbs for the important events, and make sure the statement is clear and direct.

Example:
> Soon after the resignation of the baseball commissioner, the team owners proceeded to the election of a successor.

You could fix it like this:
> Soon after the baseball commissioner resigned, the team owners elected a successor.

[1]   The recession resulted in the termination of the availability of ready cash.

[2]   It was my belief that the result of the surgery would be an improvement of her condition.

[3]   My nonpossession of funds was the cause of my nonpayment of rent.

[4]   We offered them a communication of our feelings of irritation in respect to the occurrence of the damage.

[5]   I came into receipt of a letter whose content was an indication of my boss's negative reply.

[6]   We had the intention of a return at a time appearing right to our judgment.

[7]   She became the buyer of a house whose construction occurred near the beach.

[8]   Since the discovery of antibiotics by scientists, influenza can be brought under cure.

[9]   Following their presentation of the awards, the committee attained a decision for adjournment.

[10] We have come into the realization that the printer is not presently in operation on your project.

10. QUIZ *on getting rid of excess nouns*

Fix these statements, which have too many nouns. Use verbs for the important events, and make sure the statement is clear and direct.

Example:
> An indication of a desire to remain in office was forthcoming from the baseball commissioner.

You could fix it like this:
   The baseball commissioner indicated he wanted to remain in office.

[1]   An immediate deposit of funds from your direction is now on request from our manager.

[2]   An omission of your payment will be subject to termination of your account.

[3]   Presidential confirmation of his press secretary's statement was soon in public release via the newspapers.

[4]   Student refusals regarding the surrender of parking privileges is a matter under investigation by the university administration.

[5]   The sheriff's situation was one of an absence of knowledge regarding the identity of the two men who were responsible for the commission of the holdup at the bank.

[6]   Students creating dormitory disturbances related to intense noise levels are given a reprimand.

[7]   Inconvenience resulted to the building's occupants, following your insistence on the manager's installation of new air conditioning.

[8]   A lack of clarity in the boss's communication was a source of confusion to the entire staff.

[9]   The post office issued a request whose objective was a rise in stamp prices.

[10] The individual who came into the mayor's office because of an election made a negative response to the commissioners' demands for the building of a new City Hall.

11. REVIEW QUIZ *on getting rid of excess nouns*

Same instructions as on the previous quiz.

[1]   She is in a state of sleep and our expectation is for her awakening at eight o'clock.

[2]   Encouragement was given to her by the board for the adoption of the proposal.

[3]   A lack of knowledge concerning your whereabouts was in evidence to our investigators.

[4]   My belief is a strong stand regarding the necessity for clearness of writing among professional people.

[5]   A desire for the release of more information from the father about the new house occurred among the family.

[6]   The immediate consequence of her destruction of the evidence was our report to the authorities.

[7] A reorganization of my room was an item in the weekend plan created by my mother.

[8] It was her intention that a removal of all junk be given immediate concern by myself.

[9] An end to uncleanliness of the floor and the placement of new paint on the walls were further objectives on her agenda.

[10] However, the absence of energy on my part proved to be a hindrance to this undertaking.

A.3   Making Sentences Longer

So far, we've been trying to make sentences short and simple. But as we saw at the start of this chapter, the length of your sentences depends on how hard your materials are. The usual strategy is:

USE SHORTER, SIMPLER SENTENCES
FOR HARD MATERIALS;
USE LONGER, MORE COMPLICATED
SENTENCES FOR EASY MATERIALS.

If your materials are easy to understand, you can overdo shortness and wind up with a really dull style. Suppose you had:

(22)   The day was cold. It was cloudy. The cold was bitter.

Such short sentences move the reader along at an extremely slow pace, because the materials are perfectly easy to follow. Why not say it all in one sentence?

(22a)   It was a bitterly cold, cloudy day.

After all, sentence (22a) is still pretty short, and it's easy to read, because it's talking about familiar things.

One strategy for combining short sentences to make longer ones is much the same as we used for reducing restatements and for fixing sentence fragments (see pages 22, 149, and 162), namely:

TAKE THE KEY WORDS OUT OF ONE SENTENCE
AND FIT THEM INTO ANOTHER SENTENCE.

Key words are the ones that tell us the main ideas and add something new to what was already known. To get (22a), we take the words "bitter" and "cloudy" and fit them into the first sentence. Words like "it was" are unimportant, because they don't tell us any main ideas. A few minor changes may be needed to get your new version, such as converting "bitter" to "bitterly." Here's another illustration:

(23)   Our boss refused. He was stubborn. He wouldn't open a branch office.

(23a)   Our boss *stubbornly* refused to *open a branch office.*

This time we moved "stubborn," changing it to "stubbornly," and "open a branch office." We dropped out "wouldn't," because it means the same as "refused." We added the word "to" in order to make the pieces fit together. Here too, the new sentence is still easy to read.

Another strategy should also be familiar from previous exercises:

USE LINKING WORDS TO FASTEN SENTENCES TOGETHER.

For (24), you could get either (24a) with the linking word in between or (24b) with the linking word at the start:

(24)   The soldiers left the province. They ran out of supplies.

(24a)   The soldiers left the province *because* they ran out of supplies.

(24b)   *When* they ran out of supplies, the soldiers left the province.

What was formerly a sentence by itself becomes just one *clause* inside a longer sentence. This strategy should be no problem, since we already used linking words to fix comma splices in Chapter 2, Section F.1.2.

You may need to *rearrange* your pieces a bit to fit them into just one sentence. If you have something like (25), you could make a version like (25a):

(25)   The election took place. It was November 10. The returns came in that evening. They were a disaster.

(25a)   The election *returns* on the *evening* of *November 10 were a disaster.*

Parts from various sentences now fit into one pattern. We got rid of unimportant words, such as "took place," "It was," and "came," and we added what was needed to glue the rest together, such as "on the" and "of."

You can easily get rid of words that say the same thing as other words in the final sentence. Suppose you have:

(26)   Orchids are *not easy* to grow. They're *extremely difficult*, in fact. They need special conditions.

(26a)   Orchids are extremely difficult to grow, because they need special conditions.

"Extremely difficult" takes care of whatever is said by "not easy," so we can leave the less important version out—"extremely difficult" makes a stronger statement. We worked on **streamlining** as a way to get rid of restatements in Chapter 1, Section C.3.

Combining sentences is also a useful way to get rid of a vague "this" at the start of a sentence. We tried this method in Chapter 1 (page 50). The sentence starting with "this" gets put together with the sentence before it, as in:

(27)   The crowd refused to listen to the speech. *This* angered the candidate.

(27a)   The crowd's refusal to listen to the speech angered the candidate.

(27b)   The candidate was angered when the crowd refused to listen to the speech.

If you think a version like (27a) sounds too formal, rearrange words to make a version like (27b). Rearranging is often a good idea:

(28)   We came too late for the demonstration. This was a major setback for our plans.

(28a)   *Our coming too late* for the demonstration was a major setback for our plans. [pretty formal]

(28b)   Our plans suffered a major setback *because we came too late* for the demonstration. [more usual]

Whichever method you use, you get rid of that vague "this" at the start of the second sentence.

12. EXERCISE *on combining sentences*

In the following items, the sentences are too short and choppy. Make each item into one sentence either by combining the key words from the various sentences or by using linking words. You can drop unimportant words or words that say the same thing as other words. You may need to do some rearranging and streamlining.

Example:
> We need new sockets. Three of them should do it. Our lamps aren't working. The lamps are the ones upstairs.

You could fix it like this:
> We need three new sockets for our lamps upstairs.

[1] The manager became ill. It was serious. This was at a very bad time.

[2] The employees were confused. Taxes were lowered. Then taxes were raised again.

[3] My new car is a compact. It's economical. It's roomy, too.

[4] We took three grams of the compound. We had it in a test tube. We stirred it for ten minutes. We kept it over a small flame.

[5] The state prison is still just as bad. It's a horrible place. It's unfit for human beings.

[6] The suspect had a large bruise. This told the inspectors something. He must have been in the fight.

[7] The stereo has 100 watts per channel. It has four speakers. The speakers are evenly balanced.

[8] I studied the textbook. I studied my notes too. These notes were from the lecture.

[9] It snowed in the desert. That was last year. It made the desert green in the spring.

[10] There was an auto accident last night. This shocked our whole family.

The earlier sections of this chapter should have made it clear that long sentences can be tiresome and tough to read. You shouldn't struggle to make sentences long for no good reason. Remember that longer sentences must still be *easy to under-stand*. So save your combining for times when the materials are easy or familiar.

13. QUIZ *on combining sentences*

Make each of the following items into one sentence either by combining the key words from the various sentences or by using linking words. You may need to do some rearranging and streamlining.

Example:
> This music is new. It's all done by computer. There are no musical instruments involved. There are no human voices.

You could fix it like this:
> This new music is all done by computer, with no musical instruments or human voices.

[1] Sometimes phone rates are lower. This happens on weekends and holidays. There is a difference of 60 percent.

[2] Newer computers are here. They have larger memories. They still cost the same as the old ones.

[3]   My family is going on vacation. We'll be in Hawaii. This will be during Easter.

[4]   We make screwdrivers. We take vodka. We take orange juice. We take ice cubes. We mix them all. We use a glass pitcher.

[5]   We thought of getting a smaller apartment. It should be close to the campus. This would save money.

[6]   I won't smoke cigarettes. I absolutely won't. They make me feel sick.

[7]   The general plan has mistakes in it. There are at least three. And they are major ones.

[8]   The open-air concert won't take place. It's been canceled. The weather is terrible.

[9]   You can use paint, varnish, or lacquer. This will keep the wood looking new.

[10] Orchids aren't easy to grow. This is because they're extremely sensitive. Direct sunlight is the problem.

☐ 14. REVIEW QUIZ *on combining sentences.*

Same instructions as on the previous quiz.

[1]   There are supplies in the storeroom. Use those. They are high-quality.

[2]   That season, two new movies came out. They were about how it feels to grow old. They won top awards.

[3]   Finally, the judge declared a mistrial. This meant the judgment was postponed.

[4]   Soft coal costs less. Hard coal costs more. It burns longer and hotter than soft coal.

[5]   Our town has two newspapers. One is a morning paper. One is an evening paper.

[6]   The vice-president had an operation. This was her second. It was more successful than her first.

[7]   I sent in reports. There were three of them. They were fairly detailed.

[8]   The Cornhuskers won the football game against USC. This greatly improved their chances for a record season.

[9]   Two more space flights were scheduled. They were to be in the next five years. They would be on the space shuttle.

[10] The company acquired new subsidiaries. They got a perfume factory. They got a paper mill. This was an expansion.

■ B. HOW SIMILAR SHOULD YOUR SENTENCES BE?

Another problem writers face is deciding how closely their sentences should resemble one another. If you work too hard to make every sentence exactly alike, readers will get bored. But if you work too hard to make every sentence radically different, readers will get confused. Actually, most writing falls in between—some similar sentences and some different ones.

Sentences can be similar in their **PATTERNS**—that is, in the way their words and clauses are arranged. Sentences can also be similar in their **CONTENT**—that is, how close they come to saying the same thing.

In both patterns and content, you need to consider how much similarity you want. Due to the influence of everyday talk, writers usually have two tendencies. They make their *patterns less similar* than they ought to, because talking is spontaneous and its patterns don't get so much attention. Or writers tend to make their *content more similar* than they ought to, because talking contains so many restatements (see Chapter 1, Section C.3). So we'll concentrate first on *increasing* the similarity of patterns and then on *decreasing* the similarity of content.

B.1 Making the Patterns of Your Sentences More Similar

Similar language patterns appearing together are often said to be **PARALLEL**. There is no special reason to repeat the same patterns *all the time*. However, the following strategy is often useful:

> *USE SIMILAR LANGUAGE PATTERNS WHEN YOU*
> *SAY SIMILAR THINGS.*

In talk, sudden changes of pattern probably don't get noticed. But in writing, you want to make things as clear as possible. It helps if you use the same pattern for similar things. The similarity of the pattern points out the similarity of the things more effectively. That way, the things are easier to compare or contrast. Suppose you have:

(29) It is easier *to love* all humanity than *loving* your own neighbor.

The pattern in "to love" is not the same as the pattern in "loving." When you have two different patterns like these, you usually have two ways you could make them the same. You only have to make minor changes for (29). You could either make the second item match the first (29a) or make the first item match the second (29b):

(29a) It is easier *to love* all humanity than *to love* your own neighbor.

(29b)   It is easier *loving* all humanity than *loving* your own neighbor.

Suppose you're making a list with more than two items on it, such as:

(30)   During vacation, I like *skiing*, *fishing*, and *to go* to the beach.

The third pattern, "to go," is not the same as the first two, "skiing" and "fishing." Again, only minor changes are needed. You could either make the third item match the first two items (30a) or make the first two items match the third one (30b):

(30a)   During vacation, I like *skiing*, *fishing*, and *going* to the beach.

(30b)   During vacation, I like *to ski*, *to fish*, and *to go* to the beach.

Often, though, all the possible changes are not equally good. Students generally like (30a) better than (30b). Or, to take a sample from a paper about being an actor, you might have something like (31), and you'd need to choose between (31a) and (31b):

(31)   *The clear pronunciation of your lines* and *how loud you deliver them* are very important.

(31a)   *The clear pronunciation of your lines* and *the loudness of your delivery* are very important. [with more nouns]

(31b)   *How clearly you pronounce your lines* and *how loudly you deliver them* are very important. [with more verbs]

Here, you're choosing whether to put the main ideas into *nouns* ("pronunciation," "delivery") or else into *verbs* ("you pronounce," "you deliver"). As we saw in Section A.2 of this chapter, you're generally better off using verbs for actions. So you have a good reason to pick version (31b) over (31a).

In the next illustration, it's even easier to decide which way to go. We learned about getting rid of extra words such as "something that" in Chapter 1 (see page 12). So you'd want not (32a), but rather (32b):

(32)   I need the complete printout, and the master file is something my boss wants.

(32a)   The complete printout is something I need, and the master file is something my boss wants. [too many extra words]

(32b)   I need the complete printout, and my boss wants the master file.

Here the similar patterns make it easy to compare what "I need" with what the "boss wants."

Similar patterns can be used *inside a single sentence* or *between two or more sentences*. Let's try working inside the single sentence first, since that's easier.

15. EXERCISE *on using similar patterns inside one sentence*

Fix these sentences by using similar patterns to say similar things. Try to pick the best way to fix each one.

Example:

> The man at the counter wanted to know my place of residence and what my parents' occupation is.

You could fix it like this:

> The man at the counter wanted to know where I live and what my parents' occupation is.

[1]   You can have either a boat ride along the coast, or you ride the bus over the mountains.

[2]   The instructor was the one who selected questions, and she had the job of nominating speakers.

[3]   These new pills will make your stomach relax, and the end of your headaches will come.

[4]   My father said to stay in college and that I should study law.

[5]   The secretary must attend all meetings, call the roll, and is the one who writes down all items of business.

[6]   With a four-day work week, people could spend more time with their families, and it would be possible to make more trips as well.

[7]   Congressional leaders couldn't decide whether to increase American involvement or if they should withdraw.

[8]   A sophomore needs three important qualities: persistence, being confident, and a mature outlook is good too.

[9]   In the autumn, these Indians had the customs of painting their houses, to exchange gifts, and they offered prayers for the harvest.

[10] We learned about cutting the metals and how you can shape them with heat.

Now let's try working with similar patterns *between two or more sentences.* The technique is much the same—the items are just longer. Here again, similar patterns are good for saying similar things, because they allow readers to compare and contrast more easily. Take this example:

> (33)   The sophomores visited the botanical gardens. The art gallery was the place the seniors went.

As usual, you have more than one way to fix it. The first way (33a) is better because it doesn't take as many words to get the message across:

(33a) The sophomores visited the botanical gardens. The seniors visited the art gallery. [12 words]

(33b) The botanical gardens was the place the sophomores went. The art gallery was the place the seniors went. [18 words]

Notice that you sometimes have to repeat a few words in order to make whole sentences parallel—such as "visited" in (33a). These repeats are not a major drawback if you're doing them to make similar patterns for similar things. Just try not to repeat too many words. If you have something like (34), totally similar patterns, as in (34a), give you too many repeats. Cut down on repeats while keeping the patterns as similar as you can—as, for instance, in (34b) or (34c).

(34) The big city offers a great variety of cultural activities. This variety is much less available in small towns. [patterns not similar]

(34a) The big city offers a great variety of cultural activities. The small town offers much less variety of cultural activities. [patterns similar, but too many repeats]

(34b) The big city offers a great variety of cultural activities. The small town offers much less variety. [patterns similar without so many repeats]

(34c) The big city offers a great variety of cultural activities. The small town offers much less. [patterns similar with almost no repeats]

In all versions, we still have the similar pattern of "the big city offers" versus "the small town offers." You don't have to repeat all the rest.

So far, we've been working with just two sentences. But the same thing goes for *three or more sentences*. If you had to fix (35), you could get something like (35a):

(35) The first day they attended the conference. They went sightseeing the second day. Going to the mountains was on the third day's calendar.

(35a) The first day they attended the conference. The second day they went sightseeing. The third day they went to the mountains.

You could even have more than three, though it's not terribly common.

[] **16. EXERCISE** *on using similar patterns in more than one sentence*

Fix these groups of sentences by using similar patterns to say similar things. Try to pick the best and most compact version. Remember that you shouldn't repeat too many words.

Example:

Chapter 1 deals with the French Revolution. We turn to the British Empire in Chapter 2. The American War of Independence is the focus of Chapter 3.

You could fix it like this:

Chapter 1 deals with the French Revolution. Chapter 2 turns to the British Empire. Chapter 3 focuses on the American War of Independence.

[1] Before the operation, the pain was very intense. A disappearance of pain occurred after the operation.

[2] In high school, attendance was mandatory. It's more voluntary whether you attend classes in college.

[3] Last year's season ended with a stunning victory over Georgia. A narrow loss against the same team began this year's season.

[4] The employees asked for a 10 percent raise. But a 3 percent cost-of-living adjustment is what they got. And after taxes, only a 2 percent increase was the amount they ended up with.

[5] In the first course, we learned about the construction and operation of computers. How to program them was the learning material for our second course.

[6] Americans are known for their inventiveness and technology. Abstract theories and philosophical ideas are the concerns of Europeans.

[7] First, remove the screws from the package and sort them according to size. Then, the places marked in red are where the screws should be inserted and where you should tighten them all the way.

[8] The North concentrated on industry. Agriculture was the area on which the South was focused.

[9] First, the allies used long-range guns. Next, aircraft attacks were carried out by the enemy. Finally, the allied forces were the ones who deployed middle-range missiles.

[10] Football demands general strength in all parts of the body. Specific buildup of the leg muscles is what's needed for jogging.

17. QUIZ on making similar patterns

Fix these groups of sentences by using similar patterns to say similar things, either inside one sentence or in several sentences. Try to pick the best and most compact way you can. Remember that you shouldn't repeat too many words.

Example:

The first category includes wounded veterans of foreign wars. Victims of industrial accidents go in the second category. The third category is where you put people with inherited disabilities.

You could fix it like this:

The first category includes wounded veterans of foreign wars. The second category includes victims of industrial accidents. The third category includes people with inherited disabilities.

[1] January is our coldest month. The most heat comes here in July. April is the time when the climate is most moderate.

[2] The clothes should be washed on a medium heat. A high heat is the one when you're using the dryer on them.

[3] How fast you can run is one thing to think about. But you should also consider how long your lungs can hold out.

[4] We could supply fifteen chairs from our own camp, and for fifty chairs we could go to the camp next door.

[5] Not appearing at the big game was very inconsiderate. But it was downright hostile when they didn't come to our town festival.

[6] The typewriters need new ribbons. Rolls of paper are going to have to go in the adding machines. Toner is what's needed for the copiers.

[7] It's hard enough to find the right size. But matching up the right colors is almost impossible.

[8] Material success will not give you total peace of mind. You'll be more satisfied with spiritual happiness.

[9] It's difficult to be patient with emotionally disturbed people. Being kind to violent people is even less easy.

[10] His elder brother became a lumberman. Farming was the profession his sister took up. Being a lifeguard turned out to be the job for his younger brother.

☐ 18. REVIEW QUIZ *on making similar patterns*

Same instructions as on the previous quiz.

[1] The old style required dark wood. Light wood is what is needed for the new style.

[2] Our company is happy about the speedy delivery service. But the added cost is something we are worried about. And we are undecided about what to do for extra storage space.

[3] Should I attend the meeting, or is staying away better?

[4] With the new computer, we can save on paper and fewer personnel will be needed; there also won't be so much call for filing cabinets.

[5] The classroom session dealt with the operation of the machines. How to maintain them was covered by the practical session.

[6] We have three choices: sending the invoice to the company, or we can let them send us a bill, or there's the possibility of using our credit cards.

[7] He told his mother about his acceptance into law school and that he got a scholarship.

[8] The husband works for a construction firm, a chemical company employs the wife, and a job at a steel mill is what their daughter has.

[9] The evening performances are very energetic. More relaxed is the way to describe the afternoon matinees.

[10] Surgical assistants' time is divided into three main activities. They prepare the site for the operation. Dispensing the antiseptic is something they do. And the anesthetic has to be kept ready for use.

B.2 Streamlining Sentences Whose Content Is Too Similar

STREAMLINING means reducing or combining your statements because you're saying the same thing more often than you need to. Streamlining helps remove the overlap and duplication among your statements. In Chapter 1, Sections D.3 and D.5, we practiced getting rid of extra words inside a single sentence. Now we'll be doing the same sort of thing with larger blocks of several sentences.

Because talking has so many restatements, writers naturally tend to make the content of their sentences more similar than it ought to be. Also, students are sometimes told to write so-and-so many words or to fill a certain number of pages. It's understandable if you tend to spread the same content over too many sentences, just in order to reach the quota. But in the real world, time and effort are in short supply, and so is paper. I'd much rather read something short and to the point than the same ideas spread out to make the paper look longer.

It doesn't matter if you duplicate things now and then when you're writing a new paper. The main thing is that you know how to take out the excess later on. For instance, a freshman writing a rough draft about her "problems" said pretty much the same thing twice in two sentences (36). Then, in her revision, she said it only once in one sentence (36a):*

---

* We'll look at several drafts of this paper in Chapter 4, Section B.

(36)   There are so many unknown facets involved with college. I am still uncertain as to what school might hold for me.

(36a)   I am still uncertain what unknown facets college might hold for me.

The first statement lost the empty words "There are so many." The key words
"unknown facets" and "college" got moved into the second statement.

Let's figure out how streamlining can be done in easy steps. One major strategy is:

REMOVE DUPLICATIONS AND EMPTY WORDS,
AND PUT TOGETHER WHAT'S LEFT OVER.

DUPLICATIONS are words that say pretty much the same thing over again.
EMPTY WORDS are words that don't tell us much at all, such as "someone,"
"something," "there is," "it happens that," "the fact that," and so on.

Two or more statements can be merged into just one. A good strategy for
streamlining statements is:

TAKE THE KEY WORDS OF ONE STATEMENT
AND WORK THEM INTO ANOTHER
STATEMENT.

As we've seen before (pages 149, 162, and 180), the **key words** are the parts that
carry the message and add something new to what had been said before. They are
the words that do not duplicate what other statements are saying—such as "unknown facets" and "college" in (36). Wherever it's needed, you can

---

TAKE OUT EMPTY WORDS TO MAKE ROOM
FOR KEY WORDS.

Let's see how these strategies work. Here's the opening of another student's
paper:

(37)   Both young and old go to the Alachua County Fair to have fun. People
attend the fair to have a good time and forget the little worries of everyday life.

The second statement covers about the same ground as the first. "Attend the fair"
tells us nothing we didn't know from "go to the Alachua County Fair"; and "to

have a good time" is no different from "to have fun." "People" is a pretty empty word. All you're left with as key words in the second statement is "forget the little worries of everyday life." So you work them into the first statement—for example:

(37a) Both young and old go to the Alachua County Fair to have fun and to *forget the little worries of everyday life.*

The streamlined version says just as much and uses a lot fewer words.
Let's try another one:

(38) Wishman says that criminals go free because somewhere along the line of the legal process someone *did something wrong.* Either the police investigator, the prosecutor, or the judges *made a mistake.*

This time, "made a mistake" duplicates "did something wrong." So you zero in on the key words in the second statement: "the police investigator, the prosecutor, or the judges." You can tack the key words onto the end of the first statement and get (38a); or you can put them in place of the empty word "someone" and get an even more streamlined version (38b):

(38a) Wishman says that criminals go free because somewhere along the line of the legal process someone did something wrong, *such as the police investigator, the prosecutor, or the judges.*

(38b) Wishman says that criminals go free because somewhere along the line of the legal process *the police investigator, the prosecutor, or the judges* did something wrong.

Another good strategy for streamlining statements is:

LEAVE OUT OBVIOUS MINOR DETAILS.

Many things can be taken for granted and left out, because readers would assume them anyway. There's no need to give all the little details in (39)—if you read that someone "mailed a letter at the post office," you naturally assume they made it over there and got a stamp. Once the minor details are taken out, (39a) gives just the essentials.

(39) We got in the car and drove to the post office, and when we got there, we mailed your letter after we purchased a stamp and stuck it on the envelope.

(39a) We mailed your letter at the post office.

For the same reason, (40) is an odd story. Take out the minor details and you get something more reasonable, like (40a):

(40) I suddenly realized it was finals day, so I got up out of bed, took a shower, put on my clothes, put on shoes and socks (not necessarily in that order), and ran to class like a star athlete.

(40a) I suddenly realized it was finals day, so I got up, dressed, and ran to class like a star athlete.

Unless there's some special reason, don't give obvious details, such as what you do to get dressed.

When you've overdone the details, you should streamline. Here's what a student wrote about John Steinbeck's novel *Of Mice and Men*:

(41) Lennie and George's constant moving about has turned them into drifters. They have no permanent home and they have no family. They move constantly from town to town.

Just by itself, "drifters" already means people who "have no permanent home" and "have no family" and "move constantly from town to town." The second and third statements only tell us what we know from the first statement. You should definitely streamline here. You could just leave out everything but the first statement, as in (41a); or you could beef up the first statement with a few key words from the others, as in (41b).

(41a) Lennie and George's constant moving about has turned them into drifters.

(41b) Lennie and George's constant moving *from town to town with no permanent home* has turned them into drifters.

Use your own judgment about what readers will assume, as compared to what you ought to tell them. For instance, if you're writing for children, you're more likely to give a longer description of what "drifters" do than if you're writing for adults.

When statements overlap, it may help to *circle the key words* and *draw a line through the duplications*, before you make a streamlined version. Try it on this section of a student's paper:

(42) When people see or hear something they think is humorous, they have a physical response to it. The amount of the physical response can be big or little, depending on how humorous they think it is. No matter whether the response is a big laugh or a little smile, people respond physically to humor.

When you've finished circling and drawing lines, you should have something like this:

Chapter Three / Putting Sentences Together

(42a) When people see or hear something they think is humorous, they have a physical response to it. The ~~amount~~ of the physical response can be (big or little), depending on how ~~humorous~~ they ~~think~~ it is. No matter whether the response is a big (laugh) or a ~~little~~ (smile), ~~people respond physically to humor.~~

In the second statement, only the key words "big or little" add something that the first statement didn't tell us. It's pretty obvious that "the amount of the physical response depends on how humorous they think it is"—what else would it depend on? So all you need to circle in the second statement would be "big or little." The third statement has only the key words "laugh" and "smile" to circle, since everything else there was covered in the first and second statements. The duplications include: "think"—"think," "humorous"—"humorous"—"humor," "physical response"—"respond physically," "big or little"—"big or little," and "people"—"people." Also, "the amount" is hardly needed if you say "big or little," since "amounts" always fall in some range like that. Now you can try getting all the key words into the first statement. You might have:

(42b) When people see or hear something they think is humorous, they respond physically, whether with *a big laugh or a little smile.*

Or, if you want to go from less extreme to more extreme (see pages 209–12), you could switch that last part around:

(42c) When people see or hear something they think is humorous, they respond physically, whether with *a little smile or a big laugh.*

Either way, you've streamlined the passage down to 22 words instead of the 54 words in the original (42). You've packed what there was to be said into one statement instead of spreading it all over the page.

You may not be able to get everything into just one sentence. But your strategies will still be the same: focus on key words and get rid of duplications and empty words. Suppose you have something like (43). If you circle key words and put a line through duplications, you get:

(43) Nursing offers valuable experience. ~~Nursing~~ makes you feel that you are (helping people who need it) (in times of illness). ~~Illness~~ is a (crucial) and (difficult) time. ~~People~~ (can't help themselves) and (feel cut off from the world) ~~when they're having an illness.~~

Your new version might have two sentences, as in (43a). Having just one, as in (43b), makes a pretty long sentence, like the run-ons we saw in Section A.1 of this chapter.

(43a)   Nursing offers valuable experience helping people who need it in the crucial and difficult time of illness. They can't help themselves and feel cut off from the world.

(43b)   Nursing offers valuable experience helping people who need it in the crucial and difficult time of illness because they can't help themselves and feel cut off from the world.

Either way, the result is a great improvement over the original (43). How long your sentences should be depends on how easy the materials are (see page 160).

19. QUIZ on streamlining

Streamline these passages. First, *circle key words* that carry the message and add something new to what was said in the first statement. Then *put a line through the duplications*. Finally, *make a new version* that gets the key words into just one or two sentences.

Example:
Polygamy is a marriage in which one person is married to more than one person. A husband could have more than one wife, or a wife could have more than one husband. Either way, the marriage is illegal, because it has more than two people in it.

You could fix it like this:
Polygamy is an illegal marriage in which one person is married to more than one husband or wife.

[1]   It is easy to judge the mood of a dog. It is not so easy to judge the mood of a cat. Pet owners soon find this out.

[2]   People in the caste system in India had almost no way of changing it. This meant that changes in the system to improve it didn't happen very often.

[3]   Alchemy was an early science that was a little like chemistry. Alchemists were like chemists in experimenting with combinations of elements and compounds. They were experimenting to see if new elements and compounds could be made in a laboratory.

[4]   Mental illness has become a topic of discussion in our society. People are more willing to discuss it. It's a crucial topic.

[5]   A small child might get locked in a closet. As a result, the child later suffers from claustrophobia, the fear of closed spaces. This feeling creates powerful anxieties.

[6]   According to socialism, all workers should own the factories and share the profits the factories make. The government has the job of seeing to it that the workers share the profits. The factories belong to all the workers.

[7]   Somebody has to take care of the health of animals. In our society, vet-
        erinarians are the ones who care for animals and make sure they are healthy.
        They treat large animals and small ones. A large animal could be a horse,
        and a small animal could be a parakeet.

[8]   In recent years, the growing field of real estate has been expanding. It is
        becoming very profitable to go into the field of real estate. The field offers
        good jobs that pay well.

[9]   If you pay a certain amount of money, you can fly anywhere, any place, and as
        many places as you want, with Pan Am. For that amount of money, you have
        unlimited travel in tourist class. You can travel all over for eighty days.

[10]   That year, the winter had lots and lots of snow. It snowed for weeks, and the
        temperature never got above freezing. The snow started in October and
        never stopped, not until March.

20. REVIEW QUIZ *on streamlining*

Same instructions as on the previous quiz.

[1]   Recycling is an important new way to conserve. Tin cans should be re-
        cycled. Glass should be recycled. Paper should be recycled. These materials
        are all in short supply. It doesn't make sense to put them on the junkpile
        when they're in short supply.

[2]   Courses in advanced programming have many prerequisites. You can't take
        courses in advanced programming until you've had calculus. You also need
        trigonometry before they'll let you in. And you have to have taken basic
        programming, too.

[3]   Tax lawyers are much in demand. Tax laws are complicated. Private citizens
        as well as companies are in need of tax lawyers. The laws are always changing.

[4]   Tobacco farming is very hard work. Tobacco farmers work long hours and
        don't make much money from the crop, either. The crop is tough to raise.
        It's tough to harvest and cure, too.

[5]   Our family is very close. We've always been very close. We aren't like many
        other families. Everybody treats everybody else like a good friend. You get
        the kind of advice and support from one another that you expect from good
        friends.

[6]   Rugby is a great sport. It's a team sport, and you have to work as a team.
        You're a part of the team and everyone on the team gets pretty close during
        a whole season.

[7]   I learned to fish this summer. It was pretty easy when I learned to fish.
        I learned how to get the pole ready. You need to use the right line and bait
        for it when you fish. I also learned how to find a good place where you
        should fish.

[8] The Rocky Mountains are a place of much scenery. They are breathtaking. The Rockies are unforgettable. You must see them.

[9] During World War II, many things became very scarce. You could hardly buy rubber. Sugar and coffee were hard to find. Metals such as copper were not often on the market. The reason these things were so scarce was that they were being used by the armed forces. They were being used in the war effort.

[10] The words they sing in rock music are very important. It's not at all true that the words don't matter. The words carry a message. It's an important message for the people who hear the music. It's about our life and times. It's about our glory and our madness.

■   C.   IN WHAT ORDER SHOULD YOUR SENTENCES BE?

As we've seen, you can distribute your materials over groups of sentences that are different in various ways. Sentences can be shorter or longer, depending on how hard your materials are. Sentences can also be made in similar patterns if you're saying similar things. But you don't want the content to be too similar from sentence to sentence.

Even when you've decided on the size and shape of sentence groups, you still need to decide *what order* to put your sentences in. So let's try a few common strategies writers use.

C.1 From Earlier to Later

If you're giving instructions or telling a story, you normally arrange things according to TIME. The strategy would be:

MOVE IN TIME FROM EARLIER TO LATER.

Here's an illustration from the *Florida Independent Alligator* (June 19, 1983):

(44) The storekeeper discovered the cyanide was missing. He went to the department's lab manager. The manager in turn went to his department chairman and told him. The chairman decided the same day that the police should be notified.

Each event is listed in the order things actually happened. The same strategy applies if you're giving instructions on how to do something, as in this computer manual:

(45)   Insert the diskette in the disk drive. Switch the computer on. The disk
       drive will come on and whirl a few seconds. Then, a prompt appears on
       the screen, and the computer waits for your instructions.

The manual tells you what to do and what will happen after you do it. The writer
assumes that you'll do the things in the same order in which they're mentioned,
and in a context like this it's very important that you do so.

21. QUIZ *on moving in time from earlier to later*

Make up *two or more complete sentences* about each of these topics. Mention
things in the order in which they happen or in the order in which they should
be done. If you don't know how any of these things are done, ask somebody
who does.

Example:
      how to report a fire

You could do it like this:
      First, hurry to a phone or a fire alarm box. Then get the number and
      call the fire department. Give them the exact location of the fire as best
      you can.

[1]   how to change a flat tire

[2]   what happened when I registered for classes

[3]   how to make a super-deluxe sandwich

[4]   what I did on my high school graduation night

[5]   how I came to be at this college

22. REVIEW QUIZ *on moving in time from earlier to later*

Same instructions as on the previous quiz.

[1]   how to barbecue hamburgers

[2]   the last trip I went on

[3]   how I found a place to live

[4]   my first few good experiences with music

[5]   how to get a book from the library

C.2 Cause and Effect

Frequently, you aren't so concerned about time. You want to say not just *when* things happened, but *why* they did. Here a useful strategy is:

MOVE FROM CAUSE TO EFFECT.

One student wrote about leukemia:

(46)   Healthy cells begin to divide excessively. Blood disease soon comes from this abnormal pattern and generally causes death.

He first mentions the cause ("cells divide excessively"), then the effect ("blood disease"); this effect is in turn given as a cause of "death." You can use expressions like "cause," "lead to," "result in," and the like, but you don't have to.

The reverse strategy would be:

MOVE FROM EFFECT TO CAUSE.

Sometimes you can get people's attention by starting out with something unusual or interesting. Then people will want to know what caused it to happen. This strategy is common in newspapers, such as:

(47)   Fists were flying, human bodies were thrown around, and there was a little blood spilled. The O'Connell Center presented professional wrestling last night. [*Florida Independent Alligator*, Nov. 1981]

When you are first told there was violence, you probably want to find out why. The cause was not a very usual one—it wasn't a riot, but a university event.

☐ 23. QUIZ *on cause and effect*

Organize each set of notes into *at least two complete sentences.* Be sure to put CAUSE BEFORE EFFECT. *The notes may not be in that order already!* You can use expressions like "cause," "lead to," "result in," and the like, but you don't have to.

Example:
   myth of male superiority stubbornly living on—
   men's feelings of inferiority being concealed behind the myth

You could do it like this:

> Many men conceal their feelings of inferiority behind myths. As a result, the myth of male superiority stubbornly lives on.

[1] angry mobs gathering today on the northeast side—
sudden closing of a steel plant putting people out of work

[2] freezing weather in Florida last week breaking all records—
citrus crop damage amounting to several million dollars

[3] unemployment reaching new highs—
economy stagnating in many areas such as automobile manufacturing

[4] city officials getting many complaints—
late-night disturbances taking place near campus on weekends

[5] an unknown virus from the Far East reaching the United States—
severe epidemics in large cities leading to critical emergencies

On this next part of the quiz, put EFFECT BEFORE CAUSE. *The notes may not be in that order already!* Again, be sure you make at least *two complete sentences.*

[6] the whole town filling up all at once with new students—
Greek rush getting started before the semester begins

[7] winds reaching hurricane force last night—
dramatic evacuations being carried out around New Orleans

[8] continued misunderstandings among groups in our society—
a long tradition of confrontation being hard to overcome

[9] U.S. government cutting financial aid in order to pay for the arms race—
students having to drop out of school in large numbers

[10] my desire to do well in college—
remembering failures in my childhood and wanting to prevent any more

24. REVIEW QUIZ *on cause and effect*

Same instructions as on the first part of the previous quiz.

[1] some young children's progress in schoolwork being unusually slow—
a simple loss of hearing not being detected

[2] special late hours at the library accommodating large crowds of students—
midterms going on all this week

[3] engines being damaged by overheating in brand-new cars—
defective water pumps being installed through an error at the factory

[4]   the number of illegal aliens increasing this year—
       a worsening economic picture on the domestic job market

[5]   strict new building codes being passed in California—
       a series of earthquakes doing great damage to people's homes

Same instructions as on the second part of the previous quiz.

[6]   banking services getting much faster and more efficient—
       installation of computers becoming very widespread

[7]   an all-out program getting under way to clean up and beautify the campus—
       students' parents expected to visit campus in two weeks

[8]   our rent not getting paid on time three months in a row—
       having to pay ridiculous bills for utilities in order to keep the service going

[9]   too many test planes having to make emergency landings—
       failure to check out the entire fuel system in the laboratory before installation in aircraft

[10]   price of vegetables getting out of control—
       great damage being done by hardy, pesticide-resistant insects

C.3   Statement and Evidence

Another common strategy for sentence order is:

MAKE A MAIN STATEMENT AND THEN GIVE
SOME EVIDENCE FOR IT.

Once you make your main statement, you should give people **evidence**—that is, some grounds to believe it. The **statement** is more like an opinion, whereas the **evidence** is more like obvious facts. One student wrote:

(48)   A nursing home benefits froms student volunteers. Their visits lift the spirits of elderly patients.

We are first told that the "nursing home benefits," and then we find out how the "benefit" works—by "lifting the spirits of elderly patients." The second statement says why we should believe the first one.

Following up with evidence is an especially good strategy if your main statement is surprising. Another student wrote:

(49)   Contrary to popular belief, today's society is not child-oriented. Communities keep voting down school bond issues and day-care support bills.

First, she contradicted a "popular belief" and then had to say why her own statement should be believed instead. A society can't be "child-oriented" if it "keeps
voting down" schools and day-care centers.

    You can *announce* your supporting evidence by saying "this fact is clear from,"
"we know this because," "we find evidence in," and so on, as in:

(49a)   Contrary to popular belief, today's society is not child-oriented. *This fact
is clear from* the way communities keep voting down school bond issues
and day-care support bills.

But you don't need these announcements if your evidence clearly supports your
main statement. It would certainly be annoying to have such announcements all
over the place. For instance, (50) doesn't work as well as (50a):

(50)   The recession was getting worse. *You could tell because* unemployment hit
a new record. *This fact was clear when* the number of persons collecting
welfare rose sharply. *We knew because* three people in our own family lost
their jobs. [too many announcements]

(50a)   The recession was getting worse. Unemployment hit a new record. The
number of persons collecting welfare rose sharply. Three people in our
own family lost their jobs.

Since it's plain the writer is giving evidence in (50a), there's no need for all those
announcements.

    Now suppose your main statement may be *unwelcome*. If you start right off tell-
ing people something they don't agree with, they may not pay attention to your
evidence. In that situation, a useful strategy would be:

GIVE SOME EVIDENCE FIRST AND THEN MAKE
YOUR MAIN STATEMENT.

If you wanted to lead into your statement about society and children, you could
say:

(49b)   Communities keep voting down school bond issues and day-care support
bills. Today's society must not be as child-oriented as we thought.

You could let evidence pile up and then say what conclusion you drew from it:

(51)   The invaders insisted they had acted in order to stop a major military buildup. But no political groups in the invaded country had been aware of any buildup. No large stores of weapons were found. Instead, the military installations were small and old-fashioned. Apparently, the invaders had some other motive they didn't want to admit.

The main statement that "the invaders had some other motive they didn't want to admit" is saved until several kinds of evidence have been presented. At that point, readers are more likely to believe your main statement, because they might draw the same conclusion.

☐ 25. QUIZ on statement and evidence

Make each set of notes into *two complete sentences*. Make the first one the MAIN STATEMENT, and have the second one give SUPPORTING EVIDENCE. *The notes may not be in that order already!*

Example:
    need to discover new values worth living for—
    many people full of anxiety and severely disoriented in their views on life

You could do it like this:
    Today, our society needs to discover new values worth living for. At present, many people are full of anxiety and severely disoriented in their views on life.

[1]   the need for better public transportation becoming acute—
      soaring cost of gasoline getting beyond what many people can afford

[2]   new stage in international politics beginning to be recognized—
      dissolving traditional alliances among nations

[3]   being able to take care of my daily expenses by working part-time—
      my self-reliance increasing now that I've entered college

[4]   public confidence in the national government being steadily eroded—
      large rallies in Washington protesting industrial pollution and nuclear arms
          expansion

[5]   new contracts needed to meet the dangers of inflation eating away at work-
          ers' wages—
      labor negotiations likely to be very difficult this year

On this next part, give the SUPPORTING EVIDENCE *first* and then make the MAIN STATEMENT. *The notes may not be in that order already!*

[6]   a college degree apparently less valuable than it once was—
      the number of unemployed college graduates growing

[7] an explosion of short-lived trends in women's fashions—
fashion designers in desperate need of finding some way to increase sales

[8] car racing reaching the status of a major American sport—
the number of race tracks, racing magazines, and newspaper stories growing
rapidly

[9] colder winters being recorded almost every year—
the earth headed for a new ice age

[10] the rights of women and minorities getting more and more attention—
chances improving that the Equal Rights Amendment will be ratified

▢ 26. REVIEW QUIZ on statement and evidence

Same instructions as on the first part of the previous quiz.

[1] conservative clothing trends on college campuses—
preppies thinking it's fashionable to wear their parents' clothes

[2] tuition getting higher and competition getting stiffer—
getting admitted to medical school being very difficult

[3] social work having great potential value—
easing tensions among families in the home

[4] semesters having more advantages than quarters—
students and administration going through registration only twice a year,
making less work for everybody

[5] a rash of the flu hitting the campus—
hundreds of students crowding the infirmary and absent from classes

Same instructions as on the second part of the previous quiz.

[6] "no smoking" signs appearing in all sorts of places such as buses and ele-
vators—
an increase in public awareness of the hazards of tobacco

[7] consumers waiting to see what the economy does before they make major
investments—
sales remaining very slow in real estate

[8] physicists in violent arguments about what subatomic particles there are—
particle physics in a state of tremendous confusion

[9] American corporations not spending heavily to compete with Japan in computers—
American not realizing the danger of losing out to Japan on the world
market

[10] many companies buying options to use the space shuttle—
the concept of reusable spacecraft now widely accepted

C.4 The Whole and the Parts

If you're talking about something that is made up of several parts, you could use this strategy for sentence order:

MOVE FROM THE WHOLE TO ITS PARTS.

You can mention the main thing and then tell what parts it has. You might say something like "include," "consist of," and the like, though you don't have to.
One student wrote:

(52) Quarterama is one of the largest quarter horse shows in the world. The show consists of all quarter horse classes: halter, performance, youth, and amateur classes. The average number of horses per event is about seventy-five.

This student (who in fact won the top prize for her division in the Quarterama) first tells us about the horse show and then lists the "classes" it "consists of"; after that, she goes into further detail, telling how many horses are entered in most events.

When you don't have space to mention *all* the parts of things, you can mention *some* of them—the ones that make good EXAMPLES. This student chose only two "stimuli" as illustrations:

(53) Subliminal stimuli can come in many forms. For example, death symbols such as skulls are drawn into liquor ads. The word "sex" is embedded in all kinds of pictures.

Such examples give readers a good idea of what you're talking about, so you don't have to try to provide a complete list.
Often, the parts themselves ought to be mentioned in some order. The normal strategy is:

PUT SIMILAR PARTS TOGETHER.

For instance, if you had a list of notes like (54), you could make complete sentences forming a paragraph like (54a) with the similar parts of the "job" mentioned together: first cleaning, then cooking.

(54) having a hard job when I worked as a counter person— sweeping the floor—baking the turnovers—scrubbing the counters— washing the kitchen utensils—broiling the hamburgers—frying the potatoes

(54a)   I had a hard job when I worked as a counter person. I swept the floor. I scrubbed the counters and washed the kitchen utensils. I baked the turnovers. I also broiled the hamburgers and fried the potatoes.

If you wanted to include a main heading to show how things are similar, you might get:

(54b)   I had a hard job as a counter person. *I helped clean up* by sweeping the floor, scrubbing the counters, and washing the kitchen utensils. *I helped cook* by baking the turnovers, broiling the hamburgers, and frying the potatoes.

Main headings are good if it might not be clear how your materials are organized.
   We'll work on more ways to put similar things together in Chapter 4, Section G.

27. QUIZ *on the whole and the parts*

Make these notes into *at least two complete sentences, filling in whatever words you need*. Mention the WHOLE thing first, then the PARTS. Wherever it's appropriate, *put similar parts together. The parts may not be in that order already!* You may want to put in *main headings*.

Example: see (54) and (54a).

[1]   many opportunities available for enjoying college life—
       football—dances—movies—parties—basketball—theater—skiing

[2]   thinking over several careers I might like when I graduate—
       real estate broker—builder—accountant—architect—financial consultant—housing contractor

[3]   dorm life having too many distractions—
       thin walls—loud music—annoying roommates—wild parties

[4]   New York being a city with numerous attractions—
       Ambassador Theater—Museum of Modern Art—Metropolitan Opera—Museum of the City of New York—Bronx Zoo

[5]   a new shopping mall on the west side—
       shoes—restaurants—women's fashions—bakeries—ice cream parlors—hats—snack bars

[6]   my two roommates having different tastes in their record collections—
       Pink Floyd—Loretta Lynn—Alan Parsons Project—Kenny Rogers—Willie Nelson—Emerson, Lake, and Palmer

[7]   my enjoyable high school courses still being nice to remember—
       track—drama—swimming—ballet—marching band—hockey—orchestra

[8]   always putting off things I hate to do till the last possible minute—
      paying bills—registering for classes—hassling with the bank—studying for
      a big test—getting books back to the library on time

[9]   protection of the environment being important for many areas of the United
      States—
      rivers—prairies—wildlife habitats—coastlines—lakes—forests

[10] urban planning having to deal with modern problems—
      city services—public transportation—garbage removal—buses—street
      cleaning—traffic jams—subways—air pollution control

☐ 28. REVIEW QUIZ on the whole and the parts

Same instructions as on the previous quiz.

[1]   this new car having a number of first-class special features—
      genuine leather seats—stereo tape deck—alloy wheel rims—leather steer-
      ing wheel cover—four speakers—radial tires

[2]   some courses I would have liked to drop last year—
      business administration—chemistry—American writers—physics—po-
      etry—accounting

[3]   new projects constantly going up on the northwest side of town—
      parks—apartment houses—shopping centers—family homes—supermar-
      kets—condominiums—playgrounds

[4]   my goals in life being hard to fit with one another—
      living in a fancy house—finding spiritual happiness—driving a nice car
      —knowing my true self—being in tune with nature—having a well-
      paid job

[5]   having many reasons for going to the beach—
      showing off my great body in a bathing suit—jogging—meeting people on
      the beach—swimming for exercise—having intense beach parties

[6]   living by myself at college having some advantages, but living at home hav-
      ing other advantages—
      having meals made for me—being able to stay out late—getting my mom to
      do my laundry—not having people checking up on me all the time

[7]   paying all my expenses every month being next to impossible—
      telephone—groceries—beer—electricity—pizza—water heater

[8]   today's newspaper being full of major events—
      a plane crash—a royal wedding—an earthquake—a successful space mis-
      sion—a new treatment for cancer—a mudslide

[9]   this recipe for punch having an amazing list of ingredients—
      bourbon—orange juice—gin—crushed pineapple—ginger ale—rum—
      soda water—maraschino cherries—dry ice

[10] visiting the city museum turning out to be more interesting than we'd expected—

old cars—maps showing how the town used to look—antique typewriters—pictures of Main Street around 1900—early stoves—portraits of famous citizens

C.5 Less Extreme Versus More Extreme

There are many ways to compare things. Things can be bigger or smaller, newer or older, nicer or nastier, important or unimportant, more expensive or cheaper, and so forth. The further you get from what's ORDINARY, the more EXTREME things become. This scale offers us another strategy for arranging sentences:

GO FROM LESS EXTREME TO MORE EXTREME.

If you mention the ordinary or average things earlier, the more extreme ones you mention later on come into sharp perspective. If you mention the more extreme ones first, the average ones look rather uninteresting by comparison.

For example, you could mention the smallest thing first and end with the largest:

(55) Wildlife is common throughout the northern wilderness. *White squirrels* are found in great numbers. *Geese* nest around the lakes to the west. *Grizzly bears* have been seen in the remote forests.

Or you could begin with the least unpleasant and go to the most unpleasant:

(56) If not treated, an infected appendix causes *fever, pain, blood poisoning,* and *sometimes even death.*

You want to go from minor discomfort to major calamity. The other way around would sound strange:

(56a) If not treated, an infected appendix causes *death, blood poisoning, fever,* and *sometimes even pain.*

You might also begin with the least drastic and go to the most drastic:

(57) At that point, the president still had several options. He might continue *denying any role* in the Watergate burglary, and hope the public would forget all about it. He could admit having had a *minor role* and be embarrassed. Or he could admit having had a *major role* and risk being thrown out of office.

It would be an anticlimax if you started with the most drastic and worked toward the least drastic. The word "even" can indicate that the most extreme thing is coming up, as we see in (56).

29. QUIZ on going from less extreme to more extreme

Make each set of notes into *two or more complete sentences*, going from less extreme toward more extreme. *The notes may not be in that order already!*

Example:

> several great things I want to do in my life—
> climbing Mount Everest, the highest mountain in the world—going on a wild holiday in Paris—meeting the Queen of England

You could do it like this:

> I have several great things I want to do in my life. I would like to go on a wild holiday in Paris. I would like to meet the Queen of England. And I would like to climb Mount Everest, the highest mountain in the world. [Reason: going to Paris is not as difficult as meeting the queen, and climbing Mount Everest is the most difficult of all]

[1] an unbelievable crowd checking in at the student infirmary—
students suffering—pneumonia—colds—stomach flu—tuberculosis—headaches

[2] Florida's peculiar climate hardly found anywhere else—
blazing hot sun during the summer—cloudbursts caused by the humidity—hurricanes sometimes coming in off the ocean—mild winters being due to the latitude

[3] my college's sports record being very inconsistent—
winning the state football championship last year—getting a few victories each year in tennis and swimming—usually being mediocre in basketball—becoming national hockey champions two years in a row

[4] cost of living in America rising steadily over the last fifteen years—
gasoline price having almost tripled—meat and sugar getting higher—coffee going much higher—real estate prices increasing many times over—new car prices doubling on the average

[5] you not liking what they do if you don't pay your gambling debts at a Las Vegas casino—
arranging a nearly fatal accident—sending some hired punks to rough you up a little—delivering the bill to your hotel room—embarrassing you in public

[6] recent races taking place at the Daytona race track—
a grueling competition lasting many hours—a large crowd pouring into the area—two world-famous drivers getting killed in accidents—several new speed records being set

[7] my roommate's obnoxious puppy causing all the trouble you can imagine—
almost getting us arrested by biting the sheriff's deputy—stealing a plate of hamburgers from a barbecue party—ripping up all our expensive chairs in the living room—chewing on everyone's shoes

[8] cold war stepping up again despite arms negotiations—
troops moved to the border and placed on alert—two airplanes actually shot down over neutral territory—diplomatic relations broken off

[9] a series of thefts hitting the downtown area—
a bank vault emptied of several hundred thousand dollars—parking meters getting cracked open on the streets—two liquor stores being held up at gunpoint—shoplifting in supermarkets becoming commonplace

[10] deciding to redecorate our house—
buying a new carpet for the living room—getting the couch reupholstered —tearing out the back wall to add a big game room—replacing the kitchen light

30. REVIEW QUIZ on going from less extreme to more extreme

Same instructions as on the previous quiz.

[1] several useful projects I did with my senior class—
planting trees and shrubs for three weeks in a national park—cleaning the playground at a day-care center—painting two houses in the poor section of town

[2] three of my friends managing to get steady jobs—
Kim being loan manager at a bank—Shawn working as kitchen help in a fast-food place—Carlos playing lead guitar in a top rock group

[3] bills I have to pay this week—
telephone—rent—a library book fine—a parking ticket

[4] one insane rock star from England getting crazier all the time—
threw buckets of luminous paint on the audience—shot a gun at total strangers on a New York street corner—cut the strings on his lead guitarist's instrument—walked offstage in the middle of a song

[5] my family going on a trip every summer—
relaxing at a cabin in the mountains of New Hampshire—boating all the way down the great Amazon River in Brazil—hiking from the rim of the Grand Canyon down to the bottom

[6]   a big geography test scheduled for tomorrow—
      a lot of things I still have to study—continents—cities—mountain ranges
          —countries

[7]   today's newspaper reporting all sorts of disasters—
      a collision of supertankers and a huge oil spill—an earthquake in California
          destroying a school—the worst plane crash in the history of aviation hap-
          pening in Washington, D.C.

[8]   three good reasons I have for dropping out of school—
      getting the chance of a lifetime for a great job with a construction com-
          pany—not being able to stay awake during boring lectures—losing all
          financial aid

[9]   my roommate having ways to let me know I've done something wrong—
      locking me out of the house in the middle of the night—giving me dirty
          looks—taking the good pages out of the newspaper before I get to read
          it—hiding my I.D. on a Friday evening

[10] great vacation we had in the Bahamas—
      going totally out of control at fantastic parties—going scuba diving—rent-
          ing a private yacht and sailing from island to island—relaxing on the
          beach and getting a marvelous tan

C.6   Problem and Solution

Expository writing often deals with HOW TO SOLVE PROBLEMS, as we'll see
again in Chapter 4, Section J.3. You have a PROBLEM whenever you face a
situation that might not turn out the way you'd like. So you SOLVE the problem
by getting things to turn out your way. Writing can be useful for stating what the
problem is and identifying possible solutions. In fact, describing a problem and
some solutions is often the main step in solving the problem.
    Here, the common strategy for arranging statements is:

MOVE FROM PROBLEM TO SOLUTION.

You might have just two statements, as in:

    (58)   Our stereo was sounding terrible. A new pair of speakers improved the
           sound immediately.

Or you could arrange a whole paragraph by stating the problem in a sentence or
two, and then stating the solution in another sentence or two. Here's an illustration from a paper on American history:

(59)   The British government abused the American colonies more and more. Troops were stationed in large numbers, and heavy taxes were demanded. The Americans finally decided to end British rule altogether. They declared themselves independent.

The student first stated the problem in *general* terms ("abuse") and then mentioned *specific* problems such as "troops" and "taxes." After that, we are told the solution: "to end British rule" by "declaring independence."

31. QUIZ *on going from problem to solution*

Make each set of notes into *two or more sentences*. First state the problem and then mention one or more solutions. *The notes may not be in that order already!*

Example:
America's auto industry losing money through Japanese competition— building smaller cars—providing better mileage—making prices really competitive

You could do it this way:
America's auto industry has been losing money rapidly, due to competition from Japanese imports. Detroit could relieve its woes by building smaller cars, providing better mileage, and making its prices really competitive on the market.

[1]   bicycle accidents being a severe danger to both riders and pedestrians— special bike paths and lanes being built across campus and on main streets in the town

[2]   energy consumption being far beyond what society can afford in the long run— car pools to get more people to work in fewer cars

[3]   braces being fitted to correct the teeth at the right age— crooked teeth being a serious drawback to how adolescents feel about the way they look

[4]   high unemployment rate causing anxiety among the nation's young people— more realistic and flexible job training being provided in high schools and colleges across the nation

[5]   weatherstripping put around doors—double panes installed in windows— insulation poured inside walls— noise from street traffic irritating residents

[6]   inflation in the housing market preventing many people from renting the kind of apartment they want— government price ceilings keeping rent increases within reason

[7]   my photographs turning out too dark all the time—
      finally buying a really sensitive light meter

[8]   remembering now to bend my knees and lean back during the start—
      falling on my face every time I tried to learn water skiing

[9]   unbelievable atrocities having been committed by armies during wartime—
      a convention being drawn up in Geneva in 1864 to set standards for the
        treatment of war prisoners

[10] high cost of building a house discouraging prospective home owners—
      doing as much work yourself as you can on your own house

☐ 32. REVIEW QUIZ on going from problem to solution

Same instructions as on the previous quiz.

[1]   alarm systems in rooms—security patrols in the halls—
      thefts in student housing happening far too often

[2]   long lines being a terrible nuisance during college registration—
      setting up each student to register at a specifically appointed time

[3]   feeling tense and anxious about everyday life and its demands—
      learning meditation in order to control the well-being of mind and body

[4]   getting a rough ride in my junky old car—
      replacing all the shock absorbers

[5]   learning how to use computers and finding out there's no big mystery—
      many people being intimidated by computers these days

[6]   strip mining causing whole mountain ranges to lose their soil and plants—
      passing laws to make strip mining companies fully restore the landscape
        after mining

[7]   getting a call-waiting service that signals when someone else is trying to call
        you—
      missing your calls because your telephone is busy so often

[8]   women and minorities still being denied human rights today—
      spelling out exact guidelines in the Equal Rights Amendment

[9]   the wires inside high-speed computers getting so hot they melt—
      installing powerful refrigeration units at critical points

[10] us running out of money long before the first of the month—
      writing down a record to keep track of everything we spend

General quiz

on putting statements in order

Make each set of notes into *at least two complete sentences*. You may have to change the order of the notes—for example, if you want to put similar parts together or to go from less extreme to more extreme. Also, note in the left-hand margin *what the relation is* between the two. You have the following strategies to choose from:

MOVE IN TIME FROM EARLIER TO LATER.

MOVE FROM CAUSE TO EFFECT.

MOVE FROM EFFECT TO CAUSE.

*MAKE A MAIN STATEMENT AND THEN GIVE SOME
EVIDENCE FOR IT.*

*GIVE THE EVIDENCE FIRST AND THEN MAKE YOUR
MAIN STATEMENT.*

MOVE FROM THE WHOLE TO ITS PARTS.

GO FROM LESS EXTREME TO MORE EXTREME.

MOVE FROM PROBLEM TO SOLUTION.

If you think more than one of these applies to a particular case in the quiz (and sometimes they do), note them all in the margin, using short forms: earlier/later, cause/effect, effect/cause, statement/evidence, evidence/statement, whole/parts, less/more extreme, or problem/solution.

[1]   a huge trade deficit of the United States compared to Japan—

    Japan underselling the United States in many kinds of consumer goods and

        appliances

[2]   Connors winning the first three tennis games—

    McEnroe winning the last three games

[3] students not being able to afford adequate repairs on their cars—

taking a course to learn how to make repairs themselves

[4] consumers holding back on purchases—

a continued slump in Christmas sales

[5] a truly great pizza needing all the right ingredients—

mushrooms—tomatoes—pepperoni—onions—ground beef—artichoke hearts

—tons of cheese—hot peppers

[6] my opinion that the United States is the absolute leader in space explora-

tion—

the space shuttle and Skylab being major successes not equaled anywhere

else

[7] a certain congressman being indicted on multiple counts—

believed to have extorted millions from building contractors—accused of

selling military secrets to unfriendly nations—known to have neglected

the duties of his office

[8] me forgetting appointments I've made with other people—

keeping a calendar and being sure to look at it every morning

[9] top business executives apparently being under too much stress—

the number of heart attacks and nervous breakdowns being far higher than

the average in the work force

[10] looking forward to doing some enjoyable things after I graduate—

hoping to get back into playing the guitar—intending to visit my grand-

parents in Kentucky—planning to travel around the world

Backup general quiz

34.
▼

on putting statements in order

Same instructions as on the previous quiz.

[1] tires losing traction on wet or icy pavement—

traffic accidents occurring most frequently in the winter months

[2] not liking the way I look in the mirror one bit—

trying not to eat so many pizzas or drink so much beer every night

[3] our family car having gotten an expensive major overhaul—

all four tires being replaced—the engine being totally rebuilt—the radiator

being boiled out and rustproofed—the brakes getting new pads

[4] forest fires happening every year in southern California—

vacationers not being careful with cigarettes and campfires

[5] many species of animals still inhabiting the Everglades—

herons of different colors being sighted in the sky—armadillos causing a

hazard for cars on the road—huge alligators turning up everywhere

[6] students seeming to have finally realized the importance of the electronic

revolution—

enrollment in electrical engineering growing faster than in any other field of

study

[7] rainfall being very scarce in the western U.S. in 1977 and causing severe

   drought—

rainfall being overwhelming in 1978 and causing mudslides

[8] the accommodations in my dorm being less than satisfactory, to put it

   mildly—

air conditioning making a terrible noise when it's on—not half enough

   sinks for everyone to wash and shave in the morning—almost no room to

   store your belongings—the rent being absolutely ridiculous in compari-

   son to what you get for it

[9] people filing their income tax returns at the last minute—

figuring up their taxes apparently being a job most people hate to do

[10] the spread of dangerous virus infections leading to emergencies in develop-

   ing nations—

improving public programs for sanitation and vaccination

4.
Putting Paragraphs Together

Preview

In this chapter, you'll be putting together the paragraphs in a whole paper. You'll see how to organize topics and develop them with interesting or relevant details, or support them with convincing reasons. You'll practice setting up the paragraphs in the beginning, middle, and ending of a paper. Finally, you'll work on three common types of papers: problem/solution, description, and persuasion.

We have gone over how clauses are put together inside sentences (Chapter 2), and how sentences are put together inside paragraphs (Chapter 3). Now it's time to see how paragraphs are put together inside whole papers.

■ A. TOPICS IN TALK AND TOPICS IN WRITING

A **TOPIC** is a main idea—something that holds your statements together and helps them all make sense. If you don't let readers know what your topic is supposed to be, they will have a hard time understanding or even paying attention. Here is a paragraph that was used to test people. See how well you can follow it without knowing what it's about.

> (1) The procedure is actually quite simple. First you arrange things into different groups. Of course, one pile may be sufficient, depending on how much there is to do. If you have to go somewhere else due to lack of facilities, that is the next step; otherwise you are pretty well set. It is important not to overdo things. That is, it is better to do too few things at once than too many. It is difficult to foresee any end to the necessity for this task in the immediate future.

The tests showed that people got very little out of reading this paragraph, because they didn't know the topic was "doing your laundry."

The mind works in complicated ways. If you hold an idea in mind, you'll soon think of related things. For example, if you think about "football," you'll probably get a mental picture of a football field with a game going on. You'll recall how football is played, or what happened at a game you saw. You may be able to keep this up for quite a while as ideas related to "football" pass through your mind.

This part is pretty easy. But the materials you get are not going to be very well organized. If you wrote them all down just as they came to mind, the result wouldn't look much like a paper on "football." The materials still need a clear **organization** and need to serve a **purpose**.

Suppose it was up to you to tell people how the game of football is played. You'd want to mention certain important things. Here is a transcript of a recording of a student sports enthusiast explaining the game. *

> (2) FOOTball....FOOTBALL....I said FOOTball WAS....FOOTBALL....
> the obJECTive in FOOTball..is for each team to score the most POINTS
> ....and....the TEAM with the most points wins....oKAY the FIELD is a
> hundred and twenty yards long..and....the GOALS are set one hundred
> yards aPART..at..behind each goal is a ten-yard END ZONE..in which
> ....in which you have to CROSS the goal line and go into the end zone in
> order to score points....okay..to score a point....in scoring points you can
> score six points for a TOUCHdown and you get a chance to GO for an
> EXTRA point..which is worth one MORE point....to get this you have to
> kick the ball through the UPrights

This fan's beginning was extremely general—after all, the "objective" in *any* game is "to score the most points" in order to "win." Next, he thought of the "field": how big it is and where you have to get to if you want to "score points." Then he got to the specifics of how many "points" you get for a touchdown or a field goal.

His approach was a typical one. First you pick a topic and then you break it down into parts. These parts can be further broken down as far as you need. This student began with the topic of "football" and broke it down into "field" and "scoring." He then broke the "field" down into length and divisions. He broke "scoring" down into touchdown versus field goal. Later on, he'll tell about different ways to score a touchdown. And so on.

Writing is different from speaking in the way you handle a topic. Once you have the topic and you've thought of some materials for it, you have to figure out several problems:

---

* Two dots are for a short pause, and four dots for a long pause. Stressed items are in capitals.

A.   WHAT GOES WITH WHAT?
B.   WHAT ORDER SHOULD POINTS BE IN?
C.   HOW MANY DETAILS SHOULD BE INCLUDED?

In this chapter, we'll be working on some fairly easy techniques for solving these problems. So you don't have to worry if your first batch of ideas looks messy and disorganized. We're going to start at the beginning and work through the steps until the whole paper is put together.

When you're talking, you can just string items along as they come to mind, and you can jump from one thing to another. Whoever's listening can always ask how the things you say fit together. When you write, however, you're expected to look over all your materials and figure out some sensible way to fit them all together before anyone reads the paper. If you're like most people, this job isn't terribly easy for you. So let's see what you can do to simplify it.

To start off, let's look at what that same student who was talking on tape *wrote* about football. His paper began like this:

(3)   Football is a game in which the two opposing teams defend goals at the opposite ends of a field. The object of the game is for each team to try and score more points than the other. The team with the highest score at the end of the game wins.

The field which the game is played on is 120 yards by 50 yards. The goals are set 100 yards apart. Behind each goal is a 10-yard end zone. To score, you must cross the goal line and go into the end zone. On a pass play to score a touchdown, you must be in the end zone. The sides of the field are called the sidelines. When the ball carrier steps past the sideline, the ball is dead and is put at that yardline. Yardlines are the lines going across each field.

Let's compare this written version with the talk version we looked at before. In both versions, the student opens with the "objective":

(4)   *Talk version:*   the obJECTive in FOOTball..is for each team to score the most POINTS....and....the TEAM with the most points wins

(5)   *Written version:*   The object of the game is for each team to try and score more points than the other. The team with the highest score at the end of the game wins.

We see the same materials, only put down more carefully in the written version. Just *one team*, not "*each team*," can "score the most points." The written version says that "each team" can only "*try* to score more points than the other." * The

---

* "Try" is one of the verb hedges we worked on in Chapter 1, Section D.2.2. Here, it's definitely useful in example 5.

written version adds that having "more points" makes one team win "at the end of the game"; some games, such as tennis, are over when one side scores a certain number of points, but football ends when the clock runs out. In writing, it's typical to be more careful about saying exactly what you mean.

The talk version follows the same general pattern as the written version. They both move from one part of the topic to another—namely, from the "scoring" objective to the football "field." (The student started a new paragraph in the written version at the same place he said "okay" in the talk version.) Let's make another comparison:

(6) *Talk version:* oKAY the FIELD is a hundred and twenty yards long..and ….the GOALS are set one hundred yards aPART..at..behind each goal is a ten-yard END ZONE..in which….in which you have to CROSS the goal line and go into the end zone in order to score points

(7) *Written version:* The field which the game is played on is 120 yards by 50 yards. The goals are set 100 yards apart. Behind each goal is a 10-yard end zone. To score, you must cross the goal line and go into the end zone.

Even though it's 9 words shorter, the written version includes more details. The writer gives the *width* of the field, not just the *length,* so that later on he can explain the difference between crossing the "goal line" and crossing the "sidelines." In the talk version, he wasn't thinking that far ahead. You'll also notice a small difference in how he got to the new part of his topic. While the talk version simply says "the field," the written version says "the field *which the game is played on.*" In writing, it's more customary to show just how your new idea is related to the ideas you have been dealing with just before (see Section I.2 in this chapter).

The writer then moves on to the next part of his topic, the sidelines. In the talk version, he left that part out and had to come back to it much later. In the written version, he put it right after the explanation of goal lines. The strategy here is one we practiced in Chapter 3, Section C.4: put similar parts together. Let's compare once again:

(8) *Talk version:* BY..okay..the FIELD….I said before was a HUNdred and TWENty yards….it's FIFTY yards wide….it's..the SIDES of the field are called SIDElines..and if you STEP PAST the SIDEline then the ball is dead there and is put on the YARDline….YARDLINES are the..YARDS —are the lines going across the field to let you know where you ARE

(9) *Written version:* The sides of the field are called the sidelines. When the ball carrier steps past the sideline, the ball is dead and is put at that yardline. Yardlines are the lines going across each field.

In (8), he has to repeat some things he'd "said before" in order to get the background he needs. Also, the talk version has some *inconsistencies* like the ones we saw in Chapter 1, Section E, such as: "yardlines are the yards—are the lines." In addition, the written version specifies "the ball carrier," while the talk version simply has "you" (which might be just any player on the team, if a reader didn't know better).

Here's what the two versions had to say about "points":

(10) *Talk version*: okay..to score a point....in scoring points you can score six points for a TOUCHdown and you get a chance to GO for an EXTRA point..which is worth one MORE point....to get this you have to kick the ball through the UPrights

(11) *Written version*: A touchdown is worth six points. You then get a chance to kick the ball through the uprights for an additional point.

In talk, he needed 45 words to say what he needed only 22 words to say in writing. The difference is due to the kind of **extra words** we worked on in Chapter 1. The talk version repeats the word "point" five times; the written version has it only twice. The talk version also has the word "score" three times; in the written version, the student doesn't use the word at all, assuming that if he mentions "points," everyone knows he's dealing with scorekeeping. Notice the obvious **re-stating** in the talk version: "an extra point..which is worth one more point." There the written version simply has "an additional point."

As you can see, writing about a topic requires more organizing than talking about it does. In everyday conversation, you can skip around from one thing to another, or drop something and come back to it later. In writing, your final paper should have items in a more strategic order and should fit them all into one big picture. So you probably won't get everything just right on your rough draft. Let's look at some steps for working over your draft and getting it organized.

■ B. A QUICK LOOK AT ROUGH DRAFTS

When you have something to write, you often won't know ahead of time how many drafts you'll need to go through. No paper is ever so totally refined that there's no way left to make it better. You just have to decide when the paper's good enough for the occasion.

Writing drafts and working them over can be pretty complicated. To understand how something big works, it helps to look at a little model of it first. So let's begin with two very simple drafts that a twelve-year-old in a country school wrote about the topic of "trees." He first put down whatever he could think of about trees, without following any obvious plan:

(12) Trees are very tall. Trees are green. Trees wave in the wind. Pine trees contain tar. Tar sticks to you when you sit on a stump. Trees have seeds. Trees sometimes whistle. Trees are helpful and fun.

This draft is like a slow-motion film of the mind handing out bits of knowledge about an everyday topic. We see a jumble of short statements that sound like kids' talk. However, his next version already looked better:

> (13) Trees are tall and green. They wave in the wind and whistle. The wind blows out seeds, which float to the ground to begin new trees. Trees contain tar, which sticks to you. Trees are very helpful and fun but can be dangerous.

Now the writer has sorted and arranged his materials. He took out some items: "very," "pine," "when you sit on a stump," and "sometimes." He put the remaining ideas into **groups of similar things**: (a) the appearance of trees; (b) the effects of the wind; (c) tar; and (d) overall judgment about trees. Putting similar elements into groups helped him to put his statements in a reasonable order. The statement "trees sometimes whistle," which came near the end of the first draft (12), got moved ahead in (13) to go with the "waving," because both events are caused by "wind." The revision also **streamlined** by combining statements that belong together (see also Chapter 3, Section A.3). Compare how he wrote about the appearance of trees in (14) versus (15), and about the effects of the wind in (16) versus (17):

> (14) Trees are very tall. Trees are green. [first version]
>
> (15) Trees are tall and green. [second version]
>
> (16) Trees wave in the wind. Trees sometimes whistle. [first version]
>
> (17) They wave in the wind and whistle. [second version]

In addition, the writer developed the topic by adding some more details. He used the idea of "wind" as a convenient way to lead into the idea of "seeds"; in the first draft, he had made two separate statements. Compare:

> (18) Trees wave in the wind. Trees have seeds. [first version]
>
> (19) The wind blows out seeds, which float to the ground to begin new trees. [second version]

The second version (19) mentions the life cycle of trees—an item that belongs to his topic, but got left out in his first version. He also went on to develop his overall judgment about trees at the end by including something on the unfavorable side. Compare:

> (20) Trees are helpful and fun. [first version]
>
> (21) Trees are very helpful and fun but can be dangerous. [second version]

Though some new details were added, others got removed. The writer took out some specific things: "pine" trees and "sitting on a stump"—maybe because he realized that many trees besides pines have "tar" that "sticks to you," and not just "when you sit on a stump." He threw out "very" in "very tall" (trees are different heights) and "sometimes" in "sometimes whistle" (most of his statements are true only "sometimes," so there's no reason to say it here). This way, the second version is more consistent in being very general all the way through.

Of course, the second version still isn't a great piece of writing. My point is that it is plainly better than the first, and that we can learn something by understanding why. We shouldn't underestimate what this young writer accomplished. His work was a miniature model of what skilled adult writers do with more complicated topics in long expository papers. No matter how big or small your writing project may be, the same revising strategies can help you. Once you get your materials down on paper, you start finding new ways to make them fit together. Don't worry if it takes you a while to arrive at a clear plan.

Now let's have a look at some drafts by a college freshman. The first draft wasn't made to be handed in for me to read, but I asked for it anyhow in order to examine how people organize a topic from the very beginning. The draft is called "My Problems as a Freshman," and it started out like this:

(22)   When I first entered the University of Florida, I was somewhat cautious. There are so many unknown facets involved with college. I am still uncertain as to what school might hold for me. The path I choose I know will be right for myself.

Dealing with things Mom took care of is really a drag. Not being a homebody makes me very negative towards the common household chores. There are more constructive things I would prefer to be spending time on. Who has time to sit down and wait for a load of clothes to wash? If I can get to the machine first (during the day) I'm really lucky. Another problem is a lack of change. I'm always borrowing a nickel here, a dime there just to get my wet clothes dry. Cooking can also be a major hardship. I am in a sorority. This alleviates a lot of the problems I might have had trying to cook for myself. My roommate is not in a sorority so she must cook all her meals she does not eat out. She has a hotplate she uses in our room. She does not have a car so she usually catches a bus to the store. Carrying your groceries on the bus can be embarrassing. One time when the bags ripped, cans and bottles rolled all around inside of the bus.

And so it goes on, drifting from one idea to another. By now the writer has completely gotten away from her original topic—namely, her own "problems as a freshman." Her roommate is off on a bus somewhere chasing cans and bottles. Still, the draft served as a stepping stone for getting closer to her final paper, as we'll see in a minute.

The beginning of her paper is typical in being very **GENERAL**—that is, it

gives an overall view of the situation. For example, she says that "there are so many unknown facets involved with college." A general beginning is good for showing that your topic matters to many people (see also Sections G and I.1 in this chapter).

Her beginning is also typical in being rather **ABSTRACT**—that is, it talks about things you don't directly see or feel, such as "unknown facets" and "the path I choose." An abstract beginning is good for a very broad topic such as a person's life.

However, most papers don't remain very general and abstract all the way through. There would be a danger of saying only the things everybody already knows, leaving out all your own personal experiences and contributions. More often, a paper shifts down to the **SPECIFIC**—what is the case at certain times and places—and the **CONCRETE**—what you see or feel directly. For instance, our freshman's draft shifts from "unknown facets" down to specific, concrete matters, such as the basic needs of clothing and food. "Laundry" and "cooking" are examples of things that were "unknown" to her because "Mom" had been doing them for her before. She gets even more specific and concrete by describing her struggles at the laundromat.

When she gets to "cooking," her paper runs into a little trouble—since she belongs to a sorority, "cooking" is no problem, and after all, her topic is supposed to be "problems." So she borrows her roommate's problems and gives us the specifics of what it's like getting to the store and back with no car.

Though her roommate's troubles do count as "problems," they don't really belong to our freshman's original topic. Each step in her line of reasoning must have seemed logical enough: new setting being uncertain → no Mom → laundry → cooking → roommate's hotplate → roommate getting to the store → roommate dropping groceries on the way home. But the result of all these steps was to get sidetracked from the topic.

Of course, it's not unusual for a rough draft to get sidetracked like this. Many points come to mind when you're thinking about your topic, and at least some of them you won't want to use. There's always time to decide later what's interesting or relevant and what isn't. Our freshman decided that her details about her laundry and her roommate's cooking were too specific and uninteresting to be worth including. Besides, if she stayed at that level of detail, she'd never get done telling all her problems. So she streamlined her second paragraph and got this new version:

(23)   Being away from home for the first time is an experience. The sense of security has been stripped away, along with material comforts in clothing and food.

This time, only the main points are briefly mentioned as "material comforts in clothing and food." These points are still specific examples of "unknown facets"

at college. But they aren't so specific that they'll lead her to get sidetracked in a mess of details.

Her next version of the paper went a step further. She figured people would be more interested in *everyone's* problems as a freshman, instead of just *her own* problems. By making the topic more **general**, she could also make it **relevant** for more people. So she changed her title from "My Problems as a Freshman" to "Problems That Face Freshmen." Let's see how she made her new beginning (25) more general than the old version (24):

(24)　　　　　　MY PROBLEMS AS A FRESHMAN
When *I* first entered the *University of Florida*, *I* was somewhat cautious. I am still uncertain what unknown facets college might hold for me, but the path *I* choose will be the right one.

(25)　　　　　　PROBLEMS THAT FACE FRESHMEN
Any student entering *college* for the first time is somewhat cautious about the many unknown facets of college life. *Each person* must choose the path that is right.

"I" has been changed to "any student" and "each person." "The University of Florida" has been changed to "college." She now treats her own experiences as "typical" for freshmen, which makes her topic important for more people. Just as she tossed out the details about laundromats and grocery shopping, she has now made her beginning more general.

Inspiration doesn't usually come in a sudden flash. More often, writers have to go through some messy drafts before a paper shapes up. You may have to throw some things out and put others in. You may decide you don't want so many details, or that you don't have enough. The only real trick is not to get discouraged and give up too early before your drafts are worked out. In the next sections, you'll practice some strategies that help get drafts into shape. To make the process easier, we'll follow a series of stages involved in putting a paper together.

■　　C.　TITLES

The first thing readers see in your paper is the TITLE.* In expository writing, the title should make the main topic perfectly clear. Since **EXPOSITION** means "telling what something is or something does," the title should make everyone see right away which something is involved. For instance, the title of this section here is "titles."

There are several kinds of titles you wouldn't want to use. ROUTINE titles are

---

* In a title, all words are *capitalized*, except "the," "a," "an," and short prepositions ("in," "of," "at," "with," "from," and so on); but the *first* word is always capitalized, no matter what it is. See Chapter 5, Section A. Some newspapers capitalize every word in a headline.

the ones that announce that you're just carrying out a routine assignment, and you don't really care if anyone knows what it's about. Routine titles turn up in many places—in an English class (26–27), in a business (28–30), or wherever. These titles suggest that the topic doesn't matter, because nobody would want to read it anyway:

(26)   This Week's Theme for English 101

(27)   My Comparison and Contrast Paper

(28)   Quarterly Progress Report from Division 3-J

(29)   Memorandum to All Employees

(30)   Announcements for Tuesday

Throw all such titles out, or at least put in some indication of what your specific topic is:

(27a)   Comparing *High School* with *College*

(28a)   Quarterly Progress Report *on Miniature Wire Circuits* from Division 3-J

(29a)   Memorandum to All Employees *Regarding Annual Pay Raises*

VAGUE titles are also very bad. They are so empty and general that they don't let on what the paper is about, such as:

(31)   People

(32)   Life

(33)   Our Times

(34)   An Unusual Experience

(35)   A Serious Problem

To fix these, you should again put in some indication of what your specific topic is:

(31a)   People *Facing a Serious Illness*

(32a)   Life *in a Small New England Town*

(33a)   *Living with the Threat of Nuclear War in* Our Times

(34a)   An Unusual Experience *on a Cross-Country Bicycle Tour*

(35a)   A Serious Problem *with Electric Typewriters*

MELODRAMATIC titles are also not very good for expository writing. If you're supposed to explain something, don't overdo your title in trying to grab attention, as in:

(36)   The Absolutely Strangest Fact I Ever Did Hear About Crocodiles

(37)   Dirty Work in the Transmission Shop

(38)   A Terrifying Surprise from a Defective Copying Machine

(39)   A Struggle in the Dark to Replace a Blown Fuse

(40)   Fulfilling Your Passionate Desire for a Balanced Checkbook

To fix these, be more matter-of-fact and tone them down—as in:

(36a)   A Strange Fact About Crocodiles

(37a)   Troubleshooting in the Transmission Shop

(38a)   Repairing Your Defective Copying Machine

(39a)   How to Replace a Blown Fuse

(40a)   Ways to Balance a Checkbook

LONG and CLUMSY titles waste people's time. If the title is too wordy and complicated to reveal at a glance what your paper is about, people might not bother to read the paper. Look at these:

(41)   Some Ideas I Have About the Best Way to Grow Tomatoes

(42)   A Few Preliminary Remarks on the Subject of Occupational Therapy

(43)   My Views on the Way You Should Go About Installing Air Conditioning

(44)   How It Happens That We're Making New Chemicals in Space Stations

(45)   After a Whole Lot of Hard Work We Finally Found Out Why Humans Have Two Sets of Teeth in Their Lifetime

To fix these, cut out the extra words and keep just what you need to indicate the topic:

(41a)   The Best Way to Grow Tomatoes

(42a)   Occupational Therapy

(43a)   Installing Air Conditioning

(44a)   Making New Chemicals in Space Stations

(45a)   Why Humans Have Two Sets of Teeth in Their Lifetime

You can get away from all kinds of bad titles if you just follow this strategy:

USE A SPECIFIC TITLE THAT MAKES YOUR TOPIC CLEAR.

For instance, my students wrote:

(46) Child Abuse

(47) Canine Diseases

(48) How to Fish for Trout

(49) The Evolution of Computers

(50) Advances in Chemotherapy for Cancer

You don't have to try to be *as short as possible*. The point is to be *no longer than necessary*.

■ 1. EXERCISE *on titles*

Only a few titles in the following list are good. Mark the good titles with G. Mark the bad titles with *R* for "routine," *V* for "vague," *M* for "melodramatic," or *L/C* for "long and clumsy." Then fix them. Use your imagination to supply missing information.

[1] New Trends That Are Happening These Days in the Kind of Clothes People Are Wearing in New York City

[2] My Story for English

[3] How to Fix Your Dishwasher

[4] Something I Thought Of

[5] Weekly Update

[6] Let's Get It Right When We're Going to Service a Garbage Disposal

[7] Foul Play in Chicken Farming

[8] The Easy Way

[9] Treating Nervous Tension

[10] The Grisly Death of Your Car Battery and Your Heroic Success in Getting Your Car Started Anyway

■ 2. QUIZ *on titles*

Only a few titles in the following list are good. Mark the good titles with G. Mark the bad titles with *R* for "routine," *V* for "vague," *M* for "melodramatic," or *L/C* for "long and clumsy." Then fix them. Use your imagination to supply missing information.

[1]   Setting Up Your Ham Radio

[2]   A Spectacular, Death-Defying Victory in Bringing a Cassette Tape Recorder Back to Life

[3]   My Assigned Cause and Effect Paper

[4]   Several Reasons Why It's Not Really an Awfully Good Idea to Pollute the Ocean

[5]   Three Observations

[6]   Championship Golfing

[7]   A Dastardly Encounter with a Computer Error in Your Bank Statement and Your Amazing Cleverness in Detecting It

[8]   Some Remarks of Mine on How a Newcomer Can Learn to Roller-Skate

[9]   Memo to Staff

[10] My Ideas in Regard to the Whole Subject of Abortion

☐ 3. REVIEW QUIZ on titles

Same instructions as on the previous quiz.

[1]   How It's Done

[2]   One or Two Good Ideas You Should Follow When Building a Fence

[3]   A Struggle Beyond All Human Endurance to Repair a Light Switch

[4]   A Composition for Seventh-Period English

[5]   Careers in Inorganic Chemistry

[6]   The Next Thing on My List

[7]   A Few Remarks on the Marvelous Joys You Get from Collecting Rare Insects

[8]   Financial Planning

[9]   Some Things People Are Saying Nowadays About Reforming the State Prisons

[10] My First Experience

■ D.   MAKING NOTES ABOUT A TOPIC

The first thing you'll need when you write is a topic that INTERESTS you, and one that you have a fair amount of KNOWLEDGE about. Often, you'll also need to gather and put together some additional knowledge for the paper besides what you already know—in other words, you'll need to do some **research**. You won't usually have all the details stored in your head.

One good way to get going is to MAKE NOTES about your topic. You can

---

WRITE DOWN YOUR IDEAS JUST AS THEY COME TO MIND.

Don't concentrate too much on organization at first. Just jot down your ideas as you think of them. Right now, your main job is to get some materials to work on. Even professional writers organize their topics gradually, experimenting with various combinations. Don't insist on trying for perfect organization right away.

A page of notes doesn't look the same as a formal outline. You can write down a title at the top and some parts of the topic spaced out down the page. Then you fill in the details as they come to mind. For example, here's one freshman's page of notes about "football":

```
(51)        FOOTBALL
        the football field
            size → 100 yd. by 50 yd.
            yardlines → where they are and what they're for
            sidelines
            goal lines
            goalposts
        the team
            offense and defense
            positions → linemen backs receivers
        divisions of the game
            quarters
            downs
            time out
        plays
            running
            passing
            turnovers → fumble interception
        how to score points
            touchdown
            field goal
            punt
            safety
        penalties
            against the offensive team
            against the defensive team
```

This student left some space between items to put more ideas in as he thought of them. His paper didn't follow the same order as his notes, and it contained more materials than the notes did. But at least the notes gave him a plan to use in getting his ideas in shape.

Here are the notes of the student who wrote about "Problems That Face Freshmen" (see Section B).

(52)   PROBLEMS THAT FACE FRESHMEN
  A New Environment
    Away from Home
      loss of security
      using my own judgment
    Meeting Strangers
      name, phone number
      social barriers
    Dormitories
      problems of privacy
      having to use community facilities
    Professors
      grading policies
      format of classes
    School Size
      being with friends & groups
      feeling small and insignificant
  Getting into Swing of College
    Getting up in morn.
    Odd schedules every day
    Budgeting time
    Disciplining myself
      Other attractions → time to play

She didn't include every one of these ideas in the paper. But the notes gave her a map of things she *could* write about.

Your notes can lead pretty directly to your paper. Another student wanted to write a paper on lowering the legal age for drinking alcohol in the state of Florida. Here's what he put down first in his notebook:

(53)   peer pressure
       people who get drafted and can vote should be considered adults
       less risk of a criminal record
       health hazards
       teenage parties
       criminal record leading to more serious crimes
       learn to deal with alcohol early
       greater risk of auto accidents
       danger of alcoholism

This list was not in order. It was just a catalog of some of the issues. The student then sorted and arranged the list in several ways. First, he divided his points into "reasons for" a lower drinking age and "reasons against." Second, he put related items together. And third, he arranged the items to go from less extreme to more extreme. His new set of notes looked like this:

(54)   Reasons for a lower drinking age
  learn to deal with alcohol early
  peer pressure
  teenage parties
  people who get drafted and can vote should be considered adults
  less risk of a criminal record
  criminal record can lead to more serious crimes
 Reasons against a lower drinking age
  health hazards
  danger of alcoholism
  greater risk of auto accidents

"Peer pressure" and "teenage parties" appear as fairly mild issues toward the top of the list. The most extreme issue on the "for" side is that young people who get a "criminal record" for something as petty as buying beer might not hesitate so long before attempting a more "serious crime." The most extreme issue on the "against" side is that drunken drivers cause "auto accidents" and endanger everyone, not just the drinker. Moving this way from less extreme to more extreme issues is a good strategy for building up reader interest (see also pages 209–12).

The new list then became the framework for the student's actual paper. The issues from the list were easily put in the form of complete statements. He stated the topic in the opening paragraph and said why it's important (see pages 253–54). He then included one paragraph about reasons in favor of a lower drinking age, and another paragraph about reasons against. He finished with a paragraph that again stated the topic and said why it's important, though he didn't use exactly the same words as in the first paragraph. Here's his paper:

(55)   The question of the legal drinking age is now before the legislature. This issue is important for many young people in our state. We should consider the reasons on both sides carefully.

  There are several reasons in favor of a lower age. It helps young people learn to deal with alcohol early. The peer pressure at teenage parties no longer conflicts with the law. People who are old enough to get drafted and vote should be considered adult enough to drink alcohol. They should not be threatened with a criminal record for a minor offense. In fact, a criminal record might lead them to commit more serious crimes, once they are already branded as criminals.

  On the other hand, there are several reasons against a lower drinking age. Alcohol can be a grave health hazard if consumed excessively. Too much reliance on heavy drinking leads to alcoholism. Heavy drinkers endanger not only their own health, but that of others as well. They are often responsible for auto accidents in which innocent people lose their lives.

The legal drinking age is a vital issue. It should not be decided without thoroughly considering the reasons on both sides.

The paper could be developed further by giving details on the various issues, such as statistics on criminal records or on alcoholism. But with the length it has, it is well organized because the student made, sorted, and arranged a list of ideas to use as a map of the territory. In this way, he got the topic in good shape before he wrote the actual paper.

☐ **4. QUIZ** *on making, sorting, and arranging notes*

Here are some topics. Pick one and make a page or so of notes about it. Then sort and arrange the notes in a way you could use to write a paper.

Example: See (53) and (54) in this section.

[1]   the space shuttle

[2]   finding an apartment

[3]   satellite television

[4]   junk food

[5]   buying a used car

☐ **5. REVIEW QUIZ** *on making, sorting, and arranging notes*

Same instructions as on the previous quiz.

[1]   gun control

[2]   new computer games

[3]   windsurfing

[4]   rock music

[5]   owning a horse

■   **E.   INTERESTING DETAILS**

How do you know what to put in your notes, or to include in your paper? Many of the things you know about a topic might not be worth mentioning. One major strategy is:

SELECT INTERESTING DETAILS.

INTERESTING DETAILS are those which your readers don't already know and ought to be curious about. Details should be interesting if they are *surprising, new,* or *worth remembering.* Details are not interesting if they are *obvious, well-known,* or *insignificant.* You can judge details by asking yourself if they are out of the ordinary, if they make a difference, and if they are hard to guess or predict.

Let's see if we can tell what's interesting and what isn't. Here is a list of details about taking a trip across the country. Mark the interesting ones with *yes* and the uninteresting ones with *no.*

(56)   *taking a trip*—
   climbing a high mountain
   stopping at gas stations
   walking on the rim of the Grand Canyon
   seeing a geyser erupt
   eating sandwiches
   visiting Indian villages
   checking into motels
   boating on a swift river
   checking your tire pressure

Students have usually agreed that it's interesting to hear about a high mountain, the rim of a canyon, a geyser, an Indian village, and a swift river. These places are scenic and hard to get to, and there may be danger involved. Items like gas stations, sandwiches, motels, and tire pressure, however, are just routine matters involved in taking a trip. They could hardly be the main reasons for the trip, and readers aren't likely to want you to tell about them.

☐ 6. QUIZ *on selecting interesting details*

Here are some lists of details about various topics. Mark the interesting details with *yes* and the uninteresting ones with *no.* If you can't make up your mind about an item, put a *?* by it.

[1]   *writing your life story*—
   where you grew up
   how many colds you had
   what honors you received
   which college you attended
   where you went shopping for groceries
   what major disasters you went through
   what your main goals in life are

what color toothbrushes you used
who you married
what grand dreams came true
what your astrological sign is

[2] *one doctor's career in medicine—*
she was outstanding in medical school
she saved many lives
she wore a stethoscope
she worked on cures for rare diseases
she had light brown hair
she became an expert on open-heart surgery
she looked impressive in white clothes
she established a fine reputation in her field
she tended famous people when they were ill

[3] *what you saw when you visited the nation's capital—*
art galleries
famous monuments
drugstores
the White House
the weather
the Capitol Building
newspaper stands
the subway
fashion shops
mailboxes
the Kennedy Center for the Performing Arts
slums

[4] *what you got out of attending college—*
learning about things you never even thought of before
hassling the phone company
becoming a star athlete
preparing for the well-paid job you have
sitting in laundromats
making friends for life
paying campus parking tickets
broadening your outlook on life
knowing not to eat pizza with anchovies before bedtime
developing your ability to speak with authority

[5] *the best things in the American way of life—*
garbage removal now and then
freedom to express your opinions
respect for human values
junk food on sale everywhere
a government elected by the people

daily newspapers with trivial stories
a vast and colorful landscape
commercials on television
rugged individualism of the citizens
streets with pavement on them
a new concern for the rights of women
divorce being an everyday fact of life
widespread use of Kleenex and paper towels

7. REVIEW QUIZ *on selecting interesting details*

Same instructions as on the previous quiz.

[1]   *the accomplishments of the space shuttle Columbia—*
new chemicals were made in chambers without gravity
people watched the launchings on TV
satellites were put in space by the shuttle
the shuttle goes up and down
experiments are now possible that never were before
our knowledge about outer space is advancing dramatically
it's fun to fly around way up high and enjoy the view
the shuttle can be used over and over

[2]   *the people who really matter in my life—*
my parents
the people who deliver pizza after midnight
the person I marry
the person who invented traffic lights
the people who trained me for my career
the person who figures my electricity bill
my closest friends
the people I never met at all
the people who helped me through a major crisis
the people who stole my backpack

[3]   *comparing Canada with the United States—*
Canada has postage stamps
the two countries are about the same size
Canada doesn't have a big military, while the United States spends more
    money on weapons than on anything else
Canadians watch television
Canada has the parliamentary system with a prime minister, while Ameri-
    cans have presidential elections
in Canada, French and English are both official languages
Americans drive cars
the Canadian provinces have much more home rule than the American
    states
both countries have people living in them

[4]   *what it really means to be human*—
      humans contemplate the meaning of existence
      humans get runny noses
      humans keep documents of the history of the world
      humans munch potato chips and onion dip
      humans make and record laws
      humans can control other species of animals
      humans snore when they sleep
      humans tend to keep library books out way too long
      humans build machines to increase their power

[5]   *the major benefits of modern technology*—
      we can't pass bad checks as easily because of computers
      we can put people into outer space
      we have pop-top beer cans so we don't need can openers
      we have means of traveling rapidly all over the globe
      we can cure diseases that were once incurable
      we can listen to hit songs over the radio any time of the day or night
      we can detect and prepare for major disasters such as hurricanes and earthquakes
      we can process information thousands of times faster than used to be possible
      we can use microwave ovens to make chocolate chip cookies in a fraction of the time it once took

■   F.   RELEVANT DETAILS

Another major strategy for filling in your ideas is to

SELECT RELEVANT DETAILS.

RELEVANT DETAILS are the ones your readers will need to know in order to *get something done* in a real-life situation. You should always consider how people might make use of your materials. Thus, in expository writing that explains *how to do* something, make sure that readers really can tell what to do from your explanation—how to run video equipment, how to file an income tax return, how to play tennis, or whatever. Try to anticipate possible *problems* and deal with them in your paper, explaining the things somebody might do wrong if you didn't mention them.

Here is a list of details about growing a garden. Which ones do you think are relevant for somebody who wants advice? Mark the relevant ones with *yes* and the irrelevant ones with *no.*

(57) *growing a garden—*
      how severe or mild the climate is
      how much to water and how often
      how nice the gardener's personality is
      what color the leaves should be
      how to fertilize the soil
      whether the gardener lives in a nice house
      how much sunlight the garden gets per day
      where to buy seeds and bulbs
      where to buy frozen vegetables
      when you should wear work gloves
      when you should wear braces

Students have usually agreed that matters like climate, water, leaf color, fertilizer, sunlight, seeds and bulbs, and work gloves are relevant to gardening, while personality, kind of house, frozen vegetables, and braces are not.

8. QUIZ *on selecting relevant details*

Here are some lists of details about various topics. Mark the relevant details with *yes* and the irrelevant ones with *no*. If you can't make up your mind about an item, put a *?* by it.

[1] *how to move—*
      how to protect breakable items
      how to call the power company
      how to call directory assistance
      how to wash windows
      how to move very heavy furniture
      how to get up the carpets
      how to hire a moving van
      how to flush toilets frequently
      how to pack drapes to prevent wrinkles
      how to contact the phone company to discontinue service
      how to open doors with confidence
      how to prevent rips and stains on furniture
      how to whistle while you work

[2] *how to take good care of your car—*
      change the oil every 5,000 miles
      listen only to country music on the radio
      check tire pressure regularly
      keep the glove compartment full of maps and change
      keep the engine oil at the right level
      do doughnuts in the sand or the dirt
      keep the front end in alignment

burn the rubber when you take off from a stop sign
have the car lubricated twice a year
smile when you look in the rear-view mirror
put in antifreeze before winter comes

[3]   *how to get admitted to a good college—*
read the course offerings in the catalog
have your high school transcript sent in
change your last name
file an application early
read the *I Ching* to get advice on your future
list people who will recommend you
get your hair cut very short
visit the campus and show your interest
go on a crash diet so you'll look attractive
think about what career you want to go into

[4]   *how to become a good jogger—*
eat nutritious food instead of junk
tell everybody what a great jogger you are
buy proper jogging shoes
buy good-looking jogging shorts
run on a regular basis
find a safe jogging path
feel superior to anyone who doesn't jog
be sure not to neglect your physical condition
don't smoke cigarettes
don't read *TV Guide*

[5]   *how to make new friends—*
take care of your personal appearance
be tolerant of other people and their differences
chew bubble gum all day long
listen when other people are talking
drive around in a BMW
don't always insist on having your way
participate in school events
talk about yourself all the time
drink sugar-free diet soda

◻ **9. REVIEW QUIZ** *on selecting relevant details*

Same instructions as on the previous quiz.

[1]   *how to buy a good used car—*
check the ads in the paper carefully
settle only for your favorite color of paint

believe whatever the salesperson tells you
have a good mechanic check the car
forget about gas mileage because there's no energy shortage anyway
pay attention to the resale value
notice whether previous owners treated the car well
drag race the car at stoplights
check to see if all electrical parts work
check to see if there are any good tunes on the radio
look for clues of accidents such as freshly painted fenders

[2] *how to register for the courses you really want—*
be sure you get the right information from the class schedule
look sharp when you go to register
ask your advisor what you need for your major
complain loudly about standing in line so long
sign up for whatever your best friend is taking
get to registration as early as you can
find out which instructors are good
save money by looking for courses with only a few credits
be careful when you fill out your cards

[3] *how to develop a more positive attitude about life—*
look for things to appreciate rather than to get mad about
feel sorry for yourself every chance you get
try to get things right even if it's more work
keep your fingernails well trimmed
don't worry over matters you can't do anything about
get even with people who do things you don't like
play video games every night
take good care of your health and fitness
find some hobbies you really enjoy
sit in front of the TV and watch whatever comes on

[4] *how to get a driver's license—*
fill out the application correctly
smile at the clerk
study the booklet of regulations
polish your car and mags
practice basic driving skills thoroughly
wear bright-colored clothes
work on parallel parking
practice being a pedestrian
play heavy metal rock music on your tape deck all during the road test
observe traffic signals

[5] *how to avoid being a victim of crime—*
leave a light on when you're not home
walk alone in the downtown area

carry a whistle so you can give a distress signal
try not to look attractive
hang out in bars all the time
mark your possessions so you can identify them
show off how much money you're spending
lock your bicycle when you leave it
hope nobody will bother you
memorize the local phone number to call in emergencies
try anything anywhere for a thrill

■ G. CONVINCING REASONS

If you want to *persuade* people to accept an *argument*, you have to give them convincing reasons. A reason is **CONVINCING** if it is *important and true most of the time for many people*. The reason should also *be directly related to your argument*. A reason is not convincing if it isn't true, doesn't matter much to very many people, or is not directly related to your argument.

Suppose you wanted to argue in favor of a community bond issue to finance a continuing education program that gives older people new job training. Mark the convincing reasons with *yes* and the unconvincing reasons with *no*.

(58)   *why you should vote the funds for a continuing education program—*
       training for new jobs is important to people's lives
       the school building is sometimes just standing empty anyway
       careers are changing rapidly
       people need to keep up with new developments
       money is something you should always vote for
       I had a good time in school
       education is an opportunity everyone should have
       continuing something is better than stopping it
       older people often learn better because they have a clearer idea of what
           they want

The convincing reasons are the ones that say why job training really matters: it's important to the lives of people who need to keep up with new developments at a time when careers are changing rapidly. It's also convincing to point out that older people can learn better because they have a clearer idea of what they want—this fact tells us why the program should be successful. You might also include the statement that education is an opportunity everyone should have, though you might consider this too general to be directly related to your argument.

In contrast, it's not convincing to say that the school building is sometimes standing empty, because it doesn't make sense to run a program just to fill empty rooms. The statements that money is something you should always vote for, and that continuing something is better than stopping it, don't work because they often aren't true. It's also not convincing to mention that you personally had a good time in school, because the program is for the whole community, not merely for you; you should speak for people in general.

10. QUIZ *on selecting convincing reasons*

Here are some arguments with lists of possible reasons. Mark the convincing reasons with *yes* and the unconvincing reasons with *no*. If you can't make up your mind about an item, put a *?* by it.

[1]   *why we should work to preserve endangered species—*
once a species is extinct, it can never be revived
plants and animals are as much a part of nature as people are
my little sister thinks manatees are cute
humans are altering the world in ways they barely understand
tigers can be used in advertising campaigns
living in nature's world is a responsibility we can't run away from
the creation of a plant or an animal is a major event and should be respected
I like to visit the zoo on Sundays

[2]   *why the federal government should not pile up huge debts—*
public debts heat up inflation
money is a bad thing to get involved with
the interest alone will be very hard to repay in any reasonable time
public debts lower the value of the dollar on world markets
the U.S. economy needs to be kept in a favorable balance
my family never borrows money, no matter what
dollars don't go very far these days

[3]   *why we need a council to monitor advertising practices—*
consumers have often been the victims of false advertising
advertisements make newspapers too bulky
some products being advertised are dangerous to your health
the Advertising Standards Authority in England has been a very successful
    monitor
some advertisements are not written in very good English
advertisements consistently use and portray women as subhuman objects
advertisements get on my nerves
false advertisements harm the credibility of all advertisements

[4]   *why it's worth your while to attend driver training school—*
traffic accidents cause serious injuries
the schools have to make a living too
everybody's crazy about cars these days
some traffic regulations are complicated
experienced driving instructors are better than friends and family
you can meet new people at the school

you can practice in a simulator before you get out on the road in a real car
you can find out how cars work as machines
you can find out the instructor's name

[5]   *why a poor person should be given a free trial lawyer for defense—*
lawyers are pretty good at carrying on interesting conversations
in our society, people are supposed to be equal before the law
most people are not familiar enough with the law to defend themselves
it's nice to have company when you're sitting around in a boring courtroom
the outcome of a trial depends heavily on having good legal counsel to represent you
being poor should not be an automatic disadvantage when you go to court
whether you're guilty doesn't have anything to do with whether you can
   afford a good lawyer

11. REVIEW QUIZ *on selecting convincing reasons*

Same instructions as on the previous quiz.

[1]   *why the United States should stress human rights in its dealings with foreign
nations—*
the United States wants to look good in order to attract tourist dollars
many countries are ruled by violent, repressive governments
the United States is one of the oldest and most stable democracies in the
   world
America wants to export expensive weapons systems to anyone who can
   pay
the rights of human beings should be valid in every part of the world
Americans are very kind to dogs and cats
the United States is a leader in influencing what moral standards are accepted in the world
the United States can afford to set humanitarian considerations over selfish
   interests

[2]   *why we should fund low-cost bus services in our cities—*
in many cities, current bus services are not adequate for getting to work
buying a car on credit is increasingly difficult for the average citizen
gasoline and oil are growing scarce and expensive
I enjoy riding the bus, because I had to walk to school when I was a kid
our cities are heavily congested by staggering numbers of private cars
public services should be affordable to all people who need them
bus stations are good places to hide out in

[3]   *why this candidate deserves your support—*
he has worked for useful public projects
he has a nice smile
he supports equal rights for everyone

his voting record has been consistent with his principles
he has two adorable children
his background is Irish
he grew up on a farm in the Midwest
he has never been known to sell his influence to lobbyists

[4] *why cigarette smoking should be discouraged in every way possible—*
smoking has been proven to cause fatal cancer
tobacco irreparably damages your lungs
you're breathing other people's smoke even if you don't smoke yourself
it's hard to find enough quarters for cigarette vending machines
smoking causes emphysema, which impairs the action of the heart and the
    lungs
ashtrays are inconvenient to wash
cigarettes can make you nauseous or jittery

[5] *why you should not rush into marriage until you know what it will be like—*
you need to know the person you'll be spending a major part of your life
    with
you need to order fancy wedding invitations quite a while in advance
a marriage is supposed to last
you need time to shop for outfits that will impress all your friends
a relationship demands a great deal of effort and patience if it is to work
your temperament may not be right for married life
you should build your ego by fooling around with as many people as possible

■ H. PUTTING STATEMENTS IN ORDER

In Chapter 3, Section C, we worked mainly on putting just two or three statements in order. Now we'll be working with larger numbers of statements. There
are two main strategies to follow. One is to

PUT THE MOST GENERAL STATEMENTS AT
THE BEGINNING OR AT THE END.

A statement is GENERAL if it *tells what something basically is* or if it *gives the main
ideas* that are dealt with in several other statements. A general statement makes a
good beginning or ending and shows why the topic is important to many people
(see also page 254). The other main strategy is to

PUT STATEMENTS ABOUT SIMILAR THINGS
TOGETHER.

If several statements are about the same part of your topic, group them together. Where it's useful, you can organize a group of statements to move from CAUSE to EFFECT, EARLIER to LATER, MAIN STATEMENT to EVIDENCE, and so on. Suppose the game of baseball is your topic. You could list your ideas about the game just as they come to mind:

(59)   BASEBALL
There is an infield and an outfield.
The team consists of nine players.
In the center of the infield is the pitcher's mound.
Baseball is a traditional American sport played with a ball and a bat.
A batter who swings at the ball three times and misses is put out.
It offers fun and excitement, and keeps the players in good physical condition.
There are six infielders and three outfielders.
After making a hit, the batter must pass three bases and return to home plate in order to score.
Baseball is a demanding sport, but it's worth the effort.
The catcher receives the ball if the batter doesn't get a hit.
The pitcher serves the ball to the batter.
The borders of the infield are the lines drawn along the route from home plate to first base, to second base, to third base, back to home plate.
The infielders include pitcher, catcher, three basemen, and the shortstop.
A batter is walked if four pitches are outside his reach.
In an inning, each team has a chance to bat until three players are put out.

As they stand, these statements are not in a very sensible, useful order. Here's how one student put them in order:

(60)   BASEBALL

general beginning:
Baseball is a traditional American sport played with a ball and a bat. [tells what the game basically is]
It offers fun and excitement, and keeps the players in good physical condition. [tells why it's worthwhile and important]

specific things about the field, with the most general statement first:
There is an infield and an outfield. [gives the main ideas about the field]
The borders of the infield are the lines drawn along the route from home plate to first base, to second base, to third base, back to home plate.
In the center of the infield is the pitcher's mound.

specific things about the team, with the most general statement first:
The team consists of nine players. [tells what a team is basically made of]

There are six infielders and three outfielders.
The infielders include pitcher, catcher, three basemen, and the shortstop.

specific things about a turn at bat, listing the various possible outcomes:
In an inning, each team has a chance to bat until three players are put
out. [gives the basic idea about the inning]
The pitcher serves the ball to the batter.
The catcher receives the ball if the batter doesn't get a hit.
A batter who swings at the ball three times and misses is put out.
A batter/He is walked if four pitches are outside his reach.
After making a hit, the batter must pass three bases and return to home
plate in order to score.

general ending:
Baseball is a demanding sport, but it's worth the effort. [tells again what
it is and why it's worthwhile]

Two very general statements about baseball went at the beginning—one saying
what baseball basically is and one saying why it's worthwhile. Then the student
made three groups of statements: one about the field, one about the team, and
one about a turn at bat. In each group, she put the most general statement in first
place. Finally, she put another very general statement at the end, again saying
that the game is worthwhile. Her arrangement isn't the *only* good one—you
could mention the team before the field, for instance. Just be sure you have the
most general statements toward the beginning and the end, and that you keep
similar statements together. And within a group, look for a way to arrange statements, such as general to specific, earlier to later, cause to effect, or whatever's
appropriate (see also Chapter 3, Section C). You might make minor changes in
the sentences to get them to fit together. For instance, if you have two sentences
in a row about "the batter" in (60), you might say "he" the second time.

☐ 12. QUIZ *on putting statements in order*

Put the following statements in a good order. Look for a general beginning and
ending, and make groups of similar statements. Inside each group, put the more
general statements before the more specific ones. You can make minor changes to
fit the sentences together.

Example: See (59) and (60) in this section.

[1]   FLORIDA'S ATTRACTIONS
The beaches are among the world's most famous.
Florida is a very attractive state.
Many lakes are found.
The range of wildlife is large and varied.

Disney World and Circus World are centers of entertainment.
Water is a major feature of the countryside.
Jacksonville and Miami are centers of commerce.
Some areas are well developed and densely populated.
Florida has many places of great natural beauty.
Real estate is booming.
The sun shines most of the year.
Mother Nature has been good to Florida.
The landscape has many forests and groves.
Lagoons provide for fishing and scuba diving.

[2]   PREPPY LIFE
Khaki colors are often worn.
A style of living called "prep" has become popular.
Participation in sports is widespread.
You must attend an Ivy League college.
You can wear a combination of pink and green.
There are certain types of places where you have to go.
Clothing is extremely important.
Prepsters accept the ways of their parents.
You should visit a country club frequently.
The whole life style means being conservative in every way.
The *Official Preppy Handbook* tells exactly what to do on all occasions.
You play tennis all the time, or at least look like you do.
Izod shirts, button-downs, and Sperry Topsiders are a must.
Skiing is considered "in" with the preppy set.
The best way to get in is to be born in and to use Daddy's connections all
    your life.
But you can always fake it by imitating real preppies.

[3]   PUBLIC RELATIONS
Everything depends on how you get the message across to the people.
Corporations can improve their image by contributing to charitable organi-
    zations, such as the American Red Cross and the United Fund.
Public relations is the profession of creating favorable publicity.
Corporations want to present new products with good publicity.
If the company has good relations with its employees, its relations with the
    community will benefit.
The product must be presented in ways that appeal to the customer.
A news release about a new product should state essential facts in a way
    people will remember.
No business can live without the public.
Employees appreciate it when the company consults them about major
    decisions.
Getting news to the right people at the right time has a great influence on
    your image.

[4] A CO-OP DORMITORY

There are several offices to which residents are elected.

Living in a co-op dorm has certain advantages.

A co-op dorm is a residential hall where students are in charge of the management and maintenance of the building.

Before moving in, you must consider if the co-op fits your life style.

The board of directors has weekly meetings to discuss problems and suggestions.

One advantage is the inexpensive rent.

Living in a co-op dorm has certain disadvantages.

A co-op helps students learn to be responsible for their own housing.

One disadvantage is having to do details, such as cleaning the lounge or the hallways.

People who miss their details are summoned to the meetings of the board.

The board interviews you before you are accepted as a resident.

If you miss too many details, the board kicks you out.

You must be a responsible person to live here.

The board meetings hear offenders.

Most people who live in a co-op prefer it to any other student housing.

The board of directors is the group of students who run the dorm.

[5] BOXING

Punches to the face count more points.

The boxing ring may be anywhere from fourteen feet to eighteen feet across.

A fight may vary between ten rounds and fifteen rounds.

The object in boxing is to score points by hitting the opponent.

Boxers who move around a lot prefer a larger ring.

Boxing has long been a favorite sport with the public.

The boxing ring is square and varies in size.

Punches can be either to the face or to the chest and stomach.

Boxing is a great sport for promoting physical fitness.

Fifteen rounds would be typical for a title match.

The referees determine the winner according to points.

▢ 13. REVIEW QUIZ on putting statements in order

Same instructions as on the previous quiz.

[1] THE FIDUCIARY PROFESSION

A blue-chip investment is one in which the risk is low but the capital gain is small.

The fiduciary will ask what kind of risks you want to take.

These days, it's important to protect your money against inflation.

A fiduciary is a person who invests your money for you.

Investment means making your money grow.

Higher risks mean higher profits, but the danger of losing money is also greater.

It's reassuring to know that your money is working for you all the time.

A fiduciary is usually a broker or a banker.

Buying stock in a new company is an investment in which the risk is high but the capital gain can be enormous.

[2]   DIETING

The foods you eat should be low in starch and sugar.

Dieting is not an easy task, but it's worth the effort.

It's wonderful to fit into clothes again that you had gotten too big for.

Exercise is very important.

People generally tend to view themselves as overweight.

Strenuous exercise burns up the calories you consume.

A good combination of foods is a must.

Jogging and weight lifting are two good ways to exercise your body.

It's foolish to jump into a crash diet that can damage your health.

There will always be dieting in a world so conscious of people's looks.

Dieting means controlling the food you eat in order to influence your body.

Dieting can make you feel much better about yourself and your appearance.

The foods you select should emphasize vitamins, minerals, and protein.

[3]   TOURING AMERICA

Touring the western states is essential.

You shouldn't pass up the fishing villages in Massachusetts.

The Colorado Rockies are breathtaking.

America has many sites that everyone ought to see.

You will never forget the dense forests and white sand beaches of Florida.

Arizona offers scenic deserts and the Grand Canyon.

Many picturesque towns are hidden away in the hills of Tennessee and Georgia.

The New England states should not be missed.

America is a land of scenic wonders.

The mountains in New Hampshire are impressive.

The southeastern states have a charm all their own.

California has a long and stunning coastline.

[4]   COLLEGE AND YOUR CAREER

Engineering covers a wide range of industrial uses.

Dentistry is tough and competitive, but it's very rewarding.

A college is a place to prepare for your future career.

Health-care professionals are always in demand.

Engineers are needed to build any major project, such as an office building.

Nursing is a career where you can help people in need.

Computers are the main field in electrical engineering.

A college that didn't help people find good careers would be a contradiction.

New areas of specialization are constantly opening up in surgery.

Low-cost housing must be maintained.

No citizen should be discriminated against for reasons of race, sex, or religion.

In a democracy, the government has an equal responsibility to all its citizens.

The construction of public buildings and landmarks provides valuable jobs.

Food stamps are a necessity to low-income families.

A society that cares for everyone alike is the greatest human ideal.

National parks are projects built and maintained for public recreation and relaxation.

Special support must be provided for the poor.

The government should see to it that equal rights are respected everywhere.

Public projects are a major contributor to a strong economy.

■   I. ARRANGING PARAGRAPHS

Now that we have tried arranging statements in a reasonable order, we can try arranging whole paragraphs. In everyday talk, it's all right to skip around. If you leave something out, you can supply it later. For example, the freshman who was telling how he painted his roof (see also page 143) forgot one whole part of his topic and had to start over:

(61)   first I went and I bought all the maTERials....bought two five-gallon con-
        tainers of paint....a ROLLER....a roller handle atTACHment that you
        put the ROLLER on....and....went HOME..with the maTERials....um
        ....oh....I forgot to mention about STEAM cleaning it..ALL right..let
        me start this over..first I rented a STEAM CLEANER [and so on]

In writing, however, you are expected to keep arranging the topic until your points are in a sensible order. For example, if you're giving instructions on painting a roof, you'll want to mention things in the order in which they should be done (see also page 199).

In English, everyday talk is not clearly divided into units or stages. Some people use signals like "okay" in sample (2) on page 3 to indicate when they're moving from one part of the topic to another, but such signals are not required. In writing, you mark off the parts of your topic in separate **PARAGRAPHS** by **INDENTING**—that is, by starting a new line that is set in from the left margin about a half-inch in longhand or about five spaces in typing. Each paragraph is made of sentences grouped together because they are about similar things.

The *number* of sentences in a paragraph may be anywhere from just one to a great many. In most writing, you find both long and short paragraphs. Usually, paragraphs do have more than just one sentence. A sentence would have to be very important and worth noticing to get a paragraph by itself. For example, Margaret Mead and Rhoda Metraux, in an essay "On Friendship," insert a one-sentence paragraph after describing how Europeans have problems understanding the way Americans use the word "friend":

(62)   Coming into an American home, the European visitor finds no visible landmarks. The atmosphere is relaxed. Most people, young and old, are called by first names.

        Who then is a friend?

        Even simple translation from one language to another is difficult. "You see," a Frenchman explains, "if I were to say to you in France, 'This is my good friend,' that person would not be as close to me as someone about whom I have said only 'This is my friend.'"

The short one-sentence paragraph asking "Who then is a friend?" leaps out at us. The question gets much more attention than it would if it were included at the end of the paragraph in front of it or at the beginning of the one after it—though those patterns would be perfectly all right here. Save the special effect of the one-sentence paragraph for occasions where you can really use it well.

Normally, the strategy for deciding paragraph length is to

USE PARAGRAPHS TO SHOW WHAT SENTENCES BELONG TOGETHER.

As we saw in Section H, statements about similar things should be grouped together. If you mark off one of these groups of statements as a separate paragraph, people can see right away that you are indicating a unit. So as you write, your usual strategy will be to

START A NEW PARAGRAPH WHEN YOU MOVE FROM ONE PART OF THE TOPIC TO ANOTHER.

To see how this works, we'll follow it through the whole paper. Your main divisions can simply be called the **BEGINNING**, the **MIDDLE**, and the **ENDING**. The middle is typically the longest part.

I.1 Beginning a Paper

Your **BEGINNING** should do at least two things. First, it should let people know what you're writing about. Second, it should give people a motive for reading it. So you should follow these two strategies:

BEGIN YOUR PAPER BY ANNOUNCING THE TOPIC.

BEGIN YOUR PAPER BY SAYING WHY THE TOPIC IS IMPORTANT FOR MANY PEOPLE.

For instance, one student wrote:

> (63) Although rarely spoken about by society, child abuse is one of the nation's most pressing problems today. As population continues to grow, so does the number of unwanted and unplanned children.

He made it plain right away that the paper is to be about "child abuse." He also stressed that this topic concerns "one of the nation's most pressing problems" that has not been "spoken about" nearly enough so far. He also suggests that the problem is continually growing. For all these reasons, people should feel that the topic is worth considering and reading about now.

Very often, the topic is announced in the *first sentence* of your opening paragraph. We see this done in the example on child abuse (63). Sometimes, though, a writer will use a sentence or two in order to lead into the topic, as in:

> (64) When humans wanted to increase their capacity to add beyond counting on their fingers, marking on paper, or grouping things in piles, they began making machines. These machines have developed into today's computers.

This writer saved the topic sentence until he had given us a brief historical background. He indicates that his topic of "today's computers" is part of a long tradition in human development.

These same papers that begin with examples (63) and (64) also illustrate another common strategy:

MAKE THE BEGINNING MORE GENERAL THAN THE MIDDLE OF THE PAPER.

In Section H, on putting statements in order, you were supposed to put general ones at the beginning. The reason is simple enough: *a general statement should be able to address the largest number of people.* If you start like this:

> (65) Although rarely spoken about by society, child abuse is one of the nation's most pressing problems today.

you are saying that your topic presents a very general "problem" for the whole "nation." Likewise, if your first sentence is

> (66)   When humans wanted to increase their capacity to add beyond counting on their fingers, marking on paper, or grouping things in piles, they began making machines.

you're saying something general about all "humans" and their tendency to "make machines." It's clear right away that you're concerned with people of all kinds. Then you follow up your general appeal by saying specifically what your topic will be.

Inside the opening paragraph, your sentences can be arranged according to what is more or less general. You can make the first sentence the most general, and the sentences after it more specific. You don't have to do it this way, but it's fairly common. Suppose you had some notes like this:

> (67)   *playing tennis a favorite form of recreation—*
> many benefits
> get good exercise
> relax
> meet new people

You want to make the notes into a good opening paragraph. You can do several things. You can announce the topic and say why it's important. You can also put the general before the specific. You could have:

> (68)   Playing tennis is a favorite form of recreation [names the topic]. Tennis has many benefits to offer [says why it's important]. You can get good exercise, relax, and meet new people [gives specific "benefits"].

The specific things mentioned in the opening paragraph should be the ones you plan to talk about in detail during your whole paper.

You may have more than one general sentence before you move to more specific things. Suppose your notes looked like this:

> (69)   *part-time jobs for students—*
> college expenses
> many parents not wealthy
> tuition
> books
> rent
> food

To make the notes into a good opening paragraph, you can announce the topic and say why it's important before you move to the specifics. You could do it this way:

(70)   Part-time jobs for students are in great demand today. These jobs are essential for students who have to meet their own college expenses. Many
parents are not wealthy. The students have to pay for their own tuition,
books, rent, and food.

The first sentence tells us the topic is "part-time jobs" and says that it matters to
many people because there is a "great demand" for them. The second sentence
tells us why this topic is important, that is, "essential for students." The third
sentence gives evidence why we should believe what the first two said. Then we
get the specific expenses that "students have to pay for." Here, too, readers expect that your whole paper is going to deal with the specific things mentioned in
the opening paragraph.

   If you want more details, you could also spread the specifics over several sentences. Instead of just (71), you could have (72):

(71)   The students have to pay for their own tuition, books, rent, and food.

(72)   Students must first pay tuition to get into college at all. Then they must
buy books for every course that requires them. Living on their own, students also have to earn the money for their own rent and food.

The amount of detail you include depends on how much explanation you think
your readers will need.

▢ 14. QUIZ on opening paragraphs

Now you try it. Make each set of notes into an *opening paragraph with more than
one sentence*. Be sure you **announce the topic** and say why it's **important**. Also be
sure to put the general before the specific. *The notes may not be in the order you will
use them!*

[1]   *Equal Rights Amendment getting more and more attention—*
guarantees needed in U.S. constitution
equality among human beings the greatest idea of a democratic nation
race
sex
equal pay for equal work

[2]   *housing crisis acute in large cities—*
urban renewal projects under way
tearing down slums
building public playgrounds
providing good mass transportation

[3]   *the need for exploration of outer space—*
many things to learn about the earth as a part of the universe

elements making up the stars and planets
history of the earth
future events and how they will affect the human race

[4]   *our national parks a valuable resource—*
unspoiled wilderness giving many benefits
retreat from civilization
recreation for our children
hiking for our health
understanding the place of humans in the scheme of nature

[5]   *alternative energy sources in great demand—*
high price of fossil fuel running away with us
solutions must be found as soon as possible
increased public awareness
conservation
solar energy

15. REVIEW QUIZ *on opening paragraphs*

Same instructions as on the previous quiz.

[1]   *new telephone services being offered—*
call waiting to avoid busy phones
useful ways to save time and effort
three-way calling for group conversations
call forwarding from one place to another
speed calling to dial a whole number by punching one button

[2]   *public transportation needed in crowded cities—*
traffic jams at rush hour damaging the environment and people's nerves
subways
bus lines
trains

[3]   *airlines one of our biggest industries—*
constant openings for personnel
pilots
navigators
mechanics
cabin attendants

[4]   *Europe a fascinating place to visit—*
many things worth seeing
castles
old towns
cathedrals
quaint farms

[5]   *Shakespeare one of the greatest playwrights who ever lived—*
        many things I enjoy about his plays
        unforgettable characters
        famous speeches
        beautiful language
        the feeling of watching history unfold before my eyes

I.2   Going from the Beginning to the Middle

Once you have a good opening paragraph for your beginning, you can work on
the paragraphs in the **MIDDLE**. Your opening paragraph should have made a
clear statement of an important main topic. Since the opening is normally general, your strategy for moving on to the middle of your paper is:

MOVE TO A SPECIFIC PART OF YOUR
MAIN TOPIC.

After that, you'll be moving from one part to another, and you'll usually want to
mark off each part by starting a new paragraph. Whenever you move to a new
part of your topic, your major strategy should be:

MAKE IT CLEAR HOW THE NEW PART OF THE
TOPIC IS RELATED TO THE PREVIOUS PART.

People should be able to tell right away how each new part of your paper fits with
what you've already said.

Let's see how one student did this. He moved from the main topic at the beginning to one specific part of the topic:

(73)   What makes human beings differ? This question is the focus of most de-
       velopmental psychologists. Today, most people cannot help being af-
       fected by changes throughout their lives. We change jobs, move, and
       have different problems every day.
           Infancy is the most important age in people's lives for the development
       of human nature. Children are not born with character, but develop it as
       they grow up.

The opening paragraph starts with a question the writer intends to work on. The
second sentence says who is asking the question—"developmental psychol-
ogists." The rest of the opening paragraph explains what kind of "changes" can

"affect" people's lives. In this way, the opening paragraph itself goes from general to more specific.

Then the second paragraph narrows down the topic from entire "lives" to "infancy." By saying that this "age" is crucial for the "development of human nature," the writer ties in with his opening, where he mentioned "human beings." We also have a statement of why this part of the topic is the one most worth talking about: "infancy is the most important age." The writer is offering us a motive to read on: so that we can find out why.

To make sure people see how each part goes with the rest, keep this strategy in mind:

PUT IN A TRANSITION STATEMENT
WHEREVER IT MIGHT NOT BE CLEAR
HOW A NEW SECTION GOES WITH THE REST.

A **TRANSITION STATEMENT** shows when you're moving from one part of your topic and into another, and what kind of move it is. You indicate where you've been and where you're going next. One student wrote:

(74) Many people still think of Oklahoma as a "dust bowl" like the one portrayed by John Steinbeck in *The Grapes of Wrath*. But this view is a serious mistake. The Panhandle of western Oklahoma does have wind, dust, and tumbleweeds. But it is mainly devoted to growing wheat and ranching. Irrigation systems have helped alleviate the problem of drought.

   Moreover, western Oklahoma is not typical of the whole state. Eastern Oklahoma is completely different. It has many trees, hills, and lakes, and is especially green in the springtime. [and so on]

She made a transition statement between talking about "western Oklahoma" and talking about the other parts of the state. She emphasizes that the "dust bowl" image inspired by the western Panhandle is "not typical of the whole state." This way, she sets us up for a contrast she is about to develop by telling how the rest of the "whole state" is not dusty.

Transition statements most often go at the start of a paragraph that turns to a new part of your topic. Another student wrote:

(75) People learn to play the guitar for various reasons. Many people play for enjoyment. Other people make a living as musicians. Whatever your reason is, you have to know and do certain things.

   The most basic thing to know is musical theory. You need to know how to read notes, count rhythms, and keep a beat without speeding up or slowing down. To become excellent in these areas, you need much practice and hard work.

Another important thing to know is the basics of the guitar. The playing part of the guitar consists of a neck and six strings. The strings run from low E to high E. [and so on]

Each paragraph after the first one opens with a transition statement announcing what part of the topic is coming up: "musical theory" and "the basics of the guitar."

In real-life writing, transition statements do not by any means go at the start of *every* paragraph. Sometimes, you just open a paragraph by jumping right into the next idea. Suppose the student had written:

(75a)   People learn to play the guitar for various reasons. Many people play for enjoyment. Other people make a living as musicians. Whatever your reason is, you have to know and do certain things.
   Knowing musical theory makes you able to read notes, count rhythms, and keep a beat without speeding up or slowing down. To become excellent in these areas, you need much practice and hard work.

This version doesn't use up a whole statement telling us that we'll be reading about "the most basic thing to know." Instead, we get the thing itself ("musical theory") already being related to specific ideas ("reading notes, counting rhythms, and keeping a beat"). The transition is made without a special statement to announce it.

When you write, you should always consider whether the next part of your topic will be easy to fit in with what has gone before. Whenever it might not be easy, you'll probably want to use a transition statement.

In most papers, you can't give *all* the information about an idea. But you should give *enough* to make it clear what you're dealing with. Here's a good strategy:

**WHENEVER YOUR READERS MIGHT NOT GET
THE POINT, PROVIDE A SPECIFIC
EXPLANATION OR ILLUSTRATION.**

To see how that works, let's look at the first two paragraphs of another student's paper:

(76)   Videotaping is one of many styles of photography. The images from the camera are recorded on a tape, rather than on a film. I worked with videotape equipment in high school and found it the most satisfying way to photograph.
   There are two main types of units, portable and stationary. Portable units are small and light enough to be used for recording events at outside

locations. But stationary units offer more special effects. For example, the JVC HR-6700u Vidstar offers slow motion, still framing, and single-frame advance.

The opening paragraph begins with a sentence announcing the topic—in fact, the topic is mentioned in the very first word, "Videotaping." The next sentence explains "videotaping," in case we readers don't know exactly what it is. The third sentence tells why the writer is interested in and knowledgeable about the topic. By calling it "the most satisfying way to photograph," the writer also tells us why the topic is generally important.

Then the writer marks a new paragraph and announces a more specific part of the topic: the "main types of units." He classifies these "units" into two types, "portable and stationary." Next he mentions the advantages of the first type as being "small and light," qualities we can understand without further explanation. After that, he goes on to the advantages of the second type, "special effects." Since we might not know what he means by "special effects," the writer provides very specific illustrations: "slow motion, still framing, and single-frame advance." He plans to explain each of these later on in his paper.

You need to decide what degree of detail you can afford to include. The longer a paper, the more chances you should have to include very specific explanations and illustrations. But no paper is likely to say everything about the topic. Just put in enough to make sure it's plain what you're writing about.

16. QUIZ *on moving from a general opening paragraph to a more specific paragraph in the middle*

Use these sets of notes to make an opening paragraph. Then move to a speci c part of the topic in at least one more paragraph, and provide explanations a d illustrations where you think they're needed. Make sure it's clear how the spe fic part is related to the general one. You should try putting in a transition state ent at least some of the time.

[1]   *the United States as a melting pot—*
        people from all backgrounds coming to the New World
        ethnic variety as great as in any other country in the world
        recent waves of refugees from the Caribbean
        seeking refuge from extreme poverty
        problem of riots in dense urban areas
        refugee camps dismal and overcrowded
        finding employment extremely difficult

[2]   *technology keeps advancing in our society—*
        computers becoming a necessity
        complexity of a large-scale economy not manageable any oth r way
        good careers in computing expanding all the time

operating a terminal for an airline
analyzing market trends
figuring insurance risks
bookkeeping for small businesses

[3] *nursing as a worthwhile profession—*
many health hazards to confront
contagious diseases
automobile accidents
industrial accidents
one workman fell from a construction scaffolding
very critical condition
my patient for six months
gradually regained his will to live
finally seeing him walk out
great feeling of accomplishment

[4] *music a basic need for the human spirit—*
relaxation
emotional release
important part of our culture and life style
getting the components you need to build your own stereo
amplifier
speakers
turntable
tape deck
AM/FM tuner

[5] *tuning your engine not so hard to do—*
get away from soaring repair costs
help yourself in emergencies
help others out on the highway
several main things
change spark plugs
change spark plug wires
clean out carburetor
clean and set points in distributor or replace

■ **17. REVIEW QUIZ** *on moving from a general opening paragraph to a*
more specific paragraph in the middle

Same instructions as on the previous quiz.

[1] *high school organizations and activities a worthwhile experience—*
be useful to the community
establish contacts for later life

supervise preschool children on playgrounds
work in day-care centers
organize field trips

[2] *changes in the natural environment due to human exploitation of resources*—
long-term effects on environment unknown
impact of industry a major problem
forests cleared away
soil eroded
wildlife destroyed or even made extinct

[3] *physical fitness from becoming a member of a spa*—
relax away from the noise and rush of life outside
get your body clean and balanced
sitting in the sauna
swimming in the pool
playing racquetball
playing handball

[4] *college fraternities and sororities*—
student life needs organizations
community spirit increased
companionship and support provided for strangers to the town and campus
social calendar offering many events
dances
parties
benefits for charitable causes
homecoming parade with floats

[5] *Americans becoming more superstitious*—
anxious about the future
not understanding the complexities of our society
unable to deal with pressure and tension
increase in strange practices
obeying horoscopes to the letter
consulting fortunetellers and palm readers
guessing the future from cards or coins
joining extremist cults and losing touch with reality

I.3   Deciding Where to Mark Off Paragraphs

As we saw earlier, when you're presenting a topic in writing, you use **paragraphs**
to mark off the various stages. You indicate each new paragraph by indenting its
first line—that is, by starting it farther toward the right than the rest of the lines
on the page. (In typing, you usually move over five spaces. In handwriting, anywhere between a half-inch and an inch is customary.) Normally, you should start
a new paragraph each time you move from one part of your topic to another.

Paragraphs vary in length. The place where you start a new paragraph depends more on how your topic is progressing than on how many sentences you're putting together. In expository writing, very short or very long paragraphs aren't found too often. The reason is that one part of a topic usually requires several sentences, but not a large number.

Our strategies for arranging sentences (Chapter 3, Section C) also work on a larger scale for marking off paragraphs. Moving from **earlier** to **later**, or from **cause** to **effect**, or from the **whole** to its various **parts**, or from a **main statement** to **supporting evidence**—each new element of these strategies may be an occasion to start a new paragraph. The more statements you want to make about a particular item, such as a cause, an effect, a part, or whatever, the more likely you are to give it its own paragraph. That way, the item forms a visible unit with clearly drawn borders.

Let's have a look at some ways to mark off paragraphs. The most basic strategy is:

BEGIN A NEW PARAGRAPH WHEN YOU MOVE FROM ONE PART OF YOUR TOPIC TO ANOTHER.

This strategy is only a general guideline. You still have to decide what counts as a part of your topic, as a new idea within your total plan. Sometimes the decision is pretty easy. In the essay on "friendship" by Mead and Metraux already quoted (example 62), the parts of the topic are obvious when the various countries are being contrasted. Since the paragraphs are pretty long, I'll quote only the sentences where they start:

> (77) For the *French*, friendship is a one-to-one relationship that demands a keen awareness of the other person's intellect, temperament, and particular interests. [and so on]
>
> In *Germany*, in contrast with France, friendship is much more a matter of feeling. [and so on]
>
> *English* friendships follow a still different pattern. Their basis is shared activity. [and so on]

Each paragraph opens with a statement that introduces a new part of the topic, namely one national view of "friendship": French, German, and English. This arrangement works very well, especially with the name of each nationality coming close to the start of the sentence. You don't need whole transition statements, because it's plain what transitions are being made.

The "Friendship" paper also shows this important strategy:

USE SEPARATE PARAGRAPHS TO MARK A
CONTRAST.

A **CONTRAST** happens when you go from one thing to a different thing. In (77), Mead and Metraux want to point out contrasts between views of friendship in different countries, such as France, Germany, and England. So each new paragraph marks off a contrasting unit.

Another illustration of a contrast comes from a modern version of Aristotle's *Rhetoric*:

(78)   If *you* have taken an oath before, and it conflicts with the oath you are swearing now, you must argue that *either the previous oath or the present one was brought about by force or trickery*, so you cannot be held responsible.

On the other hand, if it is your *opponent* who has sworn conflicting oaths, you must argue that *people who do not abide by their oaths undermine the whole established order.*

Aristotle first says what to do if *you* swear conflicting oaths. He then shifts to what to do if *your opponent* does the same thing. The contrast is marked by a new paragraph. Expressions like "on the other hand," "different," "in contrast," and "however" often come at the start of the new paragraph where the contrast is marked. That way, people expect the contrast, rather than more of the same. We see some of these expressions in examples (77) and (78). But sometimes the contrast may be clear enough by itself without these signals.

The "Friendship" paper (77) illustrates one more strategy:

BEGIN A PARAGRAPH WHEN YOU MOVE FROM
THE WHOLE TO THE PART, OR WHEN YOU
MOVE FROM ONE PART TO ANOTHER PART.

"Friendship" around the world is the whole idea, and friendship in each country is one of the parts. We used this same strategy for arranging statements (pages 206–09).

Here's another demonstration, from Robert Ramirez' description of a Chicano "barrio" (neighborhood) in "The Woolen Serape."

(79)   Members of the barrio describe the *entire area* as their home, but it is more than this. The barrio is a refuge from the harshness and coldness of the Anglo world.

The *tortilleria* fires up its machinery three times a day, producing steaming, round, flat slices of barrio bread. In the winter, the warmth of the factory is a woolen serape in the chilly morning hours, but in the summer, it unbearably toasts every noontime customer.

The *panaderia* sends its sweet messenger aroma down the dimly lit street, announcing the arrival of fresh, hot sugary pan dulce.

The small *corner grocery store* serves the meal-to-meal needs of customers, and the owner, a part of the neighborhood, willingly gives credit to people unable to pay cash for foodstuffs.

The *barbershop* is a living room with hydraulic chairs, radio, and television, where old friends meet and speak of life as their salted hair falls aimlessly about them.

The writer first tells us about the "entire area." After that, each paragraph deals with one part of the Chicano neighborhood—the tortilla factory, the bakery ("panaderia"), the store, and the barbershop. The new location is mentioned right at the start of every paragraph: "tortilleria," "panaderia," "corner grocery store," and "barbershop" are all in the first part of the opening sentence; we don't have full transition statements, because it's obvious where we're going. As you can see, this division sometimes makes paragraphs only one sentence long. Still, each of these sentences is packed with enough interesting details that it deserves to be a separate unit. The organization of the topic overrules the usual tendency to have paragraphs contain more than one sentence.

Another strategy also fits one we used for arranging statements (pages 198–99):

BEGIN A NEW PARAGRAPH WHEN YOU MOVE FROM EARLIER TO LATER.

If you're telling about a series of events, a new paragraph can indicate when the next event starts. An essay by Edward Peeples recounts his experiences on the topic of "humans eating pet food":

(80)   The first time I witnessed people eating pet food was among neighbors and acquaintances during my youth in the South. [and so on]

The second time occurred in Cleveland in the summer of 1953. [and so on]

The next time I ate dog food was in 1956 while struggling through a summer session in college without income for food. [and so on]

Later, while working as a hospital corpsman, I had the opportunity to ask new recruits about their home life and nutrition practices. [and so on]

By placing expressions of time—"the first time," "the second time," "the next time," and "later"—at the start of each of these paragraphs, the writer clearly leads us along from one time to the next. The paragraphs distinctly mark off the various stages.

Cause and effect also influence paragraphing:

BEGIN A NEW PARAGRAPH WHEN YOU MOVE FROM CAUSE TO EFFECT.

Here's an illustration from a passage about the election of a Hispanic mayor (*Newsweek*, July 4, 1983):

> (81)   Last week Colorado state legislator Federico Pena was elected mayor of Denver. In a city only about one-fifth Hispanic, he won less by capitalizing on his heritage than by transcending it.
>
> Across the country, the Denver results were viewed as a milestone for a minority group suddenly on the threshold of major political power.

The election in Denver was the cause of a new political outlook "across the country."

Still another strategy is like one we used for arranging statements (see pages 202–05):

BEGIN A NEW PARAGRAPH WHEN YOU PRESENT A NEW SET OF SUPPORTING EVIDENCE FOR YOUR MAIN STATEMENT.

Vernon E. Jordan, Jr., writing about the black middle class, makes his main statement and then opens a new paragraph to give us some evidence:

> (82)   The fact is that the black middle class of 1974, like that of earlier years, is a minority within the black community. In 1974, as in 1964, 1954, and in the decades stretching into the distant past, the social and economic reality of the majority of black people has been poverty and marginal status in the wings of our society.
>
> Let's look at income, the handiest guide and certainly the most generally agreed-upon measure. In 1972 the median family income—what people earn at the exact midpoint of society—was $11,549 for whites, but the black median family income was a mere $6,864.

The author backs up a controversial statement with some actual statistics on family income.

Here's another illustration. Looking back over his past "Growing Up on Long Island," Jim Brown, the football star, wrote:

> (83) As warlord of the Gaylords, I rarely had to fight, simply because my opponents almost always backed down. Still, I should have known that sooner or later I'd have to face a blade. One night in Hampstead I did.
>
> We had invited ourselves to a party being held by a rival gang. [and so on]

By indenting for a new paragraph, he lets us know he's going to give details about the time he "had to face a blade."

If your main statement might be surprising or unwelcome, you could present the evidence first and then make the statement afterward (see also page 203). This strategy would be the reverse of the one we just looked at, namely:

BEGIN A NEW PARAGRAPH WHEN YOU MOVE FROM SUPPORTING EVIDENCE TO YOUR MAIN STATEMENT.

A critical report with an unpleasant conclusion demonstrates this way of marking a paragraph:

> (84) The procedure for certification presently used in Centerville Hospital does not always provide the proper certification information. Certification cards are often missing from patients' charts or are only partially completed. The result is that cards are sometimes illegally completed by unauthorized personnel.
>
> The obvious conclusion is that the present system is defective. [and so on] [Mathes and Stevenson, *Designing Technical Reports*]

You wouldn't want to come out and say that the whole "system is defective" until you have given some good evidence. Otherwise, readers may be so annoyed or upset at the start that they won't give you a fair chance to make your point.

☐ 18. QUIZ *on deciding where to mark off paragraphs*

Sometimes you find out after you've written part of your paper that you should have divided it up into more paragraphs. Imagine that you had some passages like the following. Find *one* likely place that makes a good transition to start a new paragraph according to the strategies we've looked at in this section, and mark the place with the symbol ¶ (the customary editor's mark for a paragraph). Also indicate which strategy or strategies apply: *contrast, whole/parts, one part/another part, earlier/later, cause/effect, statement/evidence,* or *evidence/statement.* In addition, insert a transition statement that could begin the new paragraph at the point you marked, like the one in brackets in the following example.

Example:

Society is changing in several ways that do not agree with one another. Technology looks forward by speeding up the rate at which things happen, including historical events. Means of transportation get faster and faster, even beyond the speed of sound. Computers solve problems at the speed of light. ¶ [But forward is not the only direction in which our society is looking.] Our philosophies of life are slowing us down and making us look backward. We still fight wars in the same mindless spirit as the cavemen did. We still refuse to join our efforts in worldwide cooperation. We still have no consistent policy on most major social problems. CONTRAST

[1]   We live in a time of great spiritual unrest. The traditional beliefs of past generations no longer seem valid. In the Western world, young people have set out in search of something new to believe in. One sign of this trend is the growing popularity of Eastern religions. These religions are gaining acceptance among the young as an alternative to the religions of the West.

[2]   The disease spread rapidly in the hot, moist summer air. Sanitation was poor in that part of the world anyway. Hospitals were overfilled even before the epidemic broke out. Finally, the authorities recognized that a state of emergency had come. They sent a telegram to the central government asking for special forces to meet the crisis.

[3]   The status of the middle class has improved in many ways over the last fifty years. The increase in ordinary buying power has made available many commodities that few people could afford in the past, such as cars, private homes, and technological equipment. But now this picture has been darkened by inflation and unemployment. Money no longer buys the same amount of goods. And increasing numbers of once secure jobs are melting away.

[4]   The Metropolitan Museum of Art is built in the classical style, with a huge, broad staircase leading up to an impressive entrance. Inside, a solemn parade of ancient objects reminds the visitor of the grandeur and certainty of history. The Guggenheim Museum, though facing the same Manhattan avenue, barely looks like a museum at all. Inside, its dizzily spiraling walk takes the visitor past the strangest products of modern art. Great, grotesque shapes refuse to instruct or reassure, or even to inform. Here, history has no monument and no consensus.

[5]   She felt as if life had begun to close in on her. Her world was full of ene-mies, constantly plotting her doom. The most insignificant events seemed to give proof of yet another fiendish trap. One day a scrap of paper was left lying in the street near her house. It had been torn out of a child's storybook and contained the words, "The End." Here, she thought, was a sure sign that her destruction was near.

[6]   No matter how they tried, the committee couldn't change the facts. It was a difficult case, deciding whether to open criminal proceedings against a state governor. They would have to announce it to an unsuspecting public that looked on the governor as a father. After much deliberation, they released their report, and the issue almost drowned out all other issues in the news. Throughout the state, people took sides for or against the accused leader.

[7]   The northwest part of the town is anxious to represent the "good life." Houses are laundered and trimmed like children on their behavior for Sun-day school. Trees are combed, gardens are manicured, and cars are shel-lacked. Even the dogs seem to realize the dignity expected of them. The northeast part of town has its own cares. Houses are dull and anxious-looking, like workmen coming home in the dark after a long day in the fields. Trees are unkempt, gardens are madly uncontrolled like water splashed from a bucket, and cars are weary and faded. The dogs, filled with petty activity, scamper in the red dust.

[8]   It was difficult to tell how bad the damage would be. The storm continued to batter the small town most of the night with heavy rain and high winds. The temperature fell almost 30 degrees in four hours. Next morning, the scene was desolate. Of the forty houses on the waterfront, only two were still standing. A few posts were left to show where the pier had been the day before.

[9]   In its early years, the party had few supporters. Its political outlook was stag-nant. New ideas were not welcomed, and several important ones were shortsightedly rejected. Then, about two years ago, the party suddenly took on momentum. Its leaders assumed new prominence in the news media, and its membership greatly increased.

[10] The strip-mining companies moved into the canyon about a mile from our house. They announced their arrival with a series of blasts that left us with-out window panes. The plaster in the walls cracked. The concrete patio behind the garage split down the middle. Something had to be done if we wanted to save the home we had worked so many years to build. And we had very little time to do it. In a matter of days, the rains would bring slow, terrifying avalanches of mud down the hillside.

Same instructions as on the previous quiz.

[1] The coast on the Atlantic Ocean side of Florida has a large number of beaches. The sand is white and fine-grained. There are dunes covered with sea oats. Large hotels and resorts are common. The coast on the Gulf of Mexico side has fewer beaches. The sand is darker and rockier. There are lagoons with stony edges. Generally, family homes are more common than large hotels.

[2] My first year at boarding school I avidly sought acceptance. I followed every clothes fad. I belonged to every club. I tried to act just like all the other girls. My second year was just the opposite. I dressed in old, worn-out clothes. I kept away from all clubs and parties. I wanted to be as different from the other girls as I could.

[3] The situation seemed well under control. The corporation was represented in ten states. Capital holdings were large and growing. Sales were on the rise. Then the economic climate changed as suddenly as the weather. Nothing seemed to come out right. Money was invested and didn't come back. Sales were canceled again and again.

[4] None of us knew what to expect. Rumors of bankruptcy were heard in small circles. The official reports were vague and lacked the usual confidence. Personnel resigned and left quietly. All of a sudden, the news was out. Nothing was left of the giant enterprise but a few bits of office furniture and a huge stack of unpaid bills.

[5] Our society is undoubtedly at a turning point. The signs are hard to overlook. Problems are severe and solutions hard to find. Standards and values are in dispute. Public institutions come under strong criticism. For example, the role of the federal government in local affairs is rapidly changing. Cities and states are asking whether federal guidelines should be accepted and, if not, what could replace them.

[6] The atrocities committed by government police were obvious and well-known. But nothing was done to correct them. Official statements continued to deny everything. When the situation became severe enough, bands of local rebels began to attack police targets. The villagers and farmers had stood all they were going to.

[7] In the desert, real estate values stayed fairly low. The rate of construction was moderate at best. Population growth slowed down and then leveled off. On the coastline, property values soared as never before. New buildings appeared everywhere. The population increased many times over.

[8] There are many sources of confusion in American foreign policy, even among experienced diplomats. This confusion has been a problem for years. Recently, the results have become painfully clear in Central America. One part of the U.S. government does and says just the opposite of another part.

[9]   This computer is a miracle of technology. Few systems today are even close to it, and serious competition is hardly to be found at any comparable price. Just the printer in itself is a major innovation. It does all kinds of printing, graphics, and charts with a minimum of instructions.

[10]   The first year we tried to stick it out in the far north. We put up with everything we had to. We endured the terrible weather, the isolation, the lack of services, and much more. The next year, we began to lose hope. It seemed like it might be better to move south after all. The way of life was just too hard.

I.4   Ending a Paper

After you have a title, a beginning, and a middle, all you need for your paper is the conclusion. The conclusion usually looks back to the beginning, and briefly reviews the middle. The most important way to divide your paper is to organize your topic according to **GENERAL** versus **SPECIFIC**. Usually, you begin with one or more **general opening paragraphs** that state your main topic and say why it's important to many people. Then you fill in the **middle** with paragraphs about **specific parts** of your main topic. Finally, you end with one or more **general concluding paragraphs** that come back to your main topic and say again why it's important—though *not in the same words* you used in the beginning. The conclusion should also mention the **main points** you made in the middle. This organization isn't always used, but it's very common in expository writing, so we'll work on it here.

You can probably guess by now what strategies apply to concluding a paper. This one is much like the strategy for beginning your paper:

YOUR CONCLUSION SHOULD STATE THE TOPIC AGAIN, AND STRESS WHY THE TOPIC IS IMPORTANT.

That way, people will leave your paper with the topic fresh in their minds, and will feel it's been worthwhile reading about. For example, the paper on videotaping whose beginning we looked at in example (76) has this conclusion:

(85)   I think videotaping is an excellent way of expressing oneself. It can be used to tape special events in one's life, to help athletes in their games, and to teach students in schools. Videotaping can capture any occasion.

He mentions his main topic of "videotaping" and says it's important because it provides "an excellent way of expressing oneself." He also followed this strategy:

YOUR CONCLUSION SHOULD TIE THE MIDDLE TOGETHER.

You should mention in a few words what your main points were in the middle part of your paper. In (85), he reviewed his main points as "taping special events," "helping athletes," and "teaching students." The conclusion from a student's paper on drunk driving goes like this:

> (86) Alcohol combined with driving is one of the most dangerous and deadly problems we face. However, several measures are being taken against it. *Stronger penalties* are being legislated. Better means to *identify offenders* are being developed. And *treatment centers* are becoming available to help alcoholics. In the future, we may finally get this problem under control.

He uses just one sentence to name his main points from the middle of his paper: "stronger penalties," "identifying offenders," and "treatment centers." No details are needed here—just brief reminders of the issues that were raised in the middle of the paper.

Another useful ending strategy is:

LOOK BACK TO THE BEGINNING WITHOUT REPEATING IT EXACTLY.

In the student's paper on drunk driving, the **opening paragraph** began with the statement in (87); the **concluding paragraph** began with the statement in (88):

> (87) Drunk driving is a major problem in our society, because it causes more fatal auto accidents than any other factor.

> (88) Alcohol combined with driving is one of the most dangerous and deadly problems we face.

He got the same message across both times without repeating himself word for word.

Finally, this strategy is often applied in expository writing:

YOUR CONCLUSION SHOULD MOVE BACK FROM THE SPECIFIC TO THE GENERAL.

A good way to let people know you're about to conclude is to

PUT A GENERAL STATEMENT AT THE START OF YOUR CONCLUDING PARAGRAPH.

We've already seen some examples:

(89)   Alcohol combined with driving is one of the most dangerous and deadly problems we face.

(90)   I think videotaping is an excellent way of expressing oneself.

This way, people can tell you're going to finish up. You don't need to rely on worn-out signals like "in conclusion" and "I will conclude by saying."

It's also handy to

PUT A GENERAL STATEMENT AT THE VERY END OF YOUR PAPER.

This strategy is found in the same samples we've just been looking at:

(91)   Videotaping can capture any occasion.

(92)   In the future, we may finally get this problem under control.

The general statement gives your readers a feeling that you've covered the main ground and that your job is done.

Suppose you wanted to make a concluding paragraph from the notes in (93). Let's imagine your paper has already supplied the details about the various points.

(93)   growing a garden—recreation—nutrition—climate—sunlight—fertilizer—pest control—good, productive way to a healthy life

You want to start with a general statement of your topic and why it matters. Then you want to review the points you have made. Finally, you end with another general statement. You might get this:

(94)   Growing a garden is a fine source for both recreation and nutrition [general statement of topic and its importance]. You should be sure to consider such factors as climate, sunlight, fertilizer, and pest control [reviews the main points]. Your garden can provide a good, productive way to a healthy life [another general statement].

You could do it in different words, but your pattern should be like this one.

20. QUIZ on concluding paragraphs

Try making a concluding paragraph from these notes. Imagine you've already supplied details about these points in your paper. Start with a general statement of your topic and why it matters. Then review the points you've made. Finally, end with another general statement.

[1] part-time jobs for students—become self-reliant—not depend on parents for everything—college expenses—tuition—books—rent—food—major preparation for later life

[2] playing tennis—good exercise—running—swinging—improve alertness—strengthen muscle tone—relaxing and building health

[3] fraternities and sororities—student life organizations—social calendar —dances—parties—trips—football games—community spirit and companionship

[4] traveling across America—scenic attractions—mountains—deserts—prairies—rivers—beaches—appreciate nature's world

[5] computers a major advance in technology—market analysis—bookkeeping for businesses—word processing—a technology for the future

21. REVIEW QUIZ on concluding paragraphs

Same instructions as on the previous quiz.

[1] offices in student government—make a difference in dealing with campus issues—housing—parking—special events—uphold student interests with an active voice

[2] bad conditions in city centers calling for major initiatives—renovations—new buildings—rapid public transport—urban renewal a remedy against the escape to the suburbs

[3] pharmacy a valuable career—preparing remedies—filling prescriptions—giving advice on nonprescription drugs—pharmacy matters for health

[4] America a nation that worships automobiles—considered a necessity—shopping—sightseeing—social life—a movable home—a fine car the heart of the American dream

[5] gymnastics one of the most interesting sports—women train for four events —the Vault—the Parallel Bars—the Beam—the Floor Exercise—gymnastics the key to strength—coordination—agility

■ J. PUTTING THE WHOLE PAPER TOGETHER

So far, we've worked on everything from the title to the conclusion of the paper. Now let's tackle the whole thing. It might help to look at some complete papers and see how they work.

J.1 Problem and Solution Papers

One common type of expository writing is the **PROBLEM AND SOLUTION PAPER**. Expository writing is frequently intended to help people recognize and solve problems.

You have a **PROBLEM** when you face a situation that might not turn out the way you'd like. You have to **SOLVE** the problem by finding a way to make the situation work out. Writing about the problem and its possible solutions can be a big help in deciding what to do. Also, your readers might save themselves a lot of trouble by reading what you said on how to solve the problem, instead of going through a long business of trial and error on their own.

The pattern for a problem and solution paper is easy to figure out from what we've seen about papers in general. In the beginning of your paper, you state the problem and say why it matters. In the middle of the paper, you give and discuss one or more reasonable solutions. At the end of the paper, you again state the problem and stress its importance; you briefly mention your solutions; and you end with a general statement that your solution can indeed remedy the problem.

Here's a paper which works like that:

(95)   CHILD ABUSE

        Although rarely spoken about by society, child abuse is one of the nation's most pressing problems today. As population continues to grow, so does the number of unwanted and unplanned children. It is estimated that six or seven out of a hundred children will be maltreated or neglected.

        Child abuse can come in three forms: (1) passive cruelty in the neglect of children by an unloving or uneducated parent; (2) occasional cruelty in the momentary violent reaction of a frustrated or overburdened parent; and (3) consistent, deliberate cruelty in uncontrollable actions by a mentally sick parent. Simple neglect is easiest to correct. Actual abuse on the spur of the moment is more serious, but still much less so than continual abuse due to mental illness.

        Most cities and counties maintain social workers to investigate reports of child abuse. These workers are sent to the reported offenders and can make recommendations about the future of the child. If counseling fails or is rejected by a stubborn parent, the child may eventually be placed in a foster home. This solution would be called for in cases of mentally ill parents.

Some high schools and colleges are introducing programs on family planning and child care. Future parents learn what their situation may be like and how to deal with it. Abuse due to ignorance or lack of attention can be reduced in this way. Also, learning how to deal with stress reduces the likelihood of sudden, violent outbursts.

Day-care centers for children help to relieve overworked parents. Parents who don't have to feel responsible for every moment of the child's day are less likely to feel inadequate and frustrated. The day-care center also benefits the child, providing companionship with other children of the same age.

If day-care centers are not available, improved public recreation areas would be a partial solution. The child would be out of the home, relieving any tensions that might build up. Companionship with other children would again be offered. Of course, some responsible adult ought to be in the area in case of an accident.

In the future, society must get a better grip on child abuse, and stop ignoring it. Social workers for offenders, school programs for future parents, and day-care centers or public recreation areas for children are all helpful. But we must do much more. We must be ready to invest all necessary resources in solving this grave social problem.

This paper demonstrates a clear organization of the topic, "child abuse." The topic is presented in the very first sentence as "one of the nation's most pressing problems today"—an obvious indication that the topic is important. The second sentence clears up what causes the problem, "unwanted and unplanned children." The strategy here is to go **from effect to cause** (see pages 200–02). To emphasize how big the problem is, the writer tells us how many children are affected.

He then moves from the **general** to the **specific** and divides up "child abuse" into "three forms," this time going **from the whole to the parts** (see pages 206–09 and 265–66). As usual, this move is marked by starting a new paragraph. The three "forms" are arranged to go **from less extreme to more extreme** (see pages 209–12). Inserting numbers in parentheses helps keep track of the three items in the list; he could also have said "first," "second," and "third" instead. This way, we have *two opening paragraphs* to state the problem, the first one more general and the second one more specific.

The middle of the paper turns to ways for solving the problem. Each of the next four paragraphs is concerned with one possible solution for the problem of child abuse: "social workers," "school programs," "day-care centers," and "public recreation areas." By putting the solution in the *first* sentence of each paragraph—the so-called topic sentence of the paragraph—the writer shows us right away how each paragraph is related to the main topic stated at the beginning. This way, each paragraph opens with a **transition statement** (see page 259).

The follow-up sentences in each paragraph explain briefly how the solution can help. He relates some things back to the "three forms" of child abuse, for example "mentally ill parents"; "sudden, violent outbursts"; "feeling inadequate and frustrated"; "tensions building up." These reminders help strengthen the organization of the middle and fasten the whole paper together.

After surveying these four solutions in the four paragraphs, the writer moves to the concluding paragraph. As we saw in the preceding section, the conclusion should *tie the middle together* and *look back to the beginning without repeating it exactly.* The topic problem is stated again, along with a warning that we must "get a better grip" on it. The middle of the paper is briefly reviewed: "social workers for offenders, school programs for future parents, and day-care centers or public recreation areas for children." Finally, the writer makes a general statement that "we should invest all necessary resources" in solving child abuse—a reminder of how important the problem is. He also reminds us that "society" has "ignored" the problem; in the opening paragraph, he has mentioned how people "rarely speak about child abuse." Exactly because people don't want to talk about the problem, we are given a good motive for reading and thinking about it.

◻ 22. QUIZ *on problem and solution papers*

Pick one of these sets of notes and write a problem and solution paper about the topic. In the opening paragraph, state the problem and say why it's important. Use the middle paragraphs to describe the solutions. In the concluding paragraph, state the problem again and say why it matters; mention the solutions you have suggested; and then end with another general statement about solving the problem. You may want to get some further information on these topics and include it in your paper.

[1]   children disabled by diseases—multiple sclerosis—nervous disorder of brain and spinal cord—muscular dystrophy—deterioration of muscle—try to improve as much as possible—physical therapy especially vital for children— big difference for later life—treating the body—massage—whirlpool baths —ultraviolet radiation—giving patients exercises—strengthen muscles— not confined to a wheelchair—resist fatigue—improving body tone—activities that build balance and agility—games that instill a sense of success in the patients—new skills—proud of performance—need for physical therapy—give disabled children a new lease on life

[2]   recent rise in crimes on or near campus—grave situation—students, faculty, administrators alarmed—thefts—assaults—vandalism—huge increase over last ten years—new security for dorms—outside doors locked—room doors locked—night watchmen—hall patrols—new escort service across campus after dark—student volunteers—escorts with walkie-talkies—requested by phone—new lighting—sidewalks—parking lots—dorm vicinity—new hot lines—phone services twenty-four hours—call for immediate help—new courses—self-defense training—better student awareness— avoid needless risks—be alert

23. REVIEW QUIZ on problem and solution papers

Same instructions as on the previous quiz.

[1] poor living conditions in city centers—noise—pollution—overcrowding—crime—urban housing renewal projects—restoring old buildings—constructing new ones—moderate rents—well-lighted—cheerful environment—regular safety inspections—sanitation and garbage removal—increasing rapid public transit—lower cost to the citizen—less need for personal cars—less engine exhaust in the air—streets less crowded—opening civic centers—free events—meetings—dances—exhibitions—performances—keeping tax monies in the city—make a fair distribution of cost of city services—work against mass withdrawal to suburbs

[2] drunk driving—half of all auto accidents in the United States—most important factor in traffic deaths—legislating stiffer penalties—mandatory jail sentence in some states—loss of driver's license—fines—better identification of offenders—blood test methods—alcohol level in the blood—one-tenth of one percent equals driving under the influence—controlling sale of liquor—bars—stores—helping chronic alcoholics—treatment centers—other means to control feelings—medication—tranquilizers—stepping up public education via television—know how much liquor is dangerous—body weight versus amount consumed—alcohol combined with tiredness, depression, frustration—find a more responsible attitude—judge one's own condition before getting behind the wheel

J.2   Description Papers

Another common type of expository paper is the **DESCRIPTION PAPER,** which tells what something is or how it works. Usually, the writer is an expert about the topic, or at least more knowledgeable about it than the general public.

As you'd probably guess, the opening of the description paper announces what you're going to describe and why it's worth describing. The opening is usually general. But you shouldn't make it *too* general by saying totally obvious things. For example, this student's opening needs streamlining because it's too general:

(96)   Our society provides people with many hobbies. Each individual gains his own enjoyment out of the hobby they desire. Most of which are perfectly suited for the individual. My hobby is motorcycling. Riding a motorcycle is an extremely thrilling experience.

Everybody knows that "society provides many hobbies" and that people "gain enjoyment" from them. So she should have started off simply by announcing her own hobby as the topic of the paper, and by saying why it matters:

(97) My hobby is motorcycling. Riding a motorcycle is an extremely thrilling experience.

People who think your beginning is too general may decide not to read on at all, because they don't expect to find out anything new from you.

Here's a complete description paper by another student.

(98)   SURFING

Surfing is a sport that consists of three main ingredients: the surfer, the board, and the waves. You might think it doesn't take much, but any old beach bum can't just buy a board, go to the beach, and be able to surf. The sport demands considerable skills and knowledge. It brings you close to nature by tuning the motion of your body in to the motion of the sea and tides.

I'll begin with the surfer. The majority of surfers today are under six feet tall and under 150 pounds, as this size person has the best stability on a surfboard. In addition, the condition of these surfers is very good, as it takes a large amount of back, chest, and shoulder muscle to fight out against an incoming current.

Just as important is the surfboard. Today there are many different sizes, shapes, and types. There are single fins, dual fins, and quadruple fins. Most surfers agree that the multi-finned boards give more mobility to produce the radical stunts. The single fin, on the other hand, is good for learning because it gives more stability.

The length of the board varies as well as the number of fins. Most boards are under six feet. As surfers get better, they usually prefer a smaller board to maneuver more easily. However, each surfer mainly has his or her own preference for the style of the board.

The third element of surfing, which is probably the most important, is the waves. The goal of every surfer is to find the cleanest, smoothest, glassiest waves possible. The smoother the wave, the easier it is to ride and to do radical stunts.

Waves come mainly in sets, so if one good wave goes by, the next one should be as good or better. The best time to find good waves is after a storm. It helps if you wait a while to allow the waves to smooth out and become glassy. If you try to surf right after a storm, the waves will probably be choppy and hard to ride.

Land shape is another factor in finding good waves. The shape of a beach can cause a current that carries the surfer down the beach to where he or she will have to continually walk back to the best part. Also, the shape of the bottom will affect the size and shape of the waves. And you should consider how near you are to towns. Most of the best surfing spots are a good distance away from inhabited places.

As one can see, surfing has many requirements and conditions. You need the right equipment, the right weather conditions, and a knowledge of the times and places for finding good waves. The sport is a great challenge, but the experience of moving with nature is worth all the effort.

The opening paragraph is a typical one. The strategy is the usual one:

START BY ANNOUNCING YOUR TOPIC.

In his opening statement, he tells us that his topic is the "sport" of "surfing," and that there are "three main ingredients" to it. In a description paper, it's a good idea to

MENTION AT THE START WHAT THE MAIN POINTS ARE

—though you don't have to do so in the very first sentence, the way he did. However, don't go into too much detail in the opening. It's fine to mention three or four points, but not ten or fifteen. If you're writing a long paper with many points to cover, just mention a few that matter most or that illustrate the topic well.

The next strategy is again a familiar one:

SAY WHY THE TOPIC IS WORTHWHILE.

His opening paragraph not only mentions the topic and its three main points but also says why the sport of surfing should be described—namely, because it "demands considerable skills and knowledge." He makes it clear why the sport is worthwhile—"it brings you close to nature."

He then moves to the middle of the paper, where the strategy is:

USE THE MIDDLE TO COVER YOUR MAIN POINTS IN DETAIL.

Naturally, we expect this writer to deal with the "three main ingredients" he mentioned in the opening part. A helpful strategy for paragraphing is:

ANNOUNCE EACH MAIN POINT AT THE START OF A PARAGRAPH.

That way, you have a transition statement to tell people where each main point begins. In our surfing paper, we have these announcements at the start of paragraphs: "I'll begin with the surfer"; "Just as important is the surfboard"; and "The third element of surfing, which is probably the most important, is the waves." This strategy makes for a good, clear arrangement.

The transition from the beginning to the middle comes between the first and the second paragraph in the paper. Here, the writer follows this strategy for description:

MENTION RELEVANT DETAILS AND SAY
WHY THEY'RE RELEVANT.

As we saw in Section F of this chapter, RELEVANT DETAILS are the ones people need to know in order to get something done. Here, the size, weight, and physical condition of the surfer are all relevant. The student says why, too: your size and weight influence your "stability on a surfboard," and your physical condition must give you the musclepower to "fight out against an incoming current."

The third paragraph takes up a second main point, as announced in the opening sentence: "the surfboard." Here we see another important strategy for description:

CONTRAST DIFFERENT KINDS OF THINGS
THAT BELONG TO YOUR TOPIC.

The student contrasts surfboards first according to the number of fins: "single fins, dual finds, and quadruple fins." He makes it clear why the contrast is **relevant**— the "multi-finned boards give more mobility," but the "single fin gives more stability." A person who was "learning" to surf would certainly need to know all these things.

The fourth paragraph is still about surfboards. He could have included this part in the third paragraph, on the ground that all the materials are about the same thing. But he decided to make a new paragraph to keep the number of fins separate from the length of the board. He tells us the average length is "under six feet." He explains why length matters: the "smaller board" helps you "maneuver more easily." In any case, the length of your board will follow your "own preference."

The fifth paragraph moves on to his last and "most important" main ingredient, "the waves." He might have saved it for last so that he could follow this strategy:

MOVE FROM YOUR LEAST IMPORTANT POINT TOWARD YOUR MOST IMPORTANT ONE.

This tactic is the same as going from less extreme to more extreme (see pages 209–12). He describes what matters here: the best surfing requires "the cleanest, smoothest, glassiest waves possible." Again, he says why these things are relevant: "the smoother the wave, the easier it is to ride and to do radical stunts."

As you'd expect for the "most important" main ingredient, he spends more than just one paragraph on it—three, in fact. First, he describes the best waves. In the next paragraph, he tells when to look for "good waves." He opens with the general rule that "waves come mainly in sets," so that you can predict one wave from the one just before it. Then he gives us a specific "time" to look, namely "after a storm." But he includes the relevant detail that you should "wait a while," and also says why: "right after a storm, the waves will probably be choppy and hard to ride."

Now that he's told us about the kind of waves to look for and the time to do it, he tells us in a new paragraph about the places to go. He starts by mentioning "land shape" and saying that it matters because it can "cause currents." This information is relevant if you don't want to spend all your time "walking back" along the beach.

He then mentions "the shape of the bottom" as another factor in "the size and shape of the waves." Finally, he advises us to stay away from "towns," because "most of the best surfing spots are a good distance away from inhabited places."

The concluding paragraph is also typical, just like the opening one. The strategies are:

CONCLUDE BY MENTIONING YOUR TOPIC.

SAY WHY IT'S WORTHWHILE.

MENTION WHAT YOUR MAIN POINTS WERE.

He says that his topic of "surfing" is worth describing because you need to know what its "requirements and conditions" are. He reviews his three major points— "equipment," "weather conditions," and the "times and places for finding good waves." He ends up by saying once more why "the sport is worth all the effort": you get "the experience of moving with nature." This paragraph covers the same points as the opening one, but not in the same words. It would be strange and annoying if your first and last paragraphs were identical.

24. QUIZ on description papers

Pick one of the following sets of notes and write a description paper about it. In the opening paragraph, state your topic and say why it's worthwhile; also, mention what your main points will be. In the middle paragraphs of the paper, cover your main points in detail and make it clear that they're interesting or relevant. Use contrasts where they're helpful. In your concluding paragraph, state again what the topic was and why it matters, and review your main points; but don't say it the same way you said it in the opening paragraph. You may want to research additional information on your topic and include it in your paper.

[1]   inflation—process where prices keep rising—buying power eaten away—poor get poorer—due to several factors—government spending going into huge deficits—more money lavished on vast weapon systems than ever before—MX missiles a glaring example—trade deficit in regard to foreign countries—Japanese products underselling American ones here in the United States—automobiles—sound equipment—computers—machine parts—many more items—domestic wage-price spiral—wages being raised to match inflation—so-called cost-of-living raises—companies raising prices to cover the higher wages—wage earners no better off than before—time for new raises—prices go up again—never-ending cycle—"taxflation"—wage-price spiral automatically putting people in higher tax brackets—but higher wages not equaling more buying power because prices rise too—people paying more taxes on what's really the same money as before—inflation one of our nation's most serious problems today—all-out effort needed to get it under control

[2]   people needing an interesting and challenging hobby—learning to operate a ham radio—opportunities—serve the government—meet people in faraway places—several requirements you should have—understanding the basics of electricity—circuit components—resistor, conductor, capacitor—what they are and what they do—mastering Morse code—complicated patterns of dots and dashes—each pattern equal to one letter of the alphabet—handy for sending messages by cable—getting a broadcasting license—attend night classes at amateur radio clubs—different licenses you can get—"novice," "technician," "advanced"—different privileges for each—novice uses only Morse code—technician can also talk but only on one frequency band—advanced can talk on many frequencies—I recommend ham radio as a hobby—time, patience, dedication well invested

25. REVIEW QUIZ on description papers

Same instructions as on the previous quiz.

[1]   nuclear energy—a power source made by splitting atoms—harnessing the energy to make electricity—but difficulties involved—fuel not easy to get—high-grade uranium very scarce—has to be concentrated with compli-

cated techniques—supply will run out in the next thirty years—plants forced to switch to low-grade uranium—harder to purify—leave more radioactivity—heat pollution another difficulty—hot water released into lakes and rivers—fish killed—water supply depleted at a time when water systems already under a strain—waste disposal another serious difficulty—wastes remain heavily radioactive for a thousand years or more—storage sites needed far from inhabited areas—inside underground rock formations—beneath the ocean floor—safety at plants another difficulty—vast, powerful cooling systems must run at all times—a breakdown could melt the whole reactor—energy equal to several exploding atomic bombs released into the environment—millions of lives lost—nuclear energy a potential source of great power—still highly controversial—needs careful study before being developed any more

[2]   America a country worth traveling across—many unforgettable sights—a country of strong contrasts—mountains and plains—swamps and deserts—crowded cities and empty wilderness—Alaska a special place—highest mountains in the United States—long, fierce winters—short, mild summers—glaciers and snowfields—vast forests—wildlife such as seals, polar bears, reindeer—California should not be missed—Hollywood the center of the entertainment industry—home of many stars—long, rocky coastline with stunning beaches—colorful big cities with tropical gardens and trees —inland desert—Death Valley the most remote and famous—Colorado dominated by Rocky Mountains—breathtaking panoramas—great for hunting—fishing—horseback riding—skiing—mountain air good for health—these just a handful of places to visit in America—an opportunity that shouldn't be lost

J.3   Persuasion Papers

Still another common type of expository paper is the **PERSUASION PAPER**, which presents an opinion or an argument and gives reasons why we ought to agree. Usually, the writer feels strongly convinced about the opinion and wants other people to accept it as well.

The **ISSUE** is the question that your opinion is about, and writers typically pick controversial issues to persuade people about. The **ARGUMENT** is made up of your opinion plus all the materials you use to support it.

Presenting an opinion can be tricky. You have to estimate how your readers already feel about the issue. There are three major conditions you might face: (1) they strongly *agree* with you; (2) they strongly *disagree* with you; or (3) they have *no* strong feelings about the issue one way or the other. The third condition is the best one for persuading people to accept an opinion they didn't already have.

As we'd expect, the beginning of the paper should follow a strategy like this:

START YOUR PAPER BY STATING THE ISSUE
AND BY SAYING WHY IT MATTERS.

However, it's not always easy to decide just how and when your *opinion* should be presented. There are several options here. First, you could

---

START YOUR PAPER BY STATING YOUR
OPINION VERY STRONGLY.

If your topic happened to be the rights of women, your opening paragraph might state a very strong opinion like this:

(99) The rights of women are a vital issue in modern America [states the is-
      sue]. Some improvements have occurred in the last ten years. *But the con-
      dition of women is still a deplorable stain on the conscience of a nation that calls
      itself a democracy.* [strong opinion]

But if you come on this heavy at the start, you could offend uncommitted persons who don't feel so strongly about it as you. You risk losing your readers, because they haven't seen any of your reasons yet, and they might decide against you be-fore you have a real chance to persuade them. So you could use this option:

START YOUR PAPER BY STATING YOUR
OPINION IN A MILD WAY.

Then you run less risk, though you still let readers know what to expect. For a paper on the rights of women, you might start this way:

(100) The rights of women are a vital issue in modern America. Some im-
       provements have occurred in the last ten years. *But the condition of
       women is still not fully up to the standards of a democratic nation.* [milder
       opinion]

You may actually think the stronger version is closer to the truth, but the milder version is less likely to antagonize an uncommitted person.

　　If your audience might disagree with you altogether, you could be even more cautious and begin in a neutral way that doesn't take sides at all:

START YOUR PAPER BY STATING THE ISSUE, BUT SAVE YOUR OPINION UNTIL YOU'VE PRESENTED YOUR REASONS.

This time, the paper on the rights of women might open like this:

(101) The rights of women are a vital issue in modern America. Some improvements have occurred in the last ten years. *But we need to consider whether the condition of women has come up to the standards of a democratic nation.* [your opinion not yet given]

Now you're only asking a question rather than stating your own opinion about how to answer it. The conclusion would be the right time to come out with your opinion, after you've offered your evidence.

The middle of a persuasion paper follows this strategy:

PRESENT CONVINCING REASONS WHY YOUR OPINION SHOULD BE ACCEPTED.

To persuade people, you have to present **REASONS** why you have your particular opinion. These reasons should be **CONVINCING**—that is, they should be important, true, and directly related to your argument. We practiced picking convincing reasons in Section G. For example, the reasons in (102) are convincing, while the ones in (103) are not:

(102)

Opinion: The condition of women is still far from ideal.
Convincing reasons:
1. Women's wages are still far lower than those of men for the same work.
2. Women are still excluded from or discouraged from entering many occupations.
3. Women do not hold many high political offices, even though they make up the majority of American voters.
4. Women are presented in advertisements as consumable objects you can buy with material commodities.

(103) *Opinion:* The condition of women is still far from ideal.
Unconvincing reasons:
1. My mother has a chronic upset stomach.
2. Women talk too much.
3. Not every kitchen has a microwave oven.
4. Most supermarkets are not open twenty-four hours a day.

The reasons in (102) are convincing because they are related to women's rights. Women should get the same wages as men for the same work. Women and men should have the same job opportunities. A voting majority should be well represented among political leaders, such as governors or presidents. And advertising is seen by millions of people, so it should not present unfair or distorted pictures.

The reasons in (103) are not convincing because they have nothing to do with people's rights. Your mother's upset stomach is a personal problem, not a general issue. The claim that women talk too much is often not true. The number of microwave ovens and the hours of supermarkets are irrelevant, because women with equal rights would not be shut up in the kitchen or forced to do the shopping all the time.

The conclusion of a persuasion paper normally follows this strategy:

END YOUR PAPER BY STATING THE ISSUE AND YOUR OPINION ABOUT IT.

By the time you get to the end, you have given your reasons, and you can state your opinion openly, even if you didn't come out with it at the beginning. It's also a good idea to

REVIEW THE REASONS THAT SUPPORT YOUR OPINION.

This strategy is like the ones we used in the problem/solution and description papers: briefly mentioning at the end what points you've covered in the middle of your paper. For example, the paper on women's rights with the reasons outlined in (102) could have this concluding paragraph:

(104)　The condition of women in America has certainly improved in the last hundred years. But there is still a long way to go. Women do not yet have equality in their wages, their professional chances, or their representation in high political offices; and they are severely misrepresented in advertisements. We should do whatever is necessary in the future to remedy this situation.

The issue and the writer's own opinion are first stated in a couple of sentences. Then the reasons for the opinion are quickly summed up in a few key words. Finally, the writer hopes that things will change for the better "in the future."

Now let's look at a complete persuasion paper by another student and see how it's put together.

(105)

THE QUESTION OF GRADES

The practice of grading has been around in our schools and colleges for so long that it seems hard to imagine doing without it. But evidence is steadily gathering that it is not in anyone's best interests. We must look for alternative ways to evaluate students.

When you're trying to learn something, you need to know how well you're doing, and what you're doing wrong. But a grade is not an informative description or a report. It is mainly based on superficial things that are easy to find and measure—the things that make you comparable to everybody else. The things that make you a special individual with your own personal talents often get ignored.

Usually, grades are figured by counting up your mistakes. The rating shows only how much you did wrong. It gives you no credit for your positive achievements. And you're left to figure out by yourself what you should do to improve in the future.

Anything worth knowing takes quite a while to learn and perfect. You don't just suddenly take one big leap. To move up to a higher level of skills, you have to accept a temporary increase in mistakes. But grades punish you for trying to move up: more mistakes, lower grades. So you tend to stick with the old ways that are safer for getting through quizzes and tests, and you don't develop your mind the way you could.

Students are so busy taking notes and cramming for tests that no one stops to ask what it all means. The result is a jumble of isolated facts, and no understanding of the world and your place in it. You don't have time to think about how the facts fit into a large pattern, and your mind ends up like a badly disorganized encyclopedia of other people's ideas.

In modern times, major human accomplishments increasingly come from cooperative efforts. Students should learn to work together rather than to fight one another in a merciless competition for grades. We can solve the problems of the future only by sharing our knowledge, not by keeping it to ourselves.

Worst of all, grades cause students to live in constant fear of failure. Anxieties in school can severely affect your personality for the rest of your life. These anxieties are especially hard on students from disadvantaged backgrounds, for whom failure in school has the most disastrous consequences.

It is a myth that students won't do any work unless they're continually threatened and forced by grades. These tactics are necessary only when the curriculum is filled with subjects and assignments that are boring and irrelevant. Students will gladly work very hard, without being forced, on tasks that are interesting and relevant to their lives.

For all these reasons, grading should be deemphasized in favor of more detailed, humane, and meaningful evaluations. Students should be viewed as individuals, not as numbers on a scale. Students should be judged on their positive accomplishments, not just on their mistakes. Students should be allowed to work out large-scale projects that interest them, rather than being stuck with brief, standardized tasks that everyone has to do. Students should be encouraged to reach out for challenging new skills and to join in cooperative efforts. Focus should be on large, significant contexts and not on isolated facts. Anxiety and fear of failure should be relieved. Only when all these things are done can education become a truly meaningful process for the individual human being.

In the opening paragraph, she lets us know right away that the **issue** is "the practice of grading." Her opinion follows very soon: "it is not in anyone's best interests," and "we must look for alternatives." This statement is fairly strong, though she doesn't say we should abolish grades altogether.

She then offers us a series of reasons for believing her opinion. Each reason takes up its own paragraph. She argues that the "superficial things that are easy to find and measure" are "not the things that make you a special individual with personal talents." Grades usually reflect "your mistakes," not "your positive achievements." The fear of mistakes makes you shy away from trying to "move up to a higher level of skills," so that "you don't develop your mind." Instead, you end up with a clutter of "facts" and with "no understanding of the world." You don't learn to "share your knowledge" in "cooperative efforts" with other students.

These reasons all relate to qualities of the mind. By arranging them that way, she follows this strategy:

PUT SIMILAR REASONS TOGETHER.

We already practiced a strategy of this kind in Section H of this chapter.

Her next reason has more to do with personality and emotion. She stresses the "anxieties" that come from living in "fear of failure." She believes this effect to be the "worst of all." By saving it until after her other reasons, she used this strategy:

PRESENT YOUR LESS EXTREME REASONS
BEFORE YOUR MORE EXTREME ONES.

This tactic was shown in Chapter 3, Section C.5, and in the problem/solution paper in Section J.1 of Chapter 4. The description paper in Section J.2 also treated its points in order of increasing importance.

In the next paragraph, the student turns to a "myth" that is commonly used to justify the use of grades. Here, the strategy is:

ANTICIPATE POSSIBLE OBJECTIONS AND ANSWER THEM.

She argues that students don't have to be "threatened and forced by grades" unless their tasks are "boring and irrelevant." If their tasks were more meaningful, students would "work very hard, without being forced."

In the concluding paragraph, she again states her opinion: "grading should be deemphasized in favor of more detailed, humane, and meaningful evaluations." She runs over all her reasons again, usually devoting one sentence to each reason. Sometimes she packs into one sentence the key words for more than one reason—for instance: "Students should be encouraged to reach out for challenging new skills and to join in cooperative efforts." This tactic is good when you don't want your conclusion to get too long. She finishes up in an optimistic way by looking ahead to the time when "education" will be "a truly meaningful process for the individual human being." This ending corresponds to the statement at the closing of problem/solution papers, where you say the problem will be solved (Section J.1).

Whether or not we agree with this student's opinion, her paper illustrates how an argument can be organized in a persuasion paper. You state the issue and give your opinion. You offer convincing reasons why your opinion should be accepted. You deal with possible objections. Finally, you give your opinion again and sum up your reasons at the end.

☐ 26. QUIZ on persuasion papers

Pick one of the following sets of notes and write a persuasion paper about it. In the opening paragraph, state the issue and your opinion in a fairly mild way, and say why the issue matters. In the middle paragraphs of the paper, give convincing reasons for accepting your opinion and present relevant evidence. In the concluding paragraph, state the issue and your opinion in a fairly strong way, and briefly review your reasons. You may want to research additional information on your topic and include it in your paper.

[1]   poverty still an important problem despite America being a rich nation—economic recovery not reaching the poor at all—instead recovery happening at their expense—poor hit from several sides at once—food stamp program under attack—poor people depending on food stamps for basic nour-

ishment—a form of money spent only on food—welfare programs being cut back—now harder to qualify—payments losing buying power because of inflation—even school lunches reduced—loss of a vital source of daily nourishment for children from poor homes—unemployment remains high among the poor—statistics misleading—cost of living indexes and tax breaks meaningless if you don't have a job—evidence adds up to gloomy picture for the nation's poor—disgrace for the world's richest country—need to re-discover our essential human values—make the true benefits of democracy available to everyone

[2] the nation's youth barely aware of their own power—voting age lowered to eighteen in many places—young voters poorly organized so far—time for a major change—several reasons—because of the number of laws that di-rectly affect young people—the draft for military service—policies regard-ing use of marijuana—legal age to buy alcohol—financial aid bills for col-lege students—because of the open-mindedness of young people—willing to try new things—not hidebound by old-fashioned views and traditions—more honest about their life style and what it means—because of the need to maintain democracy on the broadest possible base—input from all ages and groups—opinions of young people deserve a hearing—because young people are the future managers of the world—need early preparation for the tasks ahead—too many unprepared amateurs getting into public office—all these reasons why young people should assume their true political power on the contemporary scene—some signs of improvement already—much more still to be done

27. REVIEW QUIZ on persuasion papers

Same instructions as on the previous quiz.

[1] earth's natural resources limited—fact too obvious to deny—but we live as if natural resources will never run out—headed for major disaster unless outlook changes—some waste unintentional—not noticed or planned—we don't think about what it costs to live in a throw-away culture—discard mountains of containers and packaging—toss out millions of junk-mail letters without reading—keep lights, heating, air conditioning going in all sorts of buildings—almost no one inside—other waste more deliberate—throw away anything not brand-new—think happiness means a steady flow of new cars and clothes—resent it when we don't have all this—commodi-ties not only new, but as extravagant as possible—flashy, overpowered car—can race at 120 mph—gets ten miles to a gallon of gasoline—houses show off how much they cost—electrical appliance for every job—wash dishes—bake a cake in two minutes—in the past, some areas respected as natural preserves—now society running low on resources—ready to destroy any landscape to get at minerals—even our national parks threatened—ex-ploitive industries—end of scenic wonders unmatched anywhere in the

General quiz

28.

▼

on putting your own paper together

Here are several topics, some of which were already suggested in the Quiz on Making Notes in Section D. Pick one topic and expand it into a complete paper (you could use the notes you made already). Or you may want to propose your own topic and use that. Decide which kind of paper you're going to write: problem/solution, description, or persuasion—whichever seems appropriate for the topic. Get interesting and relevant details or convincing reasons from expert people or from the library. Be sure to follow the strategies we've been practicing in the last few sections, where we looked at complete papers (J.1, J.2, and J.3).

[1]   space shuttle—reusable spacecraft—applications for science and industry—different from older spacecraft

[2]   finding an apartment—rent—deposits—location—cleaning—furniture—heating—noise—pets—pests—neighbors

[3]   satellite television—number of channels—dish antenna—programs—special-interest groups—music—arts—sports—movies

[4]   junk food a threat to our national health—low in protein—vitamins—minerals—high in sugar—fat—cholesterol—problem of overweight—heart disease

[5]   buying a used car—dealer versus private owner—cost—age—checking mechanical condition—future need for repairs—getting an outside opinion

[6]   gun control an issue of much debate—terrifying rate of violent crimes—who's protecting whom in our country, and against what

[7]   new computer games—variety of responses—special effects—images—
      sounds—odds on beating the program

[8]   shopping for groceries—following your budget—finding good nutrition—
      balancing your diet

[9]   windsurfing—equipment—board—sail—learning to stay on—picking fa-
      vorable weather—good location

[10] busing children to other schools—problems of segregated schools—merits
      of our city's plan—how it's worked out so far

Backup general quiz
on putting your own paper together

29.
▼

Same instructions as on the previous quiz.

[1] writing a computer program—computer language—format of statements—bugs—error messages—accidentally losing your program

[2] federal speed limit of 55 on all highways—imposed on all states in the United States—whether it can be realistically enforced—sheer number of violators

[3] rock music—how it's different—who plays and listens to it and why—messages in the lyrics

[4] owning a horse—proper care—cleaning—prevention of disease and lameness—preparing for a show

[5] cigarettes a grave danger—should not be allowed to advertise—addicting—health hazards—lung cancer—emphysema—blood disease

[6] setting up a stereo—amplifier—turntable—radio tuner—left and right speaker channels in phase—cables—wiring positive and negative—ground—antenna—special new equipment

[7] using robots to explore outer space—conditions dangerous for humans—photograph remote places—surfaces of Venus and Mars—moons of Jupiter—rings of Saturn

[8] violence on television should be prohibited—teaches violence to children—encourages imitation—demonstrates terrorism—gives criminals ideas—makes citizens afraid—gives a bad image of America

[9] rugby an unusual sport—players often not star athletes—builds sense of friendship both in the team and with other teams—how it's played—how the team is set up

[10] raw materials in short supply—recycling can help—glass—paper—metals—getting the public to cooperate—some initiatives that are already under way

5.

Punctuating

Preview

In this chapter, you'll try some simple strategies for deciding whether and where to put in punctuation marks. Although people differ in the ways they punctuate, punctuation has some important functions that you should know about. Punctuation allows for pauses and shows what's important. It also looks back or ahead to indicate what's ending or beginning. It can help rule out doubtful statements and can mark off lists or rows of modifiers. If you understand these functions, you should be able to punctuate clearly and confidently.

Talk has its own sound and shape. Your voice starts or stops, rises or falls, and grows louder or softer. All these variations guide and shape your statements by showing what goes with what, and what's important. *Writing*, in contrast, is not presented in sounds. All you have are PRINT VARIATIONS and PUNCTUA-TION to cover the shadings that the voice can produce in talk. These resources of writing do not match those of talk very exactly. Naturally, you'll have to make an adjustment in order to shape written statements with different means than you've been using to shape your spoken statements.

Now that printing has been established for several hundred years, some cus-toms for **varying print** have become widespread. Most of the customs for *printing* books or magazines have a corresponding custom for *typing* or *handwriting*. Printers usually work from a typed or (less often) a handwritten copy anyway.

In talk, the voice can be raised or slowed down to convey *emphasis*. In print, **ITALICS** can serve the same purpose. In typing or in handwriting, you would

UNDERLINE what you wanted to emphasize. Here are some illustrations from *Fear and Loathing in Las Vegas*, by Hunter S. Thompson:

(1)   Had we deteriorated to the level of *dumb beasts?*

(2)   "You took too *much!* Look at your *face!*"

In expository writing, italics or underlinings are good for **technical terms** that you want readers to notice and remember, as in:

(3)   The *hardware* includes the parts and wiring of the computer. The *software* is the program that sets the computer up to operate in a particular language or system.

If you mention them in your paper, **titles** of books, newspapers, journals, movies, and record albums are also italicized or underlined:

(4)   My family loves to read all sorts of things—*Gone with the Wind, The Los Angeles Times, Newsweek, Psychology Today,* you name it.

(5)   Last week, we saw *Tootsie, The Return of the Jedi,* and *The Life of Brian* on HBO.

(6)   Which Simon and Garfunkel album do you like better, *Scarborough Fair* or *Bridge Over Troubled Waters?*

Some writers prefer BLOCK CAPITALS for emphatic or technical terms, as I do sometimes in this workbook. This way is not too common, and looks odd if you use it too often on the same page.

■   A.   CAPITALIZING WORDS

CAPITAL LETTERS have two main uses. One of them is:

CAPITALIZE THE FIRST WORD IN A SENTENCE.

As we saw in Chapters 2 and 3, deciding where a sentence should begin and end isn't always easy. But once you have decided, capitalizing the first word in the sentence is no problem.

The other main use of capitals is more complicated:

CAPITALIZE NAMES.

A **NAME** is a word (or a group of words) specially used to identify *one thing* in the world, most often a particular person or place, rather than *a type of thing*. The most obvious names are **people's legal names** that appear on drivers' licenses and contracts, such as "Jimmy Carter," "Tom Bradley," "Bella Abzug," "Richard Pryor," and so on. But among small groups, people can agree to use regular words as names: "Father," "Daddy," "Mother," "Mummy," "Slim," "Tiny," "Red," and so on. The capitals show that you are using specific names rather than general words. I can write "mother" for any woman who has a child (and of course for my own mother), but I write "Mother" only if I'm using it as a name for my own mother. That's why the word is capitalized in (7), but not in (8):

(7)   I'll have to ask Mother.

(8)   I haven't seen my mother in three years.

Since "Mother" means "*my* mother," you don't capitalize it after the word "my." The same goes for "Father," "Uncle," "Grandma," "Sis," and terms for other members of your family. If you use the word as a name, capitalize it. But if you have "a," "the," "my," "your," "his," "her," "our," or "their" in front of the word, don't capitalize it.

If a name is used after a **title**, the title is capitalized too, as in "Doctor Welby" or "President Carter." These words are not always used as titles, though—you can write "a doctor" or "the president" without having anyone in particular in mind. The more formal you're being, the more likely you are to capitalize a title even when it's used without the person's name, as in:

(9)   the President of the United States

(10)   Her Honor the Judge of the Fourth Circuit Court

(11)   the Mayor of the City of Chicago

(12)   the Honorable Senator from the Great State of Tennessee

Also, words for a specific group of people—somewhere betwe names and titles—can be capitalized: "Blacks," "Chicanos," "Navajos," " ators," "Jets," "the Democrats," "the Grateful Dead," "Alpha Chi Omega," so on. Finally, the word "I" is capitalized (a leftover from early printing for .

The customs for **place names** are similar to those for **perso names**. The names of particular *buildings* and *businesses* are capitalized: "Lakes e Towers," "Hawaiian Village," the "Engineering Building," "the University rary," "Ramada Inn," "Leonardo's Pizza Palace," and so forth. You also capi ze the names of *streets*, *highways* or *freeways*, *towns*, *cities*, *states*, *countries*, c nents, and *planets*: "Wall Street," "the Coast Highway," "the Golden State eway," "Harlem," "North Hollywood," "Chicago," "Oregon," "Greece," "/ ca," "Venus," and so on. If

303

written in a series, these names go from smallest to largest, with commas in between:

(13)   McCormick Ranch, Scottsdale, Arizona, U.S.A.

(14)   Longman House, Harlow, Essex, England

Addresses are written from smallest to largest like this, but with each part on a separate line. The parts of an address don't need commas between them unless you have more than one part on the same line. For example, (15) is written in a series on one line, so commas go in between. (15a) is written in a column, so commas go only between the parts on the same line, such as city and state. Zip codes usually don't have a comma in front of them, no matter how you write the address.

(15)   Bolt, Beranek, and Newman, 50 Moulton Street, Cambridge, Mass. 02138

(15a)   Bolt, Beranek, and Newman
        50 Moulton Street
        Cambridge, Mass. 02138

Again, like people, places may have **titles**. And again, the titles can be capitalized:

(16)   the Borough of Manhattan

(17)   the City of St. Louis

(18)   the Sovereign State of Texas

(19)   Florida, the Sunshine State

(20)   Illinois, the Land of Lincoln

As with people's names, these place names have been made up by taking regular words ("city," "state," "land," and so on) and agreeing to treat them each as a name for one particular place. Also, words telling what place someone or something comes from are capitalized: "American," "European," "German," "French," "Texan," "Montanan," "New Yorker," and so on.

Other special things besides people and places may have names or titles: *pet animals* ("Lassie"), *cars* ("Pontiac," "Camaro," "Thunderbird"), *brands* ("Pepsi-Cola," "Valium"), *institutions* ("the Fire Department," "Memorial Hospital"), *school subjects* and *courses* ("Anthropology," "Advanced Inorganic Chemistry," "Swahili 100"), *books* or *documents* (*Gone with the Wind, The Curse of Lono*, "the Declaration of Independence," "the Bill of Rights"), and *works of art* ("The Man with the Hoe," "The Thinker," "The Pastoral Symphony"). The custom is to capitalize all the words in these names or titles *except* "*the,*" "*a/an,*" "*and,*" and "*or,*" plus *short prepositions* ("with," "in," "of," "on," "at," and so on). However, the *first* word of the title of a published item—book, newspaper, magazine, poem, essay, record album, or whatever—is capitalized:

(21) *On the Road*

(22) *After the Fall*

(23) *The Electric Kool-Aid Acid Test*

(24) *The Dark Side of the Moon*

Finally, some *units of time* are capitalized, but not all. The names of *days of the week* and *months* are always in capitals ("Friday," "March"), and *holidays* as well ("Halloween," "Easter," "Martin Luther King's Birthday"), but not *seasons* ("summer," "autumn").

If a name has a *hyphen* in it, capitalize the word *after the hyphen* as well as the one before. You should have "Coca-Cola," "Jensen-Healy," "the North-South Freeway," "Never-Wax Floors," "Cerwin-Vega Stereos"—not "Coca-cola," "Jensen-healy," "the North-south Freeway," and so on.

☐ 1. QUIZ *on capitalizing words*

Capitalize all necessary words.

[1] on thursday, july 4, 1776, the declaration of independence was signed in philadelphia.

[2] this christmas, daddy gave me a trans-am with a jensen stereo and daytona radials.

[3] my roommate reba sue changed her major from chemistry to computer science.

[4] as a true preppy, i'll join the boston-cambridge tennis club if mummy says so.

[5] in november, the republicans gained several seats in the u.s. senate and closed in on washington, d.c.

[6] raoul duke, the infamous gonzo journalist, was supposedly kicked out of columbia university for accidentally burning down the journalism building.

[7] at the post office, i got stuck behind some jet-setter who was mailing old issues of rolling stone to hermosa beach, california.

[8] the blues brothers, john belushi and dan aykroyd, soon made a movie, also called *the blues brothers*.

[9] on monday, september 2, mr. robert williams, secretary-treasurer of airfair inc., disappeared on his way from dallas–fort worth to san juan, puerto rico.

[10] for my english class at santa fe community college, i had to read american short stories, such as "a rose for miss emily," "the gift of the magi," and "the pump house gang."

⬜ 2. REVIEW QUIZ *on capitalizing words*

Capitalize all necessary words.

[1] on the monday after the fourth of july i went to st. augustine beach and stayed at the sheraton.

[2] the headhunters club moved in at 2100 wilshire boulevard in los angeles, california.

[3] alan parsons, who engineered the album the dark side of the moon by pink floyd, later formed the alan parsons project and released friendly card, i robot, pyramid, eve, eye in the sky, and ammonia avenue.

[4] according to scene magazine, superman iii was not as successful with american audiences as superman ii.

[5] in memory of tennessee williams, our theater department performed his play sweet bird of youth at university auditorium last july.

[6] every spring, mother's class in aerobic dance is on monday, wednesday, and friday.

[7] the crown parkway mall has sears, woolco, macy's, and penney's, all in a row.

[8] bob graham, the governor of florida, made the state legislature come back in august.

[9] the most unusual movie i saw in the year 1982 was pink floyd's the wall.

[10] the u.s. interstate was not quite finished between butte, montana, and caspar, wyoming.

■ B. SHORTENING WORDS

Another print variation is to SHORTEN words when you write them. In **ABBREVIATIONS,** you omit most of the letters and leave only enough—usually two or three—letters for the word to be recognizable. Since these shortened forms save space and effort, they are nearly always made from expressions people use a lot.

Units for measuring are a well-known example: "mph" for "miles per hour," "rpm" for "revolutions per minute," "sq. yd." for "square yard," and so on. *Time units* also qualify, such as "sec." for "second," "min." for "minute," "hr." for "hour," "Nov." for "November," and so on. With units for measuring, abbreviations are preferred if you also give a *number*. If you don't, the full forms are better. For instance, you'd write "60 mph" but "a mile in an hour," "15 min." but "wait a minute," "24 hr." but "every hour on the hour," "Nov. 24" but "last November," and so forth.

Technical terms are another example: "FM" for "frequency modulation," "EEC" for "electroencephalograph," "THC" for "tetrahydrocannabinol," and so on. Technical terms people can hardly pronounce are very likely to be abbreviated, as in "DDT" for "dichloro-diphenyl-trichloroethane."

Names or titles can also get abbreviated: "Mr." for "mister" (formerly "master"), "Ms." for "miz" (a term replacing both "miss" and "missus"), "FBI" for "Federal Bureau of Investigation," "IBM" for "International Business Machines," "UC" for "University of California," and so on.

The longer a term or name is, and the more often people have to use it, the more likely it is to be abbreviated. Most abbreviations have a fixed form, and you may need to look them up in order to find the exact spelling. Dictionaries list abbreviations either in a separate table or at the start of each letter, such as "FBI" at the start of words listed under "F."

Most abbreviations end with a *period*, especially if they might otherwise be confused with different words, such as "in." for "inch" as opposed to the preposition "in" meaning "inside." If an abbreviation comes at the *end of a sentence*, you still put *only one period* (see Section C).

CONTRACTIONS are made by putting an **apostrophe** in place of the letters left out, as in "can't" for "cannot," "I'd" for "I would," "she's" for "she is." Some very common verbs often get tacked onto the end of pronouns to make contractions: "is" and "has" become "-'s," "are" becomes "-'re," "have" becomes "-'ve," "would" and "had" become "-'d," "will" becomes "-'ll," and so on. Also, "not" becomes "-n't" when you tack it onto something: "did not" → "didn't," "should not" → "shouldn't," and so on. All these shortened versions are particularly popular in everyday usage.

The apostrophe is also used for **POSSESSIVES**—words showing who or what something belongs to—either *before* the final "-s," or, if the *word already ends in* "-s," then *after* the "-s": "Sue's roommate," but "Carlos' brother" and "all the guys' cars." Of course, there's a danger of mixing up contractions with possessives. The word "it's" is short for "it is," and is *not* the possessive "its"! Think of "his," which nobody writes with an apostrophe, and you can remember that the possessive "its" also has no apostrophe.

☐ *3. QUIZ on shortening words*

These sentences contain words that can be shortened. Some are usually *abbreviated*, and others are made into *contractions* with an *apostrophe*. Shorten whatever you think is customary.

[1] If your Volkswagen engine does not get more than 25 miles per gallon, your motor is not in tune.

[2] At that very second, three men from the Central Intelligence Agency were soaring along at 600 miles per hour in a Trans-World Airlines jet.

[3] If they had not made the room 140 square feet, we could not have put in the sofas that are 6 feet, 6 inches long.

[4] You need 2 quarts of orange juice and 2 pounds of crushed ice.

[5] On December 3, the United States Senate convened in Washington, District of Columbia.

[6] Mister and Missus Hardcastle made an appointment with Doctor Gomez for January 10.

[7] They would not be so mad if you had told them it is not safe to operate the switch.

[8] I am not sure he is the one the Federal Bureau of Investigation wants.

[9] On the last day of October, the hour is finally here when he cannot deny they are after him.

[10] The plates must be 2 yards long, 4 feet wide, and 1 inch thick. They should weigh about 120 pounds.

4. REVIEW QUIZ *on shortening words*

Same instructions as on the previous quiz.

[1] They did not realize he was not supporting the Equal Rights Amendment last September.

[2] I am complaining to the Internal Revenue Service, who did not send my tax refund.

[3] How is the United States Postal Service going to deliver mail when there is no address on the door?

[4] It is hard to imagine what our country might have become without the American Federation of Labor and Congress of Industrial Organizations.

[5] Who is the person that is a representative of International Business Machines?

[6] There is not a football team anywhere that would not have a hard time beating University of California, Los Angeles.

[7] That is the policy they are adopting at the British Broadcasting Corporation.

[8] We will join the company as soon as we have completed our Master of Arts in technical writing.

[9] The Palestine Liberation Organization has not revealed what they are planning to do in January.

[10] She is a drama major at New York University.

☐ 5. QUIZ *on apostrophes*

Insert apostrophes where they belong. Watch out for singulars and plurals.

[1] Its a pity its color is so dark.

[2] I cant tell you what theyll want when theyre finished.

[3] Gails idea was that shed copy Sybils notes.

[4] Itd be nice for Moms hamster if youd clean its cage.

[5] All the companies profits are taxed according to the governments guidelines.

[6] Nobodys a harder worker when its time to help a friend.

[7] Hed use his friends house if theyd let him.

[8] Im sure well get what weve always wanted.

[9] Mr. Ross office was moved next to the presidents, where its quieter.

[10] Alls well in the armies camps, but their morale isnt up to its usual standards.

☐ 6. REVIEW QUIZ *on apostrophes*

Insert apostrophes where they belong.

[1] Peoples ideas dont always fit with their parents ideas.

[2] Its a good bet that the plane wouldve crashed if its fuel ran out.

[3] Someones in the room where theres a light on.

[4] Most of your policies owners arent as dumb as youd think.

[5] So if its all right, wed ask for everyones opinions.

[6] Theyd like to know whats the easiest way to get to the island when theres no ferry.

[7] Manys the time weve wondered what theyd say about it.

[8] The schools leaders didnt vote the way wed expected.

[9] Ten members votes are what youd need if the committees going to change its contracts.

[10] Lets see if its time for the childrens appointments.

■ C. PUNCTUATION MARKS

There are only a few common punctuation marks you need to know. They are:

.	=	the PERIOD	!	=	the EXCLAMATION MARK
,	=	the COMMA	-	=	the HYPHEN
;	=	the SEMICOLON	—	=	the DASH
:	=	the COLON	( )	=	PARENTHESES
?	=	the QUESTION MARK	" "	=	QUOTATION MARKS

Most of the marks appear only *one at a time.* For instance, if an *abbreviation* happens to go at the *end of a sentence*, you still put *only one* **period**—not one period to mark the abbreviation and another period to mark the end of the sentence: *

(25)   The bookcase measured 75 in. by 35 in.

(26)   She moved to New Rochelle, N.Y.

You'd never have two commas, colons, or semicolons in a row.

However, **quotation marks** and **parentheses** always come in *pairs*, with at least one word in between:

(27)   Why don't you say "Hello"?

(28)   Our cafeteria served a lunch of leftover carrot greens (yecchh).

Combinations of two different marks are uncommon. You almost never put a comma right next to a colon, a semicolon, or an exclamation point, or a dash right next to a period, a comma, or a semicolon. But here too, **quotation marks** and **parentheses** are the exceptions. They appear next to the other marks pretty often, as in:

(29)   "The meeting has begun," the director said, "is there any old business?"

(30)   Her suspicions worried them (had she found out the truth?), so they called her mother (the person she trusted most!).

The position of the second quotation mark or the second parenthesis usually depends on what's being inserted. If you insert a question, then the question mark comes before the second quotation mark (29) or parenthesis (30). We'll look at these matters in detail later on (in Sections E.3 and F.2).

Punctuation is your commentary on how you want your message to be organized and understood. There are not many hard and fast "rules" for punctuation.

---

* However, you can put a *comma* after the period in an abbreviation, as in "U.S.," "lb.," "etc.," and so on.

Some writers simply use more marks than others. But it's important for you to be CONSISTENT: follow the same habits and guidelines throughout your paper.

Being consistent is easy if you adopt some general PRINCIPLES FOR PUNC-TUATING. The main thing is that your punctuating should be *motivated* by principles—that you should have a reason for using the marks you used. These principles help you punctuate according to *what you're trying to say, how you feel about the message,* and *what effect you want to create.* Once you get a grasp of these principles and motives, you should be able to punctuate with confidence.

■ D. PAUSING

One common principle for punctuating is:

PUT A PUNCTUATION MARK WHERE YOU WOULD PAUSE WHEN READING ALOUD.

Reading a piece of writing aloud is a lot different from talking in a conversation. Talk is filled with starts, pauses, and stops, as we saw from the transcripts on pages 2–4. Reading aloud is less jerky and irregular, because you're not making up your statement as you go along. Most places where you consistently pause in your reading aloud are places where you'll probably want to punctuate. If you can't decide, have other people read your passage aloud while you check where they pause.

Different marks indicate pauses of different lengths. The **period** indicates the pause at the end of a *sentence.* Except for abbreviations, a period doesn't usually appear anywhere in a sentence except at the end—and there's *only one* period there (see Sections B and C).

The **semicolon** indicates a less decisive pause than a period does. Just as a period normally marks off a *sentence,* a semicolon normally marks off an *independent clause.* As we saw in Chapter 2, Section E, an independent clause has the elements of a real sentence. So the semicolon is a special signal that the independent clause just finishing is *not* the end of the sentence, because there's another independent clause coming up. The material in the new clause will be closely related to what you just said. You might have:

(31)   The months of waiting finally paid off. I was accepted.

(31a)   The months of waiting finally paid off; I was accepted.

Version (31) with the period indicates a definite pause between the blocks of material. The semicolon in (31a) indicates that the next statement will back up or explain the first by telling how the "waiting paid off."

Be careful here, though. The semicolon gets noticed more than the period and should not be used in every other sentence.

The **comma** is the most common and the least noticeable punctuation mark. It usually signals a minor pause. Especially if you have a long sentence, you'll want to allow for a pause in it. One good place to put the comma is *between independent clauses*. The comma will go just before the *linking word* that joins the clauses. The comma shows the place for readers to pause and figure out one clause before going on to the next. You're more likely to put a comma between long and involved independent clauses, as in (33), than between short ones, as in (32).

(32)   The food was good and the prices were reasonable. [short enough to do without a comma]

(33)   The food was prepared according to the finest Italian recipes, and the prices were nonetheless astonishingly reasonable. [long enough that you need a comma]

But make sure there *is* a linking word between the independent clauses. If you put *only a comma* there, you get a **comma splice** (see Chapter 2, Section F.1). You could get:

(34)   The food was good, it was prepared according to the finest Italian recipes. [comma splice]

Dependent clauses are sometimes set off by a comma, but not always. If your dependent clause comes *first*, as in (35), you're more likely to put a comma than if the dependent clause does not come first, as in (36):

(35)   When the operators went on strike, the telephone company cut back its services. [dependent clause first, so comma used]

(36)   The telephone company cut back its services when the operators went on strike. [dependent clause not first, so comma not used]

The reason must be that the linking word marks where the clause *begins*, but not where it *ends*. So if the dependent clause comes in the first part of the sentence, the comma helps to show where the clause ends.

You can also try reading the sentence aloud and watching whether you pause between the clauses. You'd probably pause for (37) and (38), but not for (39) or (40). The commas show the difference:

(37)   The journey takes two days, now that the highway is finished.

(38)   The cities are small in the mountains, while the cities are very large along the coast.

(39)   The timer rings when the eggs are cooked.

(40)   The birds leave before it snows.

Suppose you have a sentence with *many clauses*. You can put *commas* between some of them, and a *semicolon* to divide the whole thing in half:

(41)   When the letter arrived, I was very relieved; I was accepted for college,
       though I wasn't sure my parents would let me go so far away.

The semicolon helps keep the pattern of the sentence from getting confusing.

The **dash** also indicates a pause, but the effect is different from that of the period, the comma, or the semicolon. The dash allows you to *insert any kind of a construction* without worrying about clauses, linking words, or whatever. The dash means: "I'm interrupting what I'm saying right now to bring you a message." The second dash, if there is one, means: "and now we return to what I was saying before." In a passage like:

(42)   They offered me a raise of ten cents an hour—hardly a generous move—
       and praised my good work.

you can insert your commentary inside the dashes, even though it isn't a whole clause. Periods or semicolons wouldn't work very well, since they normally follow a complete independent clause:

(43)   They offered me a raise of ten cents an hour. Hardly a generous move.
       And praised my good work. [two sentence fragments]

(44)   They offered me a raise of ten cents an hour; hardly a generous move; and
       praised my good work. [old-fashioned style]

It follows that the dash is useful for marking off short fragments. Instead of punctuating the fragment as a sentence, as in (45), set it off with a dash or two, as in (46):

(45)   Nobody could have known what would come of the incident. A declaration of war.

(46)   Nobody could have known what would come of the incident—a declaration of war.

As long as you use a dash (or a pair of dashes) to attach the words to a real sentence, you won't get a sentence fragment. (See also Chapter 2, Section F.2.)

However, dashes attract attention if used often. If they're turning up, say, in every third or fourth sentence, you should find something else to use some of the time.

7. QUIZ on marking pauses with punctuation

Use periods, semicolons, commas, or dashes to punctuate these samples. If you put a period, put capitals at the start of the sentence units you get. Be careful not to make comma splices.

Example:

> The letter was a paper covered with writing and it was all in longhand I couldn't read the language I couldn't even guess what language it was a very strange one certainly

You could do it this way:

> The letter was a paper covered with writing, and it was all in longhand. I couldn't read the language; I couldn't even guess what language it was—a very strange one, certainly.

[1] I must have had misgivings about the appointment it seemed strange terribly strange in fact

[2] I didn't know who I would be meeting no name had been mentioned I had only been given instructions by a mysterious voice over the telephone

[3] the location was a lonely place where few people lived the businesses had all shut down probably many years ago at this hour of the night it would be even lonelier than usual not a good place to go by yourself

[4] as I entered the street where I was supposed to wait I could hear the clock tower strike twelve the appointed hour

[5] at first there was nobody around no light from any of the houses I could hardly see the street

[6] then I thought I heard footsteps although I wasn't certain they sounded far away like footsteps in a dream

[7] the sound came nearer it was still muffled then as I strained to listen silence fell again

[8] my eyes gradually adjusted to the dark a little at least so I stared off in the direction where the sounds were coming from

[9] looking nervously across the way I thought I saw a shape a black outline cut out of the darkness it seemed to be watching me right back

[10] there could be no doubt it was the shape of someone in an overcoat the kind of overcoat people stopped wearing years ago

8. REVIEW QUIZ on marking pauses with punctuation

Same instructions as on the previous quiz.

[1] There was something familiar about that shape maybe I was having a hallucination but I thought I had seen it before

[2] I waited quietly until the shadow was quite close too close for comfort in fact

[3] I wished I was somewhere else but there was no way to leave now besides I wanted to clear up the whole mystery

[4] The shadow stopped I heard a voice strange and yet familiar

[5] I was suddenly reminded of an incident I had forgotten about it was long ago one day I was crossing a busy street in London about ten years earlier I'd say

[6] A Bentley pulled up beside me a stranger got out and walked up to me he handed me a letter and told me I would be contacted about it

[7] I didn't get a chance to ask any questions he got back in the car and before I knew what was happening he was gone

[8] I must have forgotten about the letter since nobody ever contacted me after all I was terribly busy at the time

[9] And now I felt sure although I couldn't say how that this dark shape had something to do with that letter something important

[10] But it didn't make sense it must have been too late by now to do anything about it

■ E. INDICATING HEAVINESS

We can use the term **HEAVINESS** to designate anything that draws special attention to a statement (or to a part of a statement) as being *strange, surprising, emphatic, complicated, difficult,* and so on. The general strategy is:

THE HEAVIER AN ELEMENT, THE MORE LIKELY IT IS TO BE SET OFF BY PUNCTUATION.

Most punctuation marks can be used in some ways to indicate heaviness. To put a **period** or a **semicolon**, for example, you should consider how heavy your materials should be for the reader. The heavier your materials, the more you'll tend to spread them out over many shorter sentences (Chapter 3, Section A).

Commas can be used for setting off a heavy part of a sentence. For example, if you open a sentence with a heavy modifier, you're likely to put in a comma. Even a short modifier like "finally" in (47) can be set off with a comma if you want to suggest strong emphasis, such as being very impatient that "the letter" took so long. (48), with no comma, is less emphatic.

(47) Finally, the letter from my college arrived.

(48) Finally the letter from my college arrived.

If an opening modifier is longer and more important, you're pretty sure to put a comma:

> (49) After an agonizing delay of three weeks, the letter from my college arrived.

We'll come back to modifiers and commas in Section I of this chapter.

E.1 Exclamation Points

One punctuation mark that obviously shows heaviness is the **exclamation point**. It follows EXCLAMATIONS (emphatic statements), such as (50), or COMMANDS, such as (51). These two sentence types don't have to be the full clauses we have in regular statements—clauses with a subject and an agreeing verb. Exclamations may not be clauses at all, as in last part of sample (50). A command has a VERB that needs no subject, as in (51)—it's usually clear who's supposed to carry out the command.

 The **exclamation point** gets a great deal of attention, and if you put it in often, its effect wears off. Writers use exclamation points mostly to report actual talk— for instance, what somebody said in a loud voice:

> (50) "You heard him!" he yelled. "The White Death!"

> (51) "Don't touch me!" he shouted. [Hunter S. Thompson, *The Curse of Lono*]

But unless they're reporting actual talk, writers have to take the responsibility themselves for being so emphatic. Most writers are reluctant to do so very often. You won't come across well if you seem to be constantly shouting at your readers or ordering them around. Many successful essays and stories don't have a single exclamation point, aside from reported talk. You need a very strong motive, such as a tense moment in a story like this:

> (52) Something is wrong—one of the cars is going out of control and skidding toward the other car! [William Allen, "A Whole Society of Loners and Dreamers"]

Perhaps too many exclamation points in advertisements have made writers cautious. You don't want to look like an overdone ad in a cheap drugstore magazine:

> (53) Imagine making $10,000 a year in your spare time! Sounds unrealistic? Not at all! Hundreds of people are doing it—and having fun!

So use exclamation points sparingly. If you're too emphatic, you're not going to convince anybody.

E.2 Question Marks

The opposite of the emphatic exclamation point is the **question mark** that follows a question. Like exclamations, questions can (but don't have to) form patterns different from those of statements. Usually, a question starts with the agreeing verb—a **helping verb** (one that you can put "not" after; see page 80); in that case, the agreeing verb is *before* the subject. However, the question mark is such an obvious signal that this pattern isn't absolutely necessary.

Question marks indicate that you aren't sure about something. Like exclamation points, question marks are most often used in writing to report actual talk, as in:

(54)   "Why," I cried the other night in despair, "out of a country of two hundred and forty million people can't we find an outstanding person to run for President?" [Art Buchwald, "America's Choices"]

Otherwise, writers use question marks to suggest that readers should ask themselves about something, or at least should stop and think about it. Here's an illustration from the essay on "Friendship" by Margaret Mead and Rhoda Metraux (already quoted on page 264):

(55)   Surely in every country people value friendship?

As writers often do, Mead and Metraux go on to answer their own question, now that they've brought it up.

Or a writer may end a paper with a question, inviting readers to think over the answer on their own:

(56)   How can the sanctity-of-life argument prevail in a society that condones death in war of young men who want to live? [Marya Mannes, "The Unwilled"]

Most students have no difficulties using question marks. It's up to you whether you consider something a question. To be safe, however, steer away from questions that are sentence fragments if you think your readers might be fussy. For example, you saw on page 313 how to prevent sentence fragments, such as the second part of (57), by using a **dash** or two, as in (58):

(57)   Where is Mankiewicz tonight? Sleeping peacefully? [Hunter S. Thompson, *Fear and Loathing on the Campaign Trail*]

(58)   Where is Mankiewicz tonight—sleeping peacefully?

Keep this point in mind for your formal writing.

9. QUIZ *on exclamation points and question marks*

Decide where to put an exclamation point or a question mark. Put in dashes and capital letters as needed.

[1]   What is the meaning of freedom

[2]   What a hard question that is

[3]   Could we answer the question simply by following our ideals would that help any or is it impossible

[4]   How the philosophers have struggled with the question those fools

[5]   And what do we have to show for it today final answers or endless confusion

[6]   When did politicians ever take advice from philosophers

[7]   In ancient times, that actually did happen doesn't that sound incredible

[8]   Famous kings would get advice from philosophers what country was that Greece perhaps

[9]   Poor fellows the kings could never agree with the philosophers what arguments they had

[10] Which side was right both of them maybe don't ask me

10. REVIEW QUIZ *on exclamation points and question marks*

Same instructions as on the previous quiz.

[1]   How could the forest fires be stopped was it too late already

[2]   The situation was growing desperate

[3]   Do you remember the great river far up north

[4]   What was its name the Peace River

[5]   Have you ever seen how big it really is unbelievable

[6]   Was it possible that the fire would be stopped by the river

[7]   Away we galloped toward the riverbank like the north wind itself

[8]   What a furious ride who knows how long it lasted

[9]   When we came to the river, we saw a raging torrent

[10] Had the fury of the fire spread to the waters of the river what a sight it was

E.3   Dashes and Parentheses

On the one hand, **dashes** can be used to insert *less heavy* materials, such as brief sidelights to a main statement, as in:

(59) "G.H.," as we called him—among ourselves, though not to his face—
was a fairly tall slim man with trim whitish-grey hair. [John Craig, "I'll
Meet You at the Y"]

On the other hand, dashes can help make materials *more heavy* since the pause
can build suspense, as in:

(60) Suddenly I heard the noise of a struggle and a shot from a pistol—and the
door flew open with a crash.

Parentheses also allow you to insert materials of all kinds. You interrupt your
statement with the left parenthesis (and continue your statement after the right
parenthesis).*
But unlike dashes, parentheses nearly always indicate that the inserted materials are not as important as what's outside them. For example, you can put alternatives inside parentheses:

(61) The hamburger and shake concept, despite its newer refinements (or lack
of refinements), can still be an impulse purchase. [Elaine Kendall, "Fast
Food"]

(62) Actors need to be told all day long how great (or beautiful, or talented, or
unforgettable) they are on stage.

Parentheses offer an option that dashes don't—you can insert *a whole sentence
with its own punctuation at the end.* That way, you can get in a statement, an exclamation, or a question inside any other sentence, as in (63), (64), and (65).
The insertion does not begin with a capital, nor does it end with a period, though
an exclamation point or a question mark at the end is okay.

(63) They apologized for bursting in at that hour (it was close to midnight)
and told us the news.

(64) The report came in on Friday (it was five days late!) and wasn't read until
Monday.

(65) She smiled slightly (did she remember after all?) and led us into the dining room.

Or you can put your statement, exclamation, or question in parentheses just by
itself, as in (66), (67), and (68). Be sure to begin with capital letter and end with

---

* Square brackets [] can be used to show when you're putting something of your own into a
quotation. Some writers use them to insert things inside parentheses: ([]). And in some fields of
study and some foreign countries, square brackets are used instead of parentheses altogether.

a period, an exclamation point, or a question mark *inside* the final parenthesis. But you can't put the insertion in the middle of a sentence. You have to start a new sentence afterward.

(66) They apologized for bursting in at that hour. (It was close to midnight.) They told us the news.

(67) The report came in on Friday. (It was five days late!) It wasn't read until Monday.

(68) She smiled slightly. (Did she remember after all?) Then she led us into the dining room.

So if you want to *continue the sentence* after an inserted exclamation or question, parentheses are definitely the punctuation to use:

(69) Though the film was shot in Morocco (of all places!), the story was set in the American West.

(70) The congressman didn't deny accepting the bribe (how could he, with the transaction recorded on film?), but he insisted he hadn't been planning to keep the money for himself.

If you use dashes, the insertion is always part of the sentence it's connected to, so you don't begin with a capital letter; for example:

(71) We were safe for the time being—but for how long?

So you wouldn't have a dash right after a period, an exclamation point, or a question mark.

11. QUIZ on dashes and parentheses

In each of the following sentences, find likely places to put in dashes or parentheses. Watch for places where a statement seems to be interrupted with an insertion.

[1] An important fact though it's often overlooked! is that many Americans live their whole lives watching television.

[2] All day long, they watch some TV show western, mystery, soap opera, whatever as if they were seeing their own lives in front of them.

[3] They'll sit through countless commercials toothpaste, soap, deodorant, anything! because they're too numb to shut off the TV.

[4] It doesn't even matter what show they're watching who could tell the difference?

[5] In every show, the main ingredients plot, dialogue, situation are taken from one basic pattern it's all the same show!

[6] After a while the viewers would you believe it? imagine themselves as characters in a television show particularly a soap opera.

[7] They copy some character they see a doctor, nurse, detective, or whatever who appeals to their imagination.

[8] They may change their habits speaking, dressing, walking, and so on just to be like the character on TV.

[9] Or they go out looking for a fantastic adventure what will it be today? that will make their lives unbearably exciting.

[10] Some even commit crimes thefts, shootings, maybe murders! because it looks so glamorous on TV.

☐ 12. REVIEW QUIZ on dashes and parentheses

Same instructions as on the previous quiz.

[1] Men, women, and children who knows why? trade their own lives for fantasy lives modeled on TV shows.

[2] They don't realize the true monotony the plots of television shows are really very uniform.

[3] Each show soap opera, murder mystery, situation comedy has the same basic setup.

[4] The show must have some crisis the more terrible, the better! that has to be met.

[5] Somebody your model character, no doubt? gets in big trouble.

[6] The show usually opens either with some crime for instance, a theft, a murder, a kidnapping or else with an accident for instance, a car wreck.

[7] You then have about thirty or sixty minutes minus the time it takes for a few dozen commercials of course! to get through all the twists and turns of the story.

[8] Finally you need a cliff-hanger ending will the good guys be saved in time?

[9] The viewer gets cranked through it all never mind what it's doing to your nerves! and is even supposed to enjoy the experience.

[10] Soon, viewers are terrified of going out on the street at all who'll be the next victim you?

Punctuation can also be used to **LOOK AHEAD**—that is, to give signals about what's coming up next.

F.1 Colons

the colon lets us know that the "reason" will be given right away. Colons are also good for introducing a list (see page 356):

> (72)   There was only one reason they could have for coming out here: to col-
> lect the overdue bill.

the colon lets us know that the "reason" will be given right away. Colons are also good for introducing a list (see page 356):

> (73)   When we open up, I have to restock the supplies: napkins, straws, salt,
> and pepper.

You can specify exactly what you're announcing—such as a "reason" in (72) or the "supplies" in (73). Or you can use a colon just to show that some explanation or details are coming up:

> (74)   The investors were very worried: they had heard rumors about bankruptcy.

Skillfully used, the colon can do the same work as a connecting phrase like "this is because" or "the reason is that." Compare (74) with this longer version:

> (75)   The investors were very worried. *The reason was that* they had heard
> rumors about bankruptcy.

You can also use a colon to save words when you announce a list of similar things (see Section J). Thus, instead of (76), you could use fewer words by adding a colon, as in (77):

> (76)   That summer we had the strangest weather ever recorded here. We had a
> long drought, then a torrential rain, and two tornados.

> (77)   That summer we had the strangest weather ever recorded here: a long
> drought, then a torrential rain, and two tornados.

As we saw in Chapter 1, saving on words is a good idea.

13. QUIZ *on announcing things with a colon*

Put colons where they fit in. Cross out the words you can save.

Example:

> We knew the children would get into trouble soon. ~~We knew they would be~~ writing on the walls, teasing the dogs, and throwing food on the floor.

You could fix it this way:

> We knew the children would get into trouble soon: writing on the walls, teasing the dogs, and throwing food on the floor.

[1] My early life was divided according to schools. These schools were kindergarten, grade school, and high school.

[2] I still remember many things about first grade. I remember the teacher's face, the room with the tall windows, and the crayon pictures on the walls.

[3] And so much of the school was dark and sad. There were the narrow stairwells, the dusty coatrooms, and the drab playground.

[4] I did well in several subjects. I did well in reading, writing, and history.

[5] I was less talented in other areas. Some of these were arithmetic, physical education, and music.

[6] In high school, a lot of things changed. I mean the social life, the clubs, and the parties.

[7] I became aware of what bothered me. I became aware of being watched, following a tight schedule every minute of the day, and being treated like a silly little kid.

[8] Only later did I realize how much we had to learn that I'll never need again. I'll never need algebra, trigonometry, and geometry.

[9] And the things we really needed weren't taught in my high school. We needed sex education, family planning, and career training.

[10] There's only one thing I have to show for it all. That is that I got a diploma.

14. REVIEW QUIZ *on announcing things with a colon*

Same instructions as on the previous quiz.

[1] Some people think high school was a great time in their lives. They think it was a time filled with parties, trips, new friends, and new discoveries.

[2] For other people, it was a solemn and difficult episode. It was an episode filled with doubt, helplessness, and defeat.

[3]   Many people had a mixture of the two sides. These people had parties, trips, and friends, but also doubts, defeats, and depression.

[4]   I don't know how I ever stood the gruesome details. What I mean is for instance checking in, checking out, cramming for tests, and then forgetting it all again.

[5]   It was like a miniature of our whole society with its weaknesses. There were conflict, prudery, hypocrisy, and aggression.

[6]   Even when you weren't in class, the school had your time planned for you. They would have home rooms, study halls, supervised recreation, anything to keep an eye on you.

[7]   The ritual of test taking was the worst of all. It included trying to find out what would be on the test, reading textbooks and notes, struggling horribly to remember it all, and then having your grade depend on a few minutes of high-pressure work.

[8]   And there was more stress ahead. There were the worries, the triumph or despair over the results, and the drama at home when grades came out.

[9]   Then there were the teachers and their special demands. They made demands for attendance, interested looks, tame ideas, and respectful silence.

[10] To keep out of trouble, you had to watch out for all sorts of things. Some of these things were staying awake, being polite, and reacting instantly when you were called on.

.F.2   Quotation Marks

Quotation marks (sometimes also called **quote marks** or **quotes**) signal something you are not actually saying yourself, at least not on that occasion of writing. You are less *responsible* for a quoted statement than you are for your own statement. The first quotation mark goes at the beginning of the quotation, and the second quotation mark goes at the end.

The most common use for quotation marks is to REPORT TALKING, as in:

(78)   At recess in the schoolyard, a Negro boy—no bigger or smaller than myself—addressed me. "You look real pretty, Sis," he said. [Jim Brown, "Growing Up on Long Island"]

The first word of the quotation (here, "You") is normally written with a **capital letter**. The capital might not be used for just one or two words taken out of a longer statement, but it would be otherwise.

You may be reporting what you yourself said or thought on some other occasion. Here George Burns quotes what he said seventy-six years before the time he's writing:

(79)   Finally, with a weak smile, I said: "Mama, I'm not in the ice business anymore." [George Burns, *The Third Time Around*]

Unless the quotation is at the very beginning of a sentence, as in (78), *a comma goes right before the quotation*. Less often, a colon is put there, as in (79).

When you're reporting talk in writing, you normally begin a *new paragraph* each time a *new speaker* starts:

(80)   I finally called my manager Irving Fein, and said, "Irving, maybe I'm making a mistake playing God."

"How can you make a mistake?" Irving replied. "They're paying you a fortune. If there's anybody who might be making a mistake, it's Warner Brothers." [George Burns, *The Third Time Around*]

In addition to quotation marks, writers usually put in signals to show who's talking, such as "I said" and "Irving replied" in (80). If there are just two speakers and it's clear who's saying what, these signals are sometimes left out, as in:

(81)   I said, "Mama, I'm now in the used bottle top business."

"I can see that," she said, without changing her expression, "with other people's bottles."

"Mama, are you mad at me?"

"No, I came up here to take a tap dancing lesson!"

"But how did you know I was up here on the roof?"

"Everybody in the building knows you're up here. How often do people see seltzer bottles flying past their windows?" [George Burns, *The Third Time Around*]

Once we know who's talking, we can figure out what "I" said and what "she" said. We just assume the two speakers are taking turns and changing whenever a new paragraph begins.

In reported talk, the first word of the quotation is usually **capitalized**. But if a quoted statement gets *interrupted* to identify the speaker, its *continuation* after the interruption doesn't have to start with a capital letter—for instance:

(82)   "I can see that," she said, without changing her expression, "with other people's bottles."

Putting punctuation near a quotation mark can be tricky. In most materials printed in the United States, * a **period** or a **comma** comes *before* the final quotation mark:

---

* This usage is preferred by the Modern Language Association, but is not followed in many scientific and technical publications, nor in most foreign countries, where nothing goes inside quotation marks except what is an actual part of the quotation.

(83)   "Mama, I'm now in the used bottle top business."

(84)   "I can see that," she said.

A **semicolon** or a **colon** always comes *after* the final quotation mark:

(85)   I was proud to be called "a professional"; I had worked very hard to deserve it.

(86)   We found out what they meant by "service charges": cleaning fees for whatever mess the previous occupants had left behind.

An **exclamation point** or a **question mark** can go either before or after the second quotation mark, depending on what you mean. If the *quotation itself is an exclamation or a question*, then the exclamation point or the question mark should go *before* the second quotation mark, as in:

(87)   "Mama, are you mad at me?"
        "No, I came up here to take a tap dancing lesson!"

But if the *writer* is the one doing the exclaiming or questioning, and the quotation itself is *not* an exclamation or a question, then the exclamation point (88) or the question mark (89) should go *after* the second quotation mark:

(88)   And those people call themselves "professionals"!

(89)   What could they mean by "service charges"?

Here's another tricky matter.* You can put one quotation between **single quotes** to go *inside* another quotation between **double quotes**. Compare:

(90)   "And those people call themselves 'professionals'!" she exclaimed.

(91)   "What do you mean by 'service charges' on this bill?" I asked.

Therefore, a quotation inside a quotation might end with *two quote marks* in a row, one *single* and one *double*, with the period (92) or the comma (93) just *before both marks*:

(92)   "Don't pay any more of these 'service charges,'" she said.

(93)   She said, "Don't pay any more of these 'service charges.'"

Fortunately, cases like these are not common.

* Single quotes are often preferred over double quotes in scientific and technical publications, as well as in Great Britain. Sometimes, double quotes are then used for a quotation inside another quotation.

15. QUIZ *on where quotation marks go*

Put in quotation marks. Watch out where they go next to other marks: period, comma, semicolon, colon, exclamation point, or question mark.

[1]   The dictionary had no such word as troddle; did he mean to write toddle?

[2]   We're leaving now, she said, but we'll be back in twenty minutes.

[3]   The sign said No admittance, but the doormat said Come In.

[4]   What should we do now? he said, we can't just wait here forever!

[5]   My roommate can't even spell words like whether, light, or fourteen!

[6]   I said, look here, the title says contact where it's supposed to say contract.

[7]   Can't you see the sign that says No Smoking in the Elevator? the doorman asked.

[8]   But somebody has changed the sign to read No Stroking, we replied.

[9]   The letters in the left-hand pile should be stamped Air Mail; the ones in the right-hand pile should be stamped Special Delivery.

[10] What good does that do? she asked, the envelopes are empty!

16. REVIEW QUIZ *on where quotation marks go*

Same instructions as on the previous quiz.

[1]   The label said Danger! and the cap said Keep Away from Children!

[2]   What a mess! I said, can't you straighten things up a little?

[3]   No, they replied, you do it yourself.

[4]   It should say This End Up on the box.

[5]   But somebody has written This End Down, I said to myself.

[6]   On July 7, 1982, a headline in the *Oregonian* read: Reagan Raps Need to Prove Sanity.

[7]   I said, maybe they mean: Reagan's Speeches Need to Prove Their Sanity.

[8]   My friend said, No, they probably mean, Reagan Criticizes the Need for a Sanity Test in a Criminal Trial.

[9]   After the accident, we changed the sign reading Freight Elevator so that it read Fright Elevator.

[10] Before we could say, Who are you? the masked man was gone.

17. QUIZ *on punctuating reported talk*

Supply punctuation and capital letters for this conversation. Watch out for places where speakers take turns.

[1] A young man opened the door, looking very sleepy what's up he asked

[2] I have to talk to you about something I replied and it's very important

[3] Not at this time of the night he said would you please come back in the morning

[4] I'm afraid I can't wait I said but I won't keep you long

[5] You won't keep me at all he said and tried to close the door

[6] Look I just told you I can't wait I insisted, holding the door open

[7] Leave me alone he shouted and get out of here
     Hey you keep quiet or I'll bring some of my colleagues to see you

[8] When he heard that he calmed down and asked me are you from the police

[9] You might call it that I replied but I'm not here on business

[10] What do you mean by the word business he asked suspiciously
     I'll tell you what I mean right now

18. REVIEW QUIZ *on punctuating reported talk*

Same instructions as on the previous quiz.

[1] I'm not here on business like in official police business I said but I do have something on my mind

[2] So let's hear it he said tell me what's up and get it over with

[3] Recently a friend of mine had what you might call a mysterious accident I said do you know what I mean

[4] He shook his head I don't know yet go on

[5] My friend was driving home late after a little party with friends

[6] What does that have to do with me he said

[7] But he never got home at all I said and do you know why not

[8] It was because his car went out of control on a perfectly straight smooth road with no other traffic on it I went on

[9] I watched him closely as I said don't you think that's a remarkable coincidence
     why do you say coincidence

[10] He was seen with you earlier that day having a pretty rough argument
downtown
who said it was rough he asked
well then how did you get that bruise on your face

F.3   Quotation Marks for Words with Special Meanings

Even when writers aren't reporting actual talk, they can put quotation marks
around *words with special meanings*. That way, we know the words are *not* being
used in their *ordinary meanings*. These quotations do not begin with a capital
letter unless there is a name or title involved.

Slang words sometimes get put in quotation marks. One student wrote:

(94)   We totally *"freaked out"* during exam week because we took too many
"*uppers.*"

This usage seems to be a bad compromise. If you think your readers won't mind
the slang words, you don't need to apologize by putting in quotation marks. But if
you think people will object to slang words, then say it some other way:

(95)   We totally *lost control* during exam week because we took too many
stimulants.

You might use quotation marks if you're quoting the slang words that somebody
said:

(96)   The accused gave the excuse that he was "super-wasted" at the time of
the fight.

Technical terms can go in quotation marks, especially if the words also have
some *everyday meaning you don't want*:

(97)   If you "crash" the system, the computer "dumps" your whole file.

You "crash" a system by making it impossible to run any programs, and the computer erases ("dumps") what's in its memory. It's not like "crashing" a car or
"dumping" garbage.

Technical terms can go in quotation marks if the terms are *unusual* or *hard to
recognize*:

(98)   An "actuarian" is someone who uses probabilities to calculate a profitable
insurance risk.

However, once you've explained a term, you can stop using the quotation marks.

Technical terms can go in quotation marks if the terms are *exaggerated* or *pompous*:

(99)   Finding the door unlocked, the campus police wrote me a "notification of security deficiency."

This way, readers can see that you aren't responsible for such high-flown language.

In general, words with special meanings should not be put in quotation marks too often in one paper. It's normal to use the marks for the *first* time, and to drop them after that. By then, people should know what meaning you intend.

19. QUIZ *on quotation marks for words with special meanings*

Put quotation marks around words with special meanings that are slang, technical, unusual, or pompous:

[1]   To fool the public, the Press Secretary made a nonoperative statement, more often known as B.S.

[2]   They announced their Gadget of the Week—a Retroflex Unscrambler for those times you decide in the midst of making scrambled eggs that you'd rather have them sunny-side up.

[3]   Three rowdies were jailed on charges of intoxication-induced misconduct.

[4]   Besides, they were charged with refusing to cooperate in the due pursuit of justice.

[5]   The regional detention center was set up for the correction of socially deficient individuals.

[6]   When the company finally sent the refund two years late, they included a note thanking us for kind and considerate patience in this unavoidable delay.

[7]   The Secretary of State explained that the missiles were needed for the peacetime deterrent factor of first-strike nuclear capacity—what ordinary people call starting a war.

[8]   According to him, bombs that terminate the human factor while preserving tangible assets make more sense, first-strike-capacity-wise.

[9]   A doctor from the hospital diagnosed a disease she preferred to call dipsomania.

[10] The computer loads the answer on nth right file and the source-on program.

Same instructions as on the previous quiz.

[1]   When the Klan had no luck with what they called a friendly warning, they came in the middle of the night to try some gentle persuasion.

[2]   President Nixon sent out his Plumbers to plug a security leak.

[3]   Before the bridal shower, she had a pre-shower to get into the mood.

[4]   This new electronic personality regulator has been praised as a miracle of the modern science of emotionology.

[5]   Its three-speed intensity function determiner puts you down, up, or in the middle of any emotion, while the environmental feedback monitor can be set to spread your emotions to other people.

[6]   A strange ailment known as Acquired Immune Deficiency Syndrome has suddenly appeared.

[7]   Today's newspaper reported a man who claims to have superhuman powers he gets from a device known as a transmagnification diode.

[8]   It also reported a trial where the defendant told the court he resisted arrest because he flipped out when he got busted.

[9]   It says here that the court gave him thirty days in jail for aggravated contravention of municipal ordinances regulating public behavior.

[10] When the defendant said the judge was putting him on and being uptight, ten days were added for failure to maintain due and proper respect toward a legal official.

■   G.   USING PUNCTUATION TO LOOK BACK

Some punctuation marks help readers to **LOOK BACK** rather than ahead. The most important mark here is the **comma** that indicates how far back to look in places where there might be more than one possibility.

G.1   Modifiers and Relative Clauses

With MODIFIERS, the usual strategy is:

> *A COMMA SUGGESTS YOU SHOULD LOOK BACK*
> *FURTHER THAN YOU WOULD WITHOUT IT.*

This strategy can help sort out what a modifier should go with. Here's an illustration with arrows to show what the modifier looks back to:

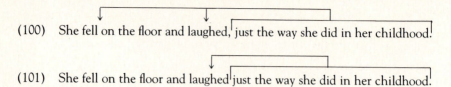

(100)   She fell on the floor and laughed, just the way she did in her childhood.

(101)   She fell on the floor and laughed just the way she did in her childhood.

Version (100) tells us that both actions, the "falling on the floor" and the "laughing," were done the same as "in her childhood." If we take the comma out in (101), we're suggesting that only the thing right before "just the way"—namely, the "laughing"—was like "her childhood."

Or take these statements, again supplied with arrows to show what the modifier goes with:

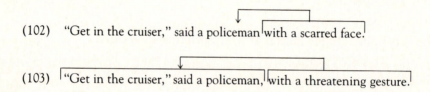

(102)   "Get in the cruiser," said a policeman with a scarred face.

(103)   "Get in the cruiser," said a policeman, with a threatening gesture.

In (102), the absence of a comma before "with" indicates that the following modifier *identifies* (singles out) the "policeman"—he's the one "with a scarred face." The modifier only looks back to the thing right before it ("policeman"). In contrast, the comma before "with a threatening gesture" in (103) looks further back: the act of saying "Get in the cruiser" was accompanied by the "gesture." A policeman always has the same face, but his gesture probably lasted only a moment.

This comma strategy can also be used to indicate what a *clause* is supposed to go with. The most important case is the **RELATIVE CLAUSE**: a *dependent clause* that "relates" to something already expressed (see also page 348). These clauses are usually introduced by **RELATIVE LINKING WORDS** like "who," "which," "that," "where," "when," "in which," "for which," and "because of which." The key position for a comma is *right before* one of those relative linking words. The first main strategy is:

**WITHOUT A COMMA, THE RELATIVE CLAUSE
SHOULD LOOK BACK ONLY TO THE
EXPRESSION JUST BEFORE IT.**

Suppose you had:

(104)   The manager told us the conditions *which* were contained in the company contract.

In (104), the absence of a comma indicates that "which were contained in the company contract" looks back only to "conditions." The other main strategy is:

WITH A COMMA, THE RELATIVE CLAUSE
SHOULD LOOK FURTHER BACK.

You might have:

(105)   The manager came two hours late to the meeting, *which* was extremely annoying.

This time, the comma tells us that it was the whole situation—the "coming two hours late"—that was "annoying," and not the "the meeting" mentioned just before the word "which."

There's something else to consider here. Some relative clauses IDENTIFY the thing they follow, and other relative clauses only DESCRIBE it. Look at these examples:

(106)   A woman who runs for mayor of New York City faces an uphill battle.

(107)   Bella Abzug, who ran for mayor of New York City, is a hard worker.

In (106), the relative clause *identifies* what sort of "woman" would face "an uphill battle." But in (107), the woman's name already identifies her; the relative clause only *describes* her. The strategy is:

MARK OFF WITH A COMMA
ONLY A RELATIVE CLAUSE THAT DESCRIBES,
NOT ONE THAT IDENTIFIES.

If the statement continues after the describing clause, put a second comma where it ends, as in (107).

If a name is very common, or if several people in one situation have the same name, you might put in an identifying clause with no comma, as in:

(108)   I don't mean the John Anderson who ran for president. I mean the John Anderson who writes psychology books.

The comma can make a big difference between two statements that otherwise look the same:

(109)   My grandfather who lives in Vermont came to visit.

(110)   My grandfather, who lives in Vermont, came to visit.

In (109), the absence of a comma indicates that the writer has more than one "grandfather" and wants to point out the one "who lives in Vermont." In (110), the commas show that the identity of the "grandfather" is taken for granted and that the writer only wants to describe him by saying where he lives; you're more likely to make a *pause* for the comma if you read the statements aloud.

21. QUIZ *on using punctuation to look back*

Decide whether a comma should go before the modifiers or relative clauses in each of the following sentences. The comma makes you look back further than you would without it. Also, use a comma only for a relative clause that describes what's ahead of it; the end of the clause gets a second comma if the statement continues after it.

[1]   George Washington who never told a lie got to be president anyway.

[2]   The office that specially requested the report never picked up the finished copy which was surprising.

[3]   In Arizona where the humidity is low old documents are preserved better than in Alabama where the humidity is very high.

[4]   He left town in the middle of the night just like we expected. In fact, he left town in the middle of a night just like tonight.

[5]   The finance companies kept after my father who never paid his bills.

[6]   We never did locate the place where the incident occurred.

[7]   He smashed that beautiful new car which made his parents furious.

[8]   The sheriff was told to look for a man with his eyes crossed.

[9] We had a big party and a sing-along with Santa giving presents to everybody.

[10] Some friends whom I saw at the party told me the bad news which I thought wasn't very good timing.

22. REVIEW QUIZ *on using punctuation to look back*

Same instructions as on the previous quiz.

[1] I had to read five books which is a strain when you're taking three other courses.

[2] I only enjoyed the book which was about the South Sea Tribes who seem to be easygoing people.

[3] The tribe which I liked most was the Trobriand Islanders who live in New Guinea.

[4] They have some customs which you wouldn't believe if I told you.

[5] If I ever get to the place where they live which seems unlikely I'll know just what to do.

[6] That would be a tangible benefit which you don't often get from college courses.

[7] I might get on a boat and sail to the South Seas just like the early explorers.

[8] A person like me wouldn't have any trouble adjusting to the life that they live on the South Sea Islands with the way I love the ocean.

[9] Anyone who can adapt to life in the tropics should leave while there's still time.

[10] You don't know when the chance will come again. It might come after you're all settled with a family and a job when you can't get away.

G.2   Punctuating Appositives

An **APPOSITIVE** is usually a noun group (a noun or a phrase built aroun(d) noun) that is simply placed after another noun group and set inside **commas.** (th)e appositive is another way to describe the same thing, but you aren't actually (ma)k-ing a statement with a verb in the middle.

Most appositives *describe* the thing they follow, rather like a describing (rel)ative clause. Compare:

(111)   The University of Florida, *one of the nation's top party schools,* i(s ge)tting better every year. [with appositive]

(111a)   The University of Florida, *which is one of the nation's top party schools*, is getting better every year. [with relative clause]

(112)   The candidate, *a wealthy real-estate salesman*, was defeated in the election. [with appositive]

(112a)   The candidate, *who was a wealthy real-estate salesman*, was defeated in the election. [with relative clause]

Appositives are easy to spot, since you wouldn't otherwise have two noun groups placed next to each other with no verb or linking word in between. The commas go where you'd pause if you were reading out loud. You put one comma *before* the appositive, and another comma *after* it, unless the sentence ends there with a period.

Only rarely does an appositive *identify* the thing it goes with. A *name* is usually involved, as in:

(113)   My *friend Cathy* has a huge sheepdog.

(114)   *Nick the Greek* won the game.

Like identifying relative clauses, these identifying appositives don't need commas. You would not pause when reading them out loud, because a pattern like "my friend Cathy" or "Nick the Greek" is treated as one unit.

The commas are most likely to get left out when the appositive is *short* and *simple*. If either the first or the second noun phrase is long and complicated, the appositive tends to take commas, no matter what kind it is. You could have:

(115)   A friend of mine at the animal shelter, *Cathy Michelson,* has an enormous sheepdog.

(116)   Nick Stavros, *the center on our city's basketball team,* won the game for us again.

On these, you would probably pause when reading out loud.

☐ 23. QUIZ *on appositives*

Put a comma before and after every appositive that needs it. Some sentences have more than one appositive.

[1]   He bought the house from Sandra Palmer a friend of his wife's.

[2]   The Jacksons our neighbors across the way decided to get rid of their old car the biggest expense they had.

[3]   Ms. Jarelsky our managing executive outlined her new plan the best one so far.

[4] Mrs. De Rocks the season's most gracious hostess mixed everyone a dry martini her famous specialty.

[5] The stranger a woman about fifty years old introduced herself as Maurine Matsumoto the city health inspector.

[6] Our doorman Gerald moved to another building the Imperial Hotel.

[7] There were only two letters one from the government and one from the electric company.

[8] Harlem a depressed area was soon recognized as a target for aid programs.

[9] John the Baptist fell into the hands of Herod the ruler of Galilee.

[10] Dreyfus a former police chief and certified lunatic demanded the assassination of Inspector Clouseau the world's worst detective.

24. REVIEW QUIZ *on appositives*

Same instructions as on the previous quiz.

[1] Hurricane David the most violent one that year was about to hit Cape Hatteras.

[2] On the Gulf Coast the other side of Florida Hurricane Frederick was building up.

[3] Mac the Finger went to Louie the King.

[4] My brother Enrico introduced us to his girlfriend the one with an eagle nose.

[5] My brother Terry and my sister Mary never got along.

[6] My roommate Melissa always plays twangy country music a real headache.

[7] Fifty dollars a huge sum in those days was out of the question.

[8] On Thursday my twentieth birthday we went to see a movie *The Return of the Jedi*.

[9] On Friday we consulted Francisca Reyes my supervisor and Stephanie Engstrom her advisor.

[10] His old car a dented Buick was still faster than his new one a shiny limousine.

■ H. CLEARING UP DOUBTFUL STATEMENTS

As we saw in Chapter 1, Section F, you can look pretty silly if you make a doubtful statement with some meaning besides the one you intended. The same effect can come from leaving out punctuation, as in (117) and (118), or from putting it in where it shouldn't be, as in (119):

(117)   Connie Was Tied, Nude Policeman Testifies [*Atlanta Journal*, June 17, 1976]

(118)   Lie Detector Tests Unreliable, Unconstitutional Hearing Told [*Hartford Courant*, Nov. 16, 1977]

(119)   It contains the richest array of gadgetry ever put into a Rolls Royce, including refrigerator, bar, ladies, vanity table, and a rear seat that reclines to form a double bed. [*Philadelphia Inquirer*, Nov. 25, 1976]

(117) left out the comma after "Nude," giving us a "Nude Policeman." (118) left out the comma after "Unconstitutional," giving us an "Unconstitutional Hearing" instead of "Unconstitutional Lie Detector Tests." In (119), the extra comma after "ladies" (where an apostrophe was needed) makes it look like "ladies" are one of the "gadgets" in a "a Rolls Royce."

Obviously, commas are important for indicating which elements should or should not go together. Our tests showed that students got confused by statements like (120) and (121) without a comma, but they had no trouble with (120a) and (121a) when the comma was put in:

(120)   Whether or not we win the game will be very exciting.

(120a)   Whether or not we win, the game will be very exciting.

(121)   When I tried to run the store detective tackled me.

(121a)   When I tried to run, the store detective tackled me.

In (120a), the comma pins down "win" as the last word of the first clause, so that "the game" is easy to put together with "will be very exciting." In (121a), the comma shows that "run" is the last word of that clause, so "the store" must go with "detective."

As we have seen (page 44), the point is not that people can't figure out what you mean. The point is that the doubtful meaning can distract people's attention from what you're trying to say. If you write:

(122)   While I vacuum another busboy in my area tables all the chairs.

nobody'd really think you were "vacuuming another busboy." But they might notice that meaning and think you were writing carelessly. Certainly, you don't want readers wandering off into weird ideas. So use commas to separate elements that shouldn't get run together.

25. QUIZ *on using commas to clear up doubtful statements*

Put commas where they're needed to clear up doubtful meanings.

[1]   Let's throw out both the shoes and the baby will never miss them.

[2]   While she was watching her swallow a flock of seagulls came and drove it away.

[3]   While the kitten was playing the piano lid fell down with a crash.

[4]   My neighbor painted the fence and all his kids had to help out.

[5]   As she was washing the trash compactor blew the main fuse.

[6]   Since I've been pulling the dandelions up my nose has been itching.

[7]   In order to read my mind must be clear.

[8]   As time marches on flat feet are becoming a less common ailment.

[9]   Every time I breathe the fire on the candle flickers.

[10] We made submarine sandwiches out of the chicken and the dog stole them all.

26. REVIEW QUIZ *on using commas to clear up doubtful statements*

Same instructions as on the previous quiz.

[1]   Just when the center went to shoot the referee blew his whistle.

[2]   Seeing the weight of the wagon the fraternity men were shoving the sorority women came to help.

[3]   As the truck driver ran over three pedestrians waved hello.

[4]   As we sat down to eat the trees dropped some twigs on our heads.

[5]   All the time my uncle was waxing and polishing his bald head was dripping with sweat.

[6]   If you're not careful how hard you stomp the woman downstairs will hear you and complain.

[7]   Whenever he's drunk his swimming pool is filled with empty bottles floating around.

[8]   Pour boiling water in the bathtub and your stomach will feel better after the bath.

[9]   Before the pilots took off the flight attendants' uniforms had to be changed.

[10] At the time we were out walking an alligator ate our neighbor's poodle.

■ I. PUNCTUATING MODIFIERS

In this section, we'll look at some reasons for using or not using commas with modifiers. We've already seen a few kinds of modifiers that take commas or dashes in Sections E and G.

I.1 Two Modifiers in a Row Before a Noun

Suppose you have *two modifiers in a row before a noun*—that is, two words that describe or specify the thing indicated by the noun. You *don't* put a **comma** between a modifier and a noun. But you must decide whether you *do* need a **comma** *between the two modifiers.*

One easy thing to consider is whether the modifiers are *movable*—that is, whether they could switch places. The main strategy is:

IF THE POSITION OF THE TWO MODIFIERS IS NOT MOVABLE, YOU DON'T NEED A COMMA BETWEEN THEM.

For instance, if one modifier applies to another modifier, you couldn't move their positions around, so don't put a comma between them:

    (123)   a *very busy* day [not: a busy very day]

    (124)   an *oddly shaped* piece [not: a shaped oddly piece]

    (125)   an *unusually high* rate [not: a high unusually rate]

Many other kinds of modifiers can't be moved around either:

    (126)   *many nice* presents [not: nice many presents]

    (127)   *some easier* jobs [not: easier some jobs]

    (128)   *more unemployed* men [not: unemployed more men]

    (129)   *fewer serious* mistakes [not: serious fewer mistakes]

    (130)   the *biggest defensive* lineman [not: the defensive biggest lineman]

    (131)   a *better amateur* dancer [not: an amateur better dancer]

    (132)   the *worst industrial* accident [not: the industrial worst accident]

    (133)   an *old iron* gate [not: an iron old gate]

    (134)   the *small silver* spoon [not: the silver small spoon]

(135)   the *yellow brick* road [not: the brick yellow road]

(136)   a *great American* tradition [not: an American great tradition]

(137)   a *dangerous chemical* compound [not: a chemical dangerous compound]

Since you can't switch any of these pairs of modifiers around, you don't put a comma between them.

You could have more than two of these unmovable modifiers in a row before the noun. You still don't need commas:

(138)   a big old stone church [not: an old big stone church or a stone big old church]

(139)   two priceless Indian earrings [not: two Indian priceless earrings or Indian two priceless earrings]

Such low rows of modifiers don't come up very often, however.

Movable modifiers, which are not as common as unmovable modifiers, follow this strategy:

IF THE POSITION OF THE TWO MODIFIERS IS MOVABLE, YOU NEED A COMMA BETWEEN THEM.

You could have:

(140)   a *difficult, complicated* assignment [OK: a complicated, difficult assignment]

(141)   a *peaceful, undisturbed* life [OK: an undisturbed, peaceful life]

(142)   *powerful, terrifying* forces [OK: terrifying, powerful forces]

(143)   *pleasing, symmetrical* designs [OK: symmetrical, pleasing designs]

(144)   a *transparent, oddly shaped* crystal [OK: an oddly shaped, transparent crystal]

You could have more than two movable modifiers before the noun. You still need commas:

(145)   solid, beautiful, durable forms [OK: beautiful, solid, durable forms or durable, beautiful, solid forms]

Suppose two modifiers are joined with a **linking word**, such as "and" or "or." The usual strategy is:

DON'T PUT A COMMA BETWEEN TWO
MODIFIERS LINKED WITH "AND" OR "OR."

You might have:

(146)   that *ridiculous and ugly* building

(147)   the *strange and terrible* saga

(148)   any *missing or unidentified* aircraft

(149)   an *earlier or later* design

However, if you link two modifiers with "but," or with any other linking word for a *contrast* (such as "though"), the usual strategy is:

PUT A COMMA BETWEEN TWO MODIFIERS
JOINED WITH A CONTRASTIVE LINKING
WORD.

You could have:

(150)   a *tiny, but very expensive* battery

(151)   an *unpleasant, although necessary* change

So if you're in doubt about two modifiers in a row before a noun, you have two things to consider. A comma does *not* go between them if their *positions are not movable* or if they are *linked with "and"* or "*or.*" A comma *does* go between them if *their positions are movable*, or if they are *linked with "but"* or with any other linking word for a *contrast*. When you have more than two modifiers in a row before a noun, use these same strategies.

☐   **27. QUIZ** *on two modifiers in a row before a noun*

Decide whether you need or don't need a comma between each of the following pairs of modifiers in a row before a noun.

[1]   We visited the extensive well-known campus with its gigantic spectacular football field.

[2]   The big orange lamps with their brilliant high-powered lights made an impressive memorable scene.

[3] The empty wooden bleachers with their long even rows looked like a big wide stepladder.

[4] They had just mowed the smooth green lawns and painted the tall white fences.

[5] Overlooking that monstrous and awesome stadium was a little tiny perch for the newscaster.

[6] The very next week they announced the first important football game and staged a special outdoor rally.

[7] There was a small but spirited crowd from the opposing team's college, carrying floppy funny-looking banners.

[8] Shrill unfriendly chants were heard, but there were no unruly or violent encounters.

[9] After a few tense moments the restless excited crowd went to the stadium to look for good empty seats.

[10] It was a rough though mostly fair game between two powerful evenly matched teams.

28. REVIEW QUIZ *on two modifiers in a row before a noun*

Same instructions as on the previous quiz.

[1] In the last few years, unemployment has become a distressing unavoidable problem.

[2] Some informed people admit that the economy is in pretty bad shape.

[3] But many worthwhile opportunities can be found if you make a long and hard search.

[4] For many highly competitive jobs, you need technical specialized skills because there is a large unskilled labor force.

[5] But you also need diversified flexible skills in case a new or undeveloped field opens up.

[6] It's a nice comforting feeling to know you can't get stuck in the same old job.

[7] Working at a tedious monotonous job makes you feel like every single day is grey rainy weather.

[8] A challenging creative job is more like a cheerful blue sky.

[9] A difficult though rewarding experience is to build a significant new invention.

[10] For example, compact little calculators came along and replaced the trusty but clumsy old slide rule.

I.2 Opening Modifiers

An **OPENING MODIFIER** is one that comes as the start of a sentence, *before the subject and its agreeing verb.* The end of the opening modifier is often marked off with a comma. The main strategy is:

> *THE LONGER AND MORE IMPORTANT THE MODIFIER IS, THE MORE LIKELY YOU ARE TO SET IT OFF WITH A COMMA.*

We can also state the strategy according to what you can observe by reading out loud:

> *THE MORE YOU TEND TO PAUSE AFTER AN OPENING MODIFIER, THE MORE LIKELY YOU ARE TO PUT A COMMA THERE.*

A *short and simple modifier* is not very "heavy" and often goes without the comma, as in:

(152)   *Then* she said a strange thing.

(153)   *After the debate* the meeting broke up.

If you read these statements aloud, you probably won't pause after "Then" in (152) or "After the debate" in (153). The comma is most likely to be left out if the *whole statement* is short and simple, as in:

(154)   Then she yawned.

(155)   After the debate I left.

Still, some short opening modifiers make you pause and do take the comma:

(156)   *However,* the final result was a failure.

(157)   *Even so,* our outlook was cheerful.

Also, a short opening modifier tends to take a comma if it's *emphatic* (see also page 315), as in:

(158)   *Finally*, the letter arrived, six weeks late!

When an opening modifier is longer and more important, a comma is probably needed:

(159)   *Later on the same day*, she said a strange thing.

(160)   *After a debate lasting far into the night*, the meeting broke up.

(161)   *Even after putting in so much work*, they felt the result was a failure.

If a sentence opens with a **dependent clause**, you usually want a comma to show where the clause stops (see Section D). You might write:

(162)   *Whenever the temperature drops*, the glass in the window clouds over.

(163)   *If you haven't already heard*, my name was taken off the list.

The comma marks the end of the dependent clause, since an **independent clause** doesn't start with a linking word (pages 124 and 126). For instance, the comma keeps you from misreading "drops the glass" in (162), or "heard my name" in (163). By marking off the modifier, you can help prevent doubtful statements (see also Section H).

29. QUIZ *on opening modifiers*

Decide whether to put a comma after the opening modifiers or clauses in these sentences. Some sentences need more than one comma.

[1]   That night the men returned.

[2]   Three days after the big robbery the suspect was arrested in New Orleans.

[3]   Coming from a rural area we appreciate Seattle.

[4]   Only moments after the fire alarm went off the roof was blazing wildly.

[5]   Once he had a nice complexion.

[6]   Being blocked at the ten-yard line our running back failed to score.

[7]   Just then the clock stopped.

[8]   As soon as the coach finished the cheerleaders ran out on stage.

[9]   After so many troubles we deserved a rest.

[10] Finally when the mayor herself went down the sewer department sent out some repair trucks.

Same instructions as on the previous quiz.

[1] Sometime early next week there'll be a major test.

[2] Fortunately I'm ready for it.

[3] Every morning I read over the assigned books.

[4] Later on in the day I go to the lab.

[5] When you get there in the evening it's not so crowded.

[6] If I'm in a hurry to finish the lab assistant will stay late.

[7] On Wednesday we all went to *2001, A Space Odyssey*.

[8] In the first scenes we see some apes discover how to use bones for weapons.

[9] Soon they go to war with other apes over a water hole.

[10] Throughout the movie the story gets lost in a surplus of special effects.

I.3   Inserted Modifiers

An **INSERTED MODIFIER** is one placed *between a subject and an agreeing verb*. As you'd expect, writers tend to

---

PUT COMMAS AROUND AN INSERTED MODIFIER THAT IS LONG, IMPORTANT, OR EMPHATIC.

If you're reading out loud, you tend to *pause* before and after an inserted modifier that calls for commas. For instance, commas aren't needed for (164), but probably are for (165), and certainly are for (166) and (167) with those long modifiers:

(164) The old warrior *still* said nothing.

(165) The old warrior, *however*, said nothing.

(166) The old warrior, *in spite of all their threats*, said nothing.

(167) The old warrior, *throughout the whole confrontation*, said nothing.

Normally, inserted modifiers don't get extremely long. It's not a good idea to crowd too many words between a subject and an agreeing verb (compare Chapter 2, Section D.1). Long modifiers are more often put in opening or final position.

If you're in doubt about whether an inserted modifier calls for commas, use this strategy:

TRY MAKING IT AN OPENING MODIFIER BY MOVING IT TO THE FRONT OF THE SENTENCE.

As we saw in Section I.2, opening modifiers usually take a comma after them. You could have:

(167a)   *Throughout the whole confrontation,* the old warrior said nothing.

Modifiers you can easily move to the opening position are also the ones that call for commas in the inserted position. Compare:

(168)   Their team, *according to the polls,* should finish in first place.

(168a)   *According to the polls,* their team should finish in first place.

In contrast, some inserted modifiers don't take commas because they can't be separated from the subject, as in:

(169)   The street *beyond the row of pine trees* takes you to the courthouse.

(170)   A child *with poor eyesight* needs help right away.

(171)   A vacationer *staying at the beach* should use a sun screen.

(172)   The instructions *printed on the label* recommend two tablets every four hours.

You wouldn't make a pause before these modifiers. They also don't move into the opening position very well. It probably wouldn't occur to you to say things like:

(169a)   *Beyond the row of pine trees,* the street takes you to the courthouse.

(172a)   *Printed on the label,* the instructions recommend two tablets every four hours.

Even so, if you do decide to move these modifiers to the front, you'll mark them off with commas.

(170a)   *With poor eyesight,* a child needs help right away.

(171a)   *Staying at the beach,* a vacationer should use a sun screen.

Only a very short modifier like "soon" could do without commas in either position:

> (173) The rains *soon* came.

> (173a) *Soon* the rains came.

Not many modifiers are that short.

RELATIVE CLAUSES start with the relative linking words "that," "which," "who," "where," or "when" (see also pages 331–35). Since they go with what's right before them, you can't move them anywhere else. So you need another way to decide whether they take commas. You should remember from Section G on "looking back" that a relative clause can either *identify* (single out) the thing before it or *describe* (give details about) the thing before it. The strategy is:

MARK OFF WITH A COMMA ONLY
A RELATIVE CLAUSE THAT DESCRIBES.

For example, the relative clause in (174) identifies which kind of "student" is meant, and it doesn't need commas:

> (174) A student *who has to work part-time* shouldn't sign up for so many courses.

However, commas should go around the relative clause in (175), because this one merely describes someone who's already identified:

> (175) The president of the student body, *who favors community projects*, attended the city council meeting.

The describing clauses make you pause before and after them when you read them out loud. The identifying clauses don't make you pause.

31. QUIZ *on inserted modifiers*

Put commas *before* and *after* the inserted modifiers that need them. Check whether you could move them to the front of the sentence, and check whether they make you pause before and after them when you read them out loud.

[1] The blood then enters the aorta.

[2] The commissioner even after his exposure in the scandal refused to resign.

[3] Any resident making noise after midnight gets reported.

[4] The tired platoon hoping the enemy was far away stopped to rest.

[5]   Robert Kilpatrick convicted of reckless driving lost his license.

[6]   The average income now seems to be leveling off.

[7]   My brother who barely passed his finals managed to graduate after all.

[8]   A diploma certainly must be worth something.

[9]   The black Ford going out of control on the last turn skidded and rolled over.

[10] The time soon came for another investigation.

32. REVIEW QUIZ *on inserted modifiers*

Same instructions as on the previous quiz.

[1]   The reporters then left the conference.

[2]   A politician who takes a clear stand risks offending some voters.

[3]   South Africa which still has minority rule was attacked at a United Nations meeting.

[4]   - Her mood often changes.

[5]   Two men seen leaving the area were arrested that evening.

[6]   The argument over income taxes will never be finished.

[7]   Our library now open every day from eight in the morning until midnight is a popular place.

[8]   Six minutes in a microwave oven will heat these enchiladas perfectly.

[9]   This cactus seldom blooms until the rainy season.

[10] A woman on horseback hardly able to say her own name arrived that same afternoon.

I.4   Final Modifiers

FINAL MODIFIERS come *after the agreeing verb.* Whereas opening modifiers tend to take a comma most of the time,

---

FINAL MODIFIERS TEND NOT TO TAKE COMMAS UNLESS THERE'S A SPECIAL REASON.

Most final modifiers are in final position because they're closely linked to the *verb,* as in (176) and (177), or else to the *object of the verb,* as in (178) and (179).

They don't need commas:

(176)   She danced the whole evening with her own husband.

(177)   The legislature reconvened *after the long holiday weekend*.

(178)   We saw the same group *performing in the Fillmore Auditorium*.

(179)   My family purchased a new house *built entirely of pine wood*.

You probably wouldn't pause before these final modifiers when reading them out loud.

As you saw in Section G,

A COMMA SUGGESTS YOU SHOULD LOOK BACK FURTHER THAN YOU WOULD WITHOUT IT.

Therefore, a comma is used if a final modifier goes with *the subject*, which is further away than the verb or the object of the verb. You could have:

(180)   The candidate left the platform, *totally at a loss for words*.

(181)   The whole village dived for cover, *hearing the bombers overhead*.

(182)   The staff took care of the injured villagers, *doing as much as they could*.

Just ask yourself what the modifier goes with, and you get the subject for your answer:

(180a)   Who was *totally at a loss for words*? The candidate.

(181a)   Who *heard the bombers overhead*? The whole village.

(182a)   Who was *doing as much as they could*? The staff.

A modifier that goes with the subject is easy to *move to the front of the sentence*:

(180b)   *Totally at a loss for words*, the candidate left the platform.

(181b)   *Hearing the bombers overhead*, the whole village dived for cover.

(182b)   *Doing as much as they could*, the staff took care of the injured villagers.

In the opening position, these modifiers usually take the comma.

If you have a **relative clause** as a final modifier, you handle it the same way you would if you had one as an inserted modifier (see Section I.3). A relative clause is set off by a comma only if it *describes what's before it*, as in:

> (183)   You see here the home of Thomas Edison, *who invented the light bulb.*

> (184)   I proceeded to Vienna, *where I enrolled in the university.*

There's no comma if it *identifies what's before it*, as in:

> (185)   We needed an operator *who knew the code.*

> (186)   We found the list *that gave all their names.*

Only the describing kind makes you pause when you're reading the statement out loud.

33. QUIZ *on final modifiers*

Put commas to mark off the final modifiers that need them. Usually, a comma is needed only if the modifier goes with the *subject* (ask who's doing what) or if the modifier is a *relative clause* that describes what's before it.

[1]   Students call in orders to the pizza places downtown.

[2]   They deliver immediately to your door using a little motorcycle.

[3]   No more news reached us the week of the invasion.

[4]   The telephone rang all day which was very annoying.

[5]   She's always doing something that will oblige her friends.

[6]   One old woman left the room very much taken aback.

[7]   The government troops were having a hard time attacked on three sides at once.

[8]   Our truck made it up the hill grinding like a cement mixer.

[9]   They just stay home every day with their cats watching old movies on TV.

[10] The papers were still on the desk written neatly in black ink.

34. REVIEW QUIZ *on final modifiers*

Same instructions as on the previous quiz.

[1]   She brought in a bottle having no label on it.

[2]   They returned the letters that didn't have enough stamps.

[3]   And so we let the watchdog go wondering what would happen next.

[4]   You get a free sundae with this dinner.

[5]   These figures were wrong which eventually ruined the whole project.

[6]   She left for California where she became an accountant.

[7]   The producer didn't give out any raises forgetting all about his promise to the actors.

[8]   We are running far behind schedule.

[9]   We thought we should apologize for the trouble that we caused.

[10] He even sent a letter to Ernest Hemingway who never replied.

General quiz

35.
▼

on opening, inserted, and final modifiers

Put in commas where they're needed. Reading out loud for pauses may help.

[1]   In the middle of the night the hurricane arrived without any warning catching us completely off guard.

[2]   Heavy rains flooding all roads prevented the passage of emergency crews into the area.

[3]   At about three o'clock in the morning a noise woke me sounding like a jet airplane outside my window.

[4]   Startled by the tremendous racket I rushed to the window knocking over a lamp.

[5]   This window which is normally hard to get open flew open this time as soon as I touched the latch dousing me with water.

[6]   Having finally got the window shut again I ran to the other side of the house trying to keep out of the way of falling objects.

[7]   Of course the power had gone out in the whole town leaving no lights anywhere.

[8]   My family had luckily gotten a supply of hurricane lamps and flashlights for just such an emergency.

[9]   Right then the roof fell in with a crash cut in half by a falling tree.

[10] I soon heard the storm growing faint and far away.

Back-up general quiz

36.
▼

on opening, inserted, and final modifiers

Same instructions as on the previous quiz.

[1] The monthly checks which usually got spent on good times kept coming all year long.

[2] Next day the weatherman very embarrassed by his wrong prediction apologized on TV.

[3] In spite of all protests game shows stayed on the air getting worse and worse.

[4] The police stunned by the theft combed the area for every trace of the robbers.

[5] However they found only a bag of clothing stashed behind a bus depot.

[6] In the autumn of the same year every tree that was blown down by the wind got replaced with a new one.

[7] Years later the park rangers still were amazed at the change in the landscape.

[8] One way or another we'll just have to find the agent who holds the title to the land.

[9] In the very next instant our old comrade who'd been hardly awake a moment before was gone from the cabin.

[10] Nevertheless I really can't understand anyone living out there considering the bleakness of the valley.

■ J. PUNCTUATING LISTS

All we have left is how to punctuate when you make **LISTS** of things in a sentence. The basic strategies are:

IN A SENTENCE, A LIST OF THREE OR MORE HAS COMMAS BETWEEN ITS ITEMS.

IN A SENTENCE, A LIST OF LESS THAN THREE HAS NO COMMAS BETWEEN ITS ITEMS.

On a list of three or more, commas should go between *all* items, including before the "and" or the "or" that normally appears in front of the *last* item, as in:

(187)   His sisters are named *Sharon, Kim, and Melanie.*

(188)   They didn't deliver *today, yesterday, or last week.*

A list with *only two items* does not usually take a comma:

(189)   His sisters are named *Sharon and Kim.*

(190)   They didn't deliver the couch *today or yesterday.*

However, a list may contain a *two-part item* linked together with "and" or "or." No comma goes *inside* the two-part item, since twos normally don't get a comma. But if the whole list has three or more items on it, commas go *around* any two-part item you have. Here's an illustration:

(191)   My job included restocking *salt and pepper,̣ napkins and straws,̣* and *ketchup and mustard.*

This writer explained that the tables at her restaurant had three brass holders: one for salt and pepper, another for napkins and straws, and a third for ketchup and mustard. She was following that setup by making a list with three two-part items. Commas don't go inside any two-part items, but only between them.

Not all writers put in a comma before the "and" or the "or" in front of the last item on a list of three or more. But you're being considerate if you do put one there. That way, people who see the comma plus "and" or "or" know that the *last* item is coming up, not just an item with *two parts* to it. (192) and (193) aren't likely to cause confusion, but (194) might:

(192)   The racing cars were *red, black,̣ and green.* [three one-part items, all separated by commas]

(193)   The racing cars were *red, black and green*, or *blue and white*. [three items separated with commas, but the second and third items each have two parts]

(194)   The racing cars were *red, black* and *green*. [three items, but no comma between the second and the third]

As long as you have commas between all items, as in (192) and (193), the list is clear. If you leave out the comma before the last item, as in (194), you blur the difference between *two items* versus *one two-part item*. That difference does matter when you want to sort out a complicated list. Compare a version with no commas (196) to one with commas (196a):

(196)   That restaurant's specials are ham and eggs spaghetti and steak and lobster.

(196a)   That restaurant's specials are ham and eggs, spaghetti, and steak and lobster.

The commas make clear what goes with what. You have three menus to choose from, and two of them have two items each.

Within one clause, you can have a *list of three or more subjects*, as in (197), or a *list of three or more agreeing verbs*, as in (198). You still put commas between the items on the list.

(197)   Our *advisor*, our *manager*, and our *editor* were likeable people.

(198)   Our advisor *came* in, *called* the meeting to order, and *read* off the list of volunteers for the day.

In contrast, you usually don't need a comma if you have only *two* subjects or *two* agreeing verbs linked with "and" or with "or."

(199)   Our *advisor* and her *husband* were likeable people.

(200)   Our *advisor came* in and *called* the meeting to order.

As usual, three is where a list begins to need commas.

A list is not likely to contain a random assortment of items. The items are almost always similar in some way—all colors of cars at a race (192), all foods on one menu (196), and so on. You might want to *announce* the list by giving a *main heading*, or a term that covers all the items, as in (201). The heading is often separated from the list items by a **colon** (see also pages 322–24).

(201)   Next, the computer carries out *several operations*: finding the file, setting it up, and printing it out.

If you want to show that your list doesn't have *all* the items under your main heading, use some words like "such as," "including," "for instance," or "for example." In that case, you'd put a **comma** after the main heading, rather than a **colon**:

(202)   Next, the computer performs *several operations*, *such as* finding the file, setting it up, and printing it out.

You can also show that the list is not complete by ending it with "and so on," "and so forth," "and the like," or "etc." This ending becomes the last item on your list, so you put a comma in front of it.

(203)   Next, the computer performs several operations, including finding the file, setting it up, printing it out, *and so on.*

You don't need any other "and" in the list, since these endings start with "and" ("etc." comes from the Latin for "*and* the others").

Now suppose you have a list whose items are so long and involved that they need *their own commas inside them.* Then you can separate the items with **semicolons**. This is one time when semicolons are not limited to appearing between independent clauses (see page 311).

(204)   Our platoon now faced three difficult options: waiting for sunrise, when the enemy might be too close; marching in the dark jungle, where we could get lost; or sending signals, which might be seen by the wrong side.

This strategy clearly shows the borders between the items. If you just used commas everywhere, the results could be confusing. When you have a main heading, put a colon after it in the usual way, as shown in (204). Then it's plain where the list starts.

37. QUIZ *on punctuating lists*

Punctuate the following sentence lists. Put commas where they are needed in lists of three or more. If there is a main heading before the list, put a colon after the heading; otherwise, don't use any colons. Use semicolons between items if the list is so complicated that its items need commas inside them.

[1]   His father and mother were very poor and couldn't help out.

[2]   My parents my brother my sister and her boyfriend all went to Disney World.

[3] Two dollars a student ID and a fee card will get you a ticket for the concert.

[4] The corporation made three changes adjusting salaries lowering deductions and creating new positions.

[5] The wood is affected by several factors such as wind sun and rain.

[6] The dining room was serving bacon and eggs either sunny-side up or over easy sausage and potatoes either french-fried or mashed steak either oven-broiled or charcoal-grilled and lobster either newburg or thermidor.

[7] Major banks are offering new services free traveler's checks interest on checking accounts automatic tellers and so forth.

[8] The tight end hesitated a moment looked around and then made a sudden dash off to the left.

[9] The new diet consists of fish and chips cornbread and salad with oil and vinegar dressing.

[10] Our puppy chewed up my slippers the ones I was very fond of tore open the sofa and scattered the stuffing bit the mailman who said he won't deliver our mail any more and did several other things that I don't even want to think about.

38. REVIEW QUIZ *on punctuating lists*

Same instructions as on the previous quiz.

[1] Two screws a wire and a small battery are needed for the next experiment.

[2] You she or I must go to the bank and get rolls of coins nickels dimes and quarters.

[3] A weightlifting set needs a bench a barbell two dumbbells and a set of weights.

[4] They looked like the three Fabulous Furry Phreek Brothers Franklin Phineas and Fat Freddy.

[5] The order listed gin and tonic vodka and orange juice vermouth and scotch and soda.

[6] I was irritated by her behavior arguing about every decision whether or not it was important changing her mood morning noon and night and insisting on watching junk on TV all the time.

[7] March April and May arrived suddenly that year stayed an instant and were gone again.

[8] The budget cuts affected schoolchildren students the elderly and the poor.

[9] The cabinet was a forest of pill bottles vitamin pills pain pills sleeping pills and stay-awake pills.

[10] The officers gave her three choices paying the usual fine right away which was impossible for her paying a larger fine over a longer period maybe a year or going to jail which was not a very inviting place.

General quiz
on punctuation

39.
▼

Provide punctuation and capital letters. You can use periods, commas, semicolons, colons, exclamation points, question marks, dashes, parentheses, quotation marks, and apostrophes. Be careful not to make any comma splices or sentence fragments.

[1]   I was out of circulation last winter I was on a special assignment a highly confidential one it began rather mysteriously as youll soon see

[2]   Id received a call it was just after midnight from Washington where my boss has his headquarters runs operations and reports back to the government

[3]   His voice was agitated and he spoke rapidly making it hard to understand him even though after all this time Im used to his ways

[4]   As soon as he said Hello how have you been I knew something was wrong he sounded scared although he himself is seldom in danger at least not as much as we are

[5]   So I said Whats wrong and expected the worst he said youll have to leave first thing in the morning but he was very vague about where I was going what I should do and why there was such a hurry

[6]   Early the next morning I my suitcase and my emergency kit were on an airplane heading for a place which most of the world never even heard of nor had I until then located far from any cities or towns

361

[7]   When we were about to arrive I saw a depressing scene no airport just trees rocks sagebrush and empty hills as far as the eye could see

[8]   I said to myself What in the world can be so important in a wasteland which has no people cities or technology of any kind Why send me here

[9]   Climbing out of the aircraft I still saw nothing not even a landing field theyll meet you soon said a crewman in a white uniform pointing out toward the west

[10] So they took off and left me a total stranger to the place sitting on a rock I wonder what Im supposed to do now I said and let my mind wander What a setup Did they expect me to walk around send a signal or just wait

362

Back-up general quiz
on punctuation

40.
▼

Same instructions as on the previous quiz.

[1] It seemed like a long time passed nobody came to meet me the sun was climbing in the sky and the wind was growing harsh

[2] Vast clouds of dust sand and twigs drifted past covering everything with a fine curtain including me and my suitcase a mournful sight in a lonely place

[3] Suddenly I saw a bright light in the distance as if some large steel object was moving at high speed toward me its engines throwing out white flame

[4] In a instant it was standing in front of me motionless metallic and mysterious It seemed to wait for me to do something But seeing the guns on its cockpit aimed in my direction I thought it would be better not to make any sudden moves

[5] Soon a voice came out over a loudspeaker talking with with a strange foreign accent though in English The voice instructed me to give the password which I did fortunately my boss had remembered to give it to me

[6] The cockpit opened still keeping its guns aimed at me and the voice said Climb in A door opened in the side of the craft revealing a narrow staircase

[7] I obeyed what else could I do Of course I had my own weapons but there wasnt much to gain from a shootout Even if I managed to survive it which

wasnt too likely I would still be alone in a hostile wilderness and would be treated like an outlaw by anyone who came along

[8]   So I walked slowly over and climbed up the staircase I was surprised to hear the sound of many voices coming from far away as if I had entered a huge hall not an aircraft Where could so many people fit in such a small space I said Soon I arrived in a room where seven people were seated on benches wearing white uniforms boots and helmets

[9]   The walls were filled with screens displaying a bewildering array of events The voices Id heard came from there Were glad to see you said one of them in a voice with the same accent that Id heard before wont you make yourself at home

[10] I hope you didnt have to wait too long for us someone else said We had an unfortunate encounter with some unfriendly forces very unfriendly We have to be more careful who sees us if we dont want trouble As they were talking they handed me a folder with some papers Hmm my assignment i thought who knows what theyre going to ask me to do

6.

Spelling

Preview

Although spelling will always be more or less troublesome to many people, it will help you to know what the typical problems are. In this chapter, you'll see some common trouble spots that you can watch for in your writing.

One thing you really don't have to worry about when you talk is how to **SPELL**. If you're like most people, you've already noticed that spelling English words can be a real pain in the class. You have to be very alert to get every letter right. Misspellings can be disasters:

(1) County Parks Resent Shakespeare [present] [*Van Nuys* (Calif.) *News*, July 22, 1975]

(2) New Orleans Will Get Force of 50 State Supersops [supercops] [*Cumberland* (Md.) *News*, May 18, 1979]

(3) School homecoming queer is a former football player [queen] [*Frederick* (Md.) *Post*, Oct. 16, 1979]

(4) Better Bull Is Aim of University [bill] [*New Orleans Times-Picayune*, May 13, 1973]

(5) Kinney plans to increase the number of uninformed sergeants by 14. [uniformed] [*Sacramento Bee*, Sept. 3, 1972]

Knowing how to *say* and *use* a word is no guarantee that you can *spell* it. You can try to remember rules like "'i' before 'e,' except after 'c,' or when sounded like 'ay,' as in 'neighbor' and 'weigh.'" But there aren't very many "rules" like this one—certainly not enough to cover all the hard-to-spell words in English.

Or you can try to remember *what the word looks like*, at least well enough to tell whether it looks right when you write it down. But no matter what you do, you'll have to check the dictionary sometimes. Even professional writers do.

While you write, your attention is probably on other things besides just spelling. So you should check for correct spelling when you read back over your writing.

Although good spellers may not know *every word*, they do know *what sorts of words are likely to cause trouble*. If you know where to expect misspellings, you can watch for them. So to help you be on your guard, let's look at what sorts of words are particularly likely to get misspelled. These misspellings in the right-hand column are taken from students' papers; the correct spellings are in the left-hand column.

■ A.   LONG WORDS WITH MANY SYLLABLES

If a word has many letters or syllables, people tend either to leave out or to add some; for example:

CORRECT	STUDENTS WROTE
maintenance	maitenance, maintainance
possibility	possibity
convenience	convience
penetrates	petrates
specialties	specialities
opponents	oppents
bronchopulmonary	bronchopulmory
ventilation	ventilalation

The length of these words makes the slip-up harder to see. Also, it is easy to get confused by letters or syllables that appear more than once in a word. Try reading the long words aloud very slowly, like you did when you were a kid, saying every letter you see. That way, you're more likely to notice what's wrong

■ B.   WORDS WHERE LETTERS MIGHT BE DOUBLED

We just saw how letters or syllables that appear more than once in a word cause trouble. Doubled letters are particularly touchy. On the one hand, a writer may insert double letters where they shouldn't be:

CORRECT	STUDENTS WROTE
slick-bodied	slick-boddied
habit	habbit
propels	propells
sheriff	sherriff
heavily	heavilly

On the other hand, a writer may not put double letters where they should be:

CORRECT	STUDENTS WROTE
misspell	mispell
roommate	roomate
embarrassed	embarassed
occurrence	occurence
parallel	paralell

Check your dictionary whenever you're not sure whether or not to double a letter.
letter.

■ C. WORDS WITH INDISTINCT SOUNDS

Many words contain unstressed syllables where all you hear is an indistinct sound like "uh." It's hard to know what letters should go there. Students often guess wrong:

CORRECT	STUDENTS WROTE
permanent	permenant
separate	seperate
residence	residance
definite	definate

It helps to know another form of the word with a different emphasis (see page 373). If you think of "finite," for example, you'll find it easy to spell "definite."

A similar danger comes up when a vowel is next to one of the four "resonants"—"l," "m," "n," and "r." These sounds are somewhere between vowels and consonants. An "l" or an "r," especially, can blend with the vowel sound, so that it's hard to tell from saying the word whether the vowel comes before or after. Here, too, students get the spelling wrong sometimes:

CORRECT	STUDENTS WROTE
libel	lible
title	titel
proportion	porportion
prescribe	perscribe
particular	preticular

Sometimes students can't tell if there's even supposed to be a vowel next to the "l" or "r." They may leave the vowel out where it's needed or put it in where it isn't:

CORRECT	STUDENTS WROTE
bachelor	bachlor
accidentally	accidently
lightning	lightening
interest	intrest
interfere	intefere

These problems are natural enough, since "l," "m," "n," and "r" are like vowel sounds and mingle with them easily.

Clusters of letters with "s" also tend to get rearranged:

CORRECT	STUDENTS WROTE
contrast	contrats
instance	intsance
convicts	convics

When I asked a class to give directions for getting off the Interstate, several students wrote "exist" for "exits" over and over.

■ D. WORDS THAT OFTEN APPEAR TOGETHER

If two words frequently appear together, students may run them together:

CORRECT	STUDENTS WROTE
a lot	alot
a little	alittle
at least	atleast
no one	noone
all over	allover
all right	allright

Conversely, students sometimes make two or more words out of one:

CORRECT	STUDENTS WROTE
without	with out
whenever	when ever
nevertheless	never the less
upstanding	up standing

When you check the dictionary, look first for the version written as one word; if it's not there, assume that you're dealing with more than one word.

■ E. WORDS YOU DON'T USE VERY OFTEN

When you have to spell a word that you don't run into very often, you're less able to tell if it looks right or not. So watch out for unusual words like these:

CORRECT	STUDENTS WROTE
bifocals	biofocals
retina	retinia
Ophelia	Olpheleia
fluorinated	florinated

Words like these you really need to look up, but you might not find them at all if your spelling is way off. You can ask someone who is likely to know the word.

■ F. WORDS THAT SOUND THE SAME BUT LOOK DIFFERENT

You should be especially careful when two words are not spelled the same way but still sound alike:

INTENDED WORD	STUDENTS WROTE
affect [verb]	effect [noun]
accept	except
it's [= it is]	its
you're [= you are]	your
they're [= they are]	there
principal	principle
brake	break

Words that sound *almost* the same also get mixed up:

INTENDED WORD	STUDENTS WROTE
lose	loose
personal	personnel
whether	weather

These similar-sounding words can lead you to make some pretty strange statements if you're not careful:

(6) Gorillas Vow to Kill Khomeini [guerillas] [*Monessen* (Pa.) *Valley Independent*, Sept. 28, 1981]

(7) Nationwide Heroine Crackdown Includes Arrest of Three Here [heroin] [*Gainesville* (Fla.) *Sun*, Oct. 8, 1976]

■ G. SHORT, COMMON WORDS THAT LOOK LIKE EACH OTHER

Short, common words that look like each other often get switched. You don't notice it because you don't pay much attention to those words. Of course, they're easy to spell by themselves, since you practice them all the time. The danger is that you'll use the wrong one. Many students interchange words like "and/are," "than/that," "or/of/on," "in/is/it," "a/as/at," "to/too," "there/their," and so on. Students wrote:

(8) What we know about *is* is by reconstruction. [it]

(9) The obstacles are far *to* great at present. [too]

(10) The first impact of an idea *of* theory is little. [or]

(11) They contribute a large part *is* scientific theory. [in]

(12) They will soon need *a* least twice the resources. [at]

(13) *There* usefulness is a benefit to humankind. [their]

Here, too, it helps to read over your writing very carefully.

■ H. WORDS WITH UNPRONOUNCED LETTERS

As if you didn't have enough troubles, many English words contain letters that are never pronounced. Student writers naturally tend to leave those letters out:

CORRECT	STUDENTS WROTE
acquire	aquire
mortgage	morgage

stretched	streched
hustle	hussle
autumn	autum
parliament	parlament

Try to remember which words like these you have trouble with and make a special effort to spell them correctly.

■ I. WORDS THAT CAN CHANGE THEIR FORMS TO ADD ENDINGS

The basic form of a word sometimes changes when you have to add something onto the end (see also page 89). You should be careful about forming plurals of nouns, particularly nouns ending in "-o," "-s," "-sh," or "-y." An extra "e" may be needed:

BASIC FORM	GOES TO
tomato	tomatoes
loss	losses
wish	wishes
fly	flies
lady	ladies

Be careful also about adding "-s," "-ed," "-er," "-ing," or "-able/-ible" to verbs. For one reason, you may have to *double the final consonant* in order to keep the vowel short:

BASIC FORM	GOES TO
hop	hopped
kid	kidder
dig	digging
forget	unforgettable

For another, you may have to worry about whether you have a "soft c" (as in "cent") or a "hard c" (as in "can't"), and a "soft g" (as in "George") or a "hard g" (as in "glory"). Normally, the "soft c" or "g" comes *only before* "e," "i," *or* "y," *

---

* Even so, a "hard g" sound can come before "e," "i," and "y" if the "g" is *doubled*: "tagged," "rigging," "groggy," and so on.

while the "hard" sounds come before any other letter. So if a word ends in "-ce" or "-ge," drop the "-e" if you add "-ing" or "-ed":

BASIC FORM	GOES TO
race	racing
spice	spiced
rage	raging
lounge	lounging

Students' mistakes show that endings do cause problems:

CORRECT	STUDENTS WROTE
copies	copys
tomatoes	tomatos
stopped	stoped
tries	trys
policing	policeing
bridging	bridgeing

Good dictionaries list all the changes a word stem can have. Others list only those changes that don't take the form that you'd expect. The real cheapies don't list any changes. It pays to get a good dictionary and use it whenever you're not sure how to add an ending.

■ J. SIX STRATEGIES FOR SPELLING

As you can see from the examples, there are plenty of traps in spelling. Don't be embarrassed when you fall into them like everybody else. Keep this strategy in mind:

EXPECT MISSPELLINGS AND
WATCH FOR THEM.

Since you have enough other things to worry about when you're writing your draft, your next strategy should be:

GO BACK AND CHECK FOR SPELLING
WHEN YOU'RE FINISHED WRITING

—particularly if spelling often gives you trouble. This strategy will help you spot slip-ups that you were too busy to notice while you were in the middle of writing. By rereading your paper later, you'll see more accurately what's on the page, and you'll be more aware of what you're not sure about.

You may remember that a certain word causes trouble, but not how it ought to be spelled. One memory aid is:

COMPARE DIFFERENT FORMS OF THE WORD.

This strategy is good for a word with an indistinct sound. Try to think of a related form where the doubtful part of your word is clear enough for you to tell the spelling from the sound. For example, to decide which of the two possibilities on the left is correct, try thinking of the word on the right:

TO DECIDE	THINK OF
who's or whose?	who *is*
receive or recieve?	reception
their or *thier*?	*they*
suspicious or suspiscious?	suspect
definite or defanate?	finite
competition or compatition?	compete
competitive or competative?	competition

The distinct form helps for remembering the indistinct one. Of course, this strategy works only in certain cases, because not all troublesome words have related forms.

Everyone follows this strategy now and then:

IF YOU'RE IN DOUBT,
USE A GOOD DICTIONARY.

But what if you don't have a dictionary handy, or you can't find the word in the dictionary because your spelling is way off? Then you should

ASK SOMEONE WHO KNOWS.

As a last resort, say it some other way and don't use the word at all. But try to stay away from this dodge, because you should make full use of your stock of words.

373

One more strategy is good for "problem words"—that is, words you misspell often:

PUT A LIST OF YOUR PROBLEM WORDS IN A
NOTICEABLE PLACE.

Make the list in large, colorful letters and put it where you'll see it often, such as on the door of the refrigerator. Just seeing the words every day will give you a good mental image of how they ought to look.

NAME _____ CLASS _____ DATE _____

Quiz

1.
▼

on finding and fixing misspellings

Read the following passages, looking for the kinds of spelling dangers we have been discussing. Mark every word that looks suspicious to you, and check it in the dictionary if you're in any doubt. Then correct all misspellings.

[1]   Some times when your travling thorough the dark, you run into car troubel. Is might be the carburater, the raidiator, or the alternanator. Afterall, a car needs alot of maintenence in the engin, aswellas in things like baterys, axels, and winsheild wiper's. A untimly brake down at night it bad whether in the middle of no where can be a preticularly horrable occurence.

[2]   Engineering is a fasinating feild. I leads to alot of specilization's, suchas mecanics, electricicity, areadynamics, and computors. To keep instep with technolology, every body should have at aquaintance with enginering. You must be perpared, how ever, four struggleing through unresonably difficult requirments, forinstance, chemestry, calculus, and thermodymanics.

[3]   Because or a computor error, I was compeled to enrol in a sociolgy course. I had to learn allabout forms of goverment, both domestic and foriegn. The goverment of the Untied States is devided into three branchis: executata-tive, legeslative, and judicical. This arangement keeps power seperated. Foriegn goverments are not atall setup the same. In Europ, their's parlamen-tary rule, where the presidant is only a figurhead and the real power it held

by a chancelor, usualy the leader of the majoraty party in parlament. The chancelor can be dismised at anytime by a vote of no confidance, and than some one else has to takeover.

Review quiz
on finding and fixing misspellings

2.
▼

Same instructions as on the previous quiz.

[1] Last year I dicided to particepate in the compitition for homecomeing queeen. Haveing been in the Miss Misissipi compitition preiviously, I felt confidant that I had a resonable oportunity to atain the the titel. The principal dificulty would be the interveiws, where they interogate you about you're personel belief's. My perculiar veiws on sociaty are'nt alwys apperciated.

[2] My freinds in Talahassee took us to the zoo. Bioligy was my favorate subject in highschool, so we were asured of a goodtime. We inspected the aviary and then preceded to the large mamals: gorilas, chimpanzeees, orangetangs, cheatas, giraffs, rhinoceruses, and hippopopotamuses. Finely, we arived at the highpoint for us Gators: the aligator santuary, where we payed our respecks.

[3] My favorit job was manageing a garden supplie store. I weighted on cos-tumers and insulted about there problems. I tended the green house to keeptrack of things suchas humidifires and fertalizors. I put lables on all the flower beds and made sure the names did'nt get mispelled. We had

flowers like lielacks, dafodills, crissanthamums, patoonias, peeonys, mary-golds, and violence. We also carryed friut treees, forexample, appels, pairs, peeches, cumquots, tangereens, and avocacadoes. I injoyed these task's verymuch.

Index
of
Terms

A 4
B 5
C 6
D 7
E 8
F 9
G 0
H 1
I 2
J 3